Mason-Dixon
KNITTING
Outside the Lines

Mason-Dixon
KNITTING
Outside the Lines

**PATTERNS, STORIES, PICTURES, TRUE CONFESSIONS,
TRICKY BITS, WHOLE NEW WORLDS, AND FAMILIAR ONES, TOO**

Kay Gardiner and Ann Shayne

PHOTOGRAPHY BY GALE ZUCKER

POTTER
CRAFT

NEW YORK

Copyright © 2008 by Kay Gardiner and Ann M. Shayne

Photographs © 2008 by Gale Zucker

Published in the United States by Potter Craft, an imprint of
the Crown Publishing Group, a division of Random House,
Inc., New York.

www.crownpublishing.com
www.pottercraft.com

POTTER CRAFT and CLARKSON N. POTTER are
trademarks, and POTTER and colophon are registered
trademarks of Random House, Inc.

Library of Congress Cataloging-in-Publication Data is available
upon request.

ISBN: 978-0-307-38170-5

Printed in China

BOOK DESIGN BY CHALKLEY CALDERWOOD

The author and publisher would like to thank the
Craft Yarn Council of America for providing the yarn weight
standards and accompanying icons used in this book. For
more information, please visit www.YarnStandards.com.

10 9 8 7 6 5 4 3 2 1

First Edition

To our mothers

Lill Gardiner

Helen Allen Meador

Contents

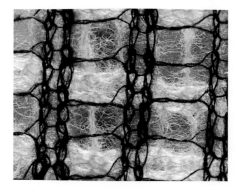

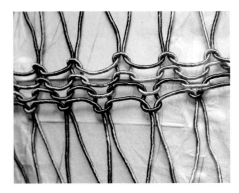  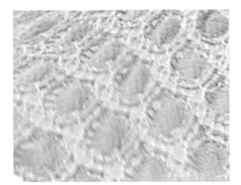

Introduction

The Secret of Knitting, Revealed

We begin where we always begin, with Mason-Dixon Rule Number 1:
Knitting is spoze to be fun. Of course, the longer we knit, the more the definition of
fun expands. What makes knitting fun? We've been lugging this question around
like Linus with his blanket. It starts to sound like some kind
of religious question. Why are we here? Why are we doing this?
Why didn't we spend more time on math homework?

Sorry. But really: What makes knitting fun? Upon contemplation, and list making, and extreme amounts of coffee, we have concluded that *fun* is many things. Things that seem at once contrary. Consider these:

Simple and Complex. Have you noticed something? It's getting easier. The more we knit, the more we learn. We keep discovering new tricks, and it means we are making things that not long ago we never would have dreamed of making.

You can get pretty far down the road with a knit stitch. Throw in a purl, and a new vista opens. Beyond that, we have unearthed some stitches in this book that pretty much took our breath away when we first discovered them. So crazy. And such a fine puzzle to work.

The Familiar and the New. A silhouette, a yarn, a technique. These are the familiar elements of just about any knitting project. We have discovered, again and again, that if you mess around with one of them, cool things happen. Alter the fit of a familiar sweatshirt, for example, and the dumpy garment of last resort becomes a daily sweater. Begin with that most basic sweater, a cardigan, but make it in the filmiest yarn you can find. All of a sudden, you have a piece you can wear all sorts of ways. Make a blanket for a baby, but use Fair Isle to keep it fun.

Economy and Luxury. We have never forgotten that the roots of knitting are humble, that the first person who picked up sticks and string was hoping to beat back the cold or otherwise avoid wearing poorly cured animal skins. Those first knitters were hanging out with the Mother of Invention, driven by necessity. The transformation that has occurred with knitting—the way this humble craft has become the pastime of people who do it for fun—is a curiosity that seems topsy-turvy to us. We have made our share of stuff that uses extravagant yarn, and it can be thrilling to finish a delicate shawl in a spectacular lace. But simple materials and familiar techniques always call us back.

Function and Ornament. Use your handknits. Make them beautiful and interesting, that's all. We are really happy when we've made something that has a function in our lives, and that's something we have kept in mind as we cooked up projects for this book.

Process and Product. In some cases, the projects you see here are the result of hair-raising odysseys into the dark side of knitting. We have been on a couple of trips that can only be called grueling slogs through the swamp of reality—where fantasy holds up exactly as long as it takes to find a pair of needles and a ball of yarn. But still and all, it is when things are not going according to plan that we are most engaged. Finding a way out of the woods is a great, absorbing game.

In the following five chapters, we pile all these elements into projects that we very much hope will challenge, intrigue, and surprise you. Some of these ideas are Kay's, some Ann's, and some are from our friends whose creativity has really knocked us out.

1 DECORATING YOURSELF:

A collection of things to make for your most demanding yet forgiving client—yourself.

2 THE FAIREST ISLE OF ALL:

A sort of knitting you may never have considered.

3 COVERING THE SMALL HUMAN:

The delights of pint-sized knits and the evolving challenge of knitting for youngsters after they have discovered free will.

4 OCCASIONAL KNITTING:

The special occasions in life often inspire a burst of knitting.

5 THE SOPHISTICATED KITCHEN:

Did you really, actually think that we would leave without including new uses for dishcloth cotton? Did you really?

That feeling of accomplishment—of doing something we didn't quite know we could do—continues on these quiet adventures we take when we hunker down with a bit of knitting. As we tested out ideas, we were on a constant quest for new things to try, challenges to stretch your skills. And, always, we aimed for projects that allow you to elaborate on the pattern, to make it your own.

Our guarantee: There is nothing in this book that you cannot do. Nothing. If you try something in here, and you can't do it, then we'll happily take your yarn off your hands and help you find a new hobby. (Warning: it may involve woodworking.) We wouldn't put it in here if we thought you couldn't do it. We include all these projects because we hope that you will find them fun.

There it is, the secret of knitting: The longer you knit, the more fun it gets.

Chapter One

Decorating YOURSELF

Ann ✳ Is it just me, or does it seem like everybody else in the world is a better dresser? Now that I have no choice but to call myself a grown-up, I have been thinking about grooming. Natural splendor is no longer carrying the day; I have *got* to get busy.

There's a friend I see around town. We'll call her Madame X. Madame X dresses at such a fine level of detail that I spend most of my time with her pondering whatever ensemble she has cooked up. She has Outfits. Suits. Pantsuits. Blouses. Skirts and dresses and scarves and belts and heels and pocketbooks. I've never seen her wear the same shoes twice. Things are snappy. Things are kicky.

On one morning, while we sat drinking coffee, I realized in a flash that Madame X doesn't dress herself; she decorates herself. She's not tracking down her least-bad-fitting pair of blue pants, the way I do. She's operating under the same impulse that leads a person to hang stuff on a Christmas tree. It's not profound, or important, or efficient. It's fun. It's pretty. I'd never thought about this.

When people put a lot of effort into what they're wearing, I have always concluded that they must be shallow, vain, or boring. I never entertain the possibility that they're simply having fun. But during my visit with Madame X, I realized that she goes to her closet every morning with a little thrill: "It's time to decorate me!"

I'm not wearing enough handknits. That's what Madame X says to me every time I see her. "Why don't you wear your handknits? Surely you have a ton of 'em. Why wouldn't you wear them *all the time*?"

It's a fair question, if a painful one. My guess is that Madame X's question comes mostly because, in her mind, I knit so often that I must have nothing but handknits in my closet. To her, it defies explanation how I could have clothes that are not knitted.

She has a point. For all the knitting I've done, I remain remarkably undecorated. And I have a feeling that many fellow knitters are going through the day without consideration for their self-decoration. So, underdecorated knitters of the world, this chapter's for us. Go ahead—think about all the people you have knitted for. Now (it's not disloyal to do this) just forget about them for a minute. Give yourself a little decoration. These are projects that you can wear for years to come. You don't have to make them for the niece who's graduating from high school or the best friend who just had a birthday. We realize that you are likely to do this anyway, but still.

Make these things for the one you know best: yourself.

A Haze of Knitting

Let's start with one of the great mystery fibers: mohair. Mohair is weird. It's a fiber full of paradox. It's lightweight but surprisingly warm. It can be spun so finely that you can barely see it—but that fine yarn can create a substantial fabric of bright, bright color.

It can become a shawl so light that you can hardly weigh it. And it can make a blanket so warm that you could use it to insulate your attic. You wouldn't want to insulate your attic, though, because mohair is so pretty. It's not like anything else, which is why we turn to kid mohair for two highly decorative projects.

When One Cardigan Is Not Enough

Ann ✳ I have a confession to make. I love a fine-gauge, store-bought cardigan more than just about anything. If you shop after Christmas and catch a cashmere cardigan on deep discount, you have a piece of clothing you can wear virtually every day. So light, and so warm, it's a delicious little treat. It is not, however, a handknit. It does not even vaguely look like a handknit—nobody ever asks, "Did you knit that?" As a daily, hard core knitter, it bothered me to be so devoted to a knitted garment that I did not make myself. Short of knitting cashmere on 00000 needles, I didn't really see a way around this problem.

That is, I didn't see a way around this problem until one recent afternoon. Kay and I were in the same room together, which is rare. We have our ongoing, baroque correspondence, and we have become used to hearing the shocking sound of each other's voices on the telephone. Still, we do live a thousand miles apart, so most of our cogitating takes place in the ether of the Internet.

Anyway, we were hanging out, knitting, and studying a specimen I had caught at a local department store, a real prize that I bought the minute I saw it. It was a simple cardigan, but it was striking for the way it layered two colors of mohair, making the most of mohair's translucent yet vibrant color properties. We thought, as we always think, *Wouldn't it be just great to knit one of those ourselves?*

We quickly decided that getting such a cool layered effect would be possible only by knitting two whole sweaters of mohair, which seemed extreme even for us. And two layers of mohair are strikingly warm. Like, a delivery guy could use this cardigan to keep the pizzas hot.

But what if one of the sweaters were already made? What if you made a loosely structured layer to wear over a cardigan you already owned? What if you made a cozy for your cardigan?

A surrounded cardigan. A protective cardigan cover. A cardigan cozy.

This delicate bit of frosting works as a layer over a cardigan or as an extremely airy companion to a camisole. A party cozy. The cables almost disappear, leaving just a trace of a pattern. It's decoration, pure and simple.

CARDI COZY

We have had to keep the samples for this airy cardigan, knit from the top down, under lock and key. Everybody who sees this wants it.

SIZE
XS (S, M, L, XL, XXL)

FINISHED BUST MEASUREMENT
38 (40, 42, 45, 49, 53)" (96.5 [101.5, 106.5, 114, 124.5, 134.5]cm)

MATERIALS
- **1** super fine
- 2 balls Rowan Kidsilk Haze, 70% mohair, 30% silk, ¾ oz (25g), 229 yd (210m), in gray
- Size 8 (5mm) needles, or size needed to obtain gauge
- Stitch holders
- Tapestry needle

GAUGE
16½ stitches and 21 rows = 4" (10cm) in stockinette stitch

DIFFICULTY
Whatever trickiness the slim yarn gives you, the fact that you can crank a sweater out of two balls of yarn will turn that frown upside down.

PATTERN NOTES
This pattern uses a specific type of increase to form the raglan sleeve seams. Once you have worked it on a couple of rows, you will recognize the "seam stitch" when you come to it. The idea is to work across the piece until you get to the seam stitch, where you will work the increase as follows, depending on whether you are working a knit or purl row:

(k1, yo, k1): Work these 3 stitches into a single stitch—knit 1 but leave the stitch on the left needle, move yarn over needle from front to back, knit 1 into the stitch on the left needle.

(p1, yo, p1): Work these 3 stitches into a single stitch—purl 1 but leave stitch on the left needle, yarn over, purl 1 into the stitch on the left needle.

The Cardi Cozy has a single cable running down each Sleeve and Front and the center Back. Unlike typical cables, there are no purl background stitches; the cables simply rise from the mohair mist of the stockinette fabric.

c7f: cable 7 front—slip next 4 stitches to cable needle and hold at front, k3, k4 from cable needle.

c7b: cable 7 back—slip next 3 stitches to cable needle and hold at back, k4, k3 from cable needle.

Cardigan

Cast on 41 (41, 43, 47, 49, 55) stitches. Purl 1 row.

Row 1 (RS) kfb, (k1, yo, k1), k7 (7, 7, 9, 9, 11), (k1, yo, k1), k21 (21, 23, 25, 25, 27), (k1, yo, k1), k7 (7, 7, 9, 9, 11), (k1, yo, k1), kfb—51 (51, 53, 57, 59, 65) sts.

Row 2 p3, (p1, yo, p1), p9 (9, 9, 11, 11, 13), (p1, yo, p1), p23 (23, 25, 25, 27, 29), (p1, yo, p1), p9 (9, 9, 11, 11, 13), (p1, yo, p1), p3—59 (59, 61, 65, 67, 73) sts.

Row 3 kfb, k3, (k1, yo, k1), k11 (11, 11, 13, 13, 15), (k1, yo, k1), k25 (25, 27, 27, 29, 31), (k1, yo, k1), k11 (11, 11, 13, 13, 15), (k1, yo, k1), k3, kfb—69 (69, 71, 75, 77, 83) sts.

This is a project to wear two ways: with a cardigan or on its own.

Row 4 p6, (p1, yo, p1), p13 (13, 13, 15, 15, 17), (p1, yo, p1), p27 (27, 29, 29, 31, 33), (p1, yo, p1), p13 (13, 13, 15, 15, 17), (p1, yo, p1), p6.

Rows 5–8 Continue to increase 10 stitches on every RS row and 8 stitches on every WS row as set, ending with a WS row—113 (113, 115, 119, 121, 127) sts.

Row 9 (RS) kfb, k12, (k1, yo, k1), k8 (8, 8, 10, 10, 12), c7f, k8 (8, 8, 10, 10, 12), (k1, yo, k1), k15 (15, 16, 16, 17, 18), c7f, k15 (15, 16, 16, 17, 18), (k1, yo, k1), k8 (8, 8, 10, 10, 12), c7b, k8 (8, 8, 10, 10, 12), (k1, yo, k1), k12, kfb—123 (123, 125, 129, 131, 137) sts.

Rows 10 and 11 Work increases as set—141 (141, 143, 147, 149, 155) sts.

Sizes XS, S, and M only Row 12 and all following WS rows: Purl, without doing increases. Increase on RS rows only.

Sizes L, XL, and XXL only Continue to increase at raglans on every row as set 0 (8, 9) times more, from then on increase on every row on back and fronts only, and increase on the sleeves on every RS row.

Row 15 Cast on 3 stitches, work rest of row as set, with increases as given for your size.

Row 16 Cast on 3 stitches, work rest of row as set for your size. These 2 rows with cast-on stitches at the beginning mark the end of the front neck shaping. From now on, increases are only worked at the raglans, increasing as given above for your size, slipping the first stitch of each row to give a neat selvedge.

All Sizes Row 19 Insert cables on fronts, 11 stitches in from front edge, as follows: Slip 1, k10, c7b, work to last 11 stitches as set for your size, c7f, work to the end of the row. The 5 cables now repeat on every following tenth row.

Continue to increase as given for your size until there are 59 (61, 63, 65, 69, 73) stitches in each sleeve section. Continue increasing on fronts and back ONLY (as given below) until there are 79 (83, 87, 91, 99, 107) stitches in the back portion of the body (between the stitches where the [k1, yo, k1] increases are worked), ending with a WS row.

Increase on fronts and back only, as follows:

Knit to seam stitch, yo, knit seam stitch, knit sleeve stitches, knit seam stitch, yo, knit across back stitches to seam stitch, yo, knit seam stitch, knit across sleeve stitches, knit seam stitch, yo, knit to the end. Work a WS row.

Sleeve (make 2)

Next row k41 (43, 45, 47, 51, 55) for left front, knit the next 61 (63, 65, 67, 71, 75) stitches for the sleeve (sleeve stitches and 2 "raglan" stitches); turn. Put the remaining stitches for the back, right sleeve, and right front onto a holder; cast on 2 (2, 4, 4, 6, 6) stitches for underarm gusset, p61 (63, 65, 67, 71, 75); turn, put remaining stitches onto a holder for left front. Now work on the sleeve stitches only—63 (65, 69, 71, 77, 81) sts.

Keeping the cable pattern correct as set, work 5 rows straight, then decrease 1 stitch at each side of the next and every following 6th (6th, 6th, 5th, 5th, 5th) row until there are 35 (35, 35, 39, 39, 39) stitches or until the sleeves are the length of your "undercardigan" or your actual arms. Work a further 6 rows straight, ending with a RS row. The sleeve measurement from neckline to cuff should be approximately 27 (27½, 27½, 27¾, 28, 28)" (69 [70, 70, 70.5, 71, 71]cm). Bind off loosely.

Slip the stitches for the back onto another holder, cast on 2 (2, 4, 4, 6, 6) stitches, knit the remaining sleeve stitches, and turn. Now work on these sleeve stitches only, completing the right sleeve to match the left.

Body

Slip the stitches for the left front onto the needle, rejoin the yarn at the underarm, cast on 2 (2, 4, 4, 6, 6) stitches, knit

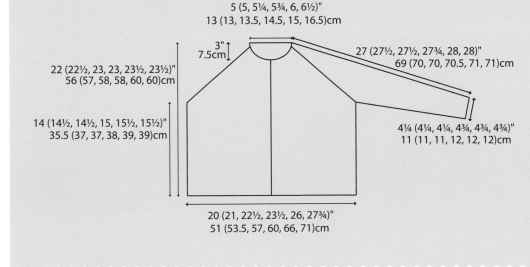

5 (5, 5¼, 5¾, 6, 6½)"
13 (13, 13.5, 14.5, 15, 16.5)cm

3"
7.5cm

27 (27½, 27½, 27¾, 28, 28)"
69 (70, 70, 70.5, 71, 71)cm

22 (22½, 23, 23, 23½, 23½)"
56 (57, 58, 58, 60, 60)cm

14 (14½, 14½, 15, 15½, 15½)"
35.5 (37, 37, 38, 39, 39)cm

4¼ (4¼, 4¼, 4¾, 4¾, 4¾)"
11 (11, 11, 12, 12, 12)cm

20 (21, 22½, 23½, 26, 27¾)"
51 (53.5, 57, 60, 66, 71)cm

across the back stitches, cast on 2 (2, 4, 4, 6, 6) stitches, knit across the right front stitches—165 (173, 185, 193, 213, 229) sts. Look at what you've just done: it's a seamless body!

Next row (WS) p41 (43, 47, 49, 53, 57), k1, p81 (85, 89, 95, 105, 113), k1, purl to end. The knit stitches (purl stitches on the RS) provide a mock side seam.

Work even on these stitches, keeping cable pattern correct, until the fronts and back measure 14 (14½, 14½, 15, 15½, 15½)" (35.5 [37, 37, 38, 39, 39]cm) down the "side seam" or until your cardi is the length you would like. Bind off loosely and evenly.

Finishing

Sew the sleeve seams. Weave in ends. Work 1 row of single crochet around the neck if you wish. (We did.) There is no need to leave a pile of sweater pieces piled in a corner of your closet for six months while you wait for the gumption to seam them together. The sweater is done.

We suggest that you wear clothes under the Cardi Cozy. But if you want to get all freaky on us, well … let the Courvoisier flow.

We put the question to the readers of masondixonknitting.com, and as usual, their answers were fascinating.

"Mostly I look at a pattern and ask myself, 'How much presence of mind does this require?' "

"Patterns that are completely unforgiving of mistakes. I hate when I misplace one little stitch and I have to rip back to fix it!"

"I realize this is a sort of hubris, but when anyone cries 'This is hard!' my reaction tends to be 'Why? What's the worst part?' I'm sure that if the steps are taken one at a time, there are resources and patience enough to take on any task."

"Nothing's hard, but plenty of things are tiresome. I truly lack the patience for complicated patterns."

"Nothing, in my opinion, is harder than something that is boring."

"It turns out that garter stitch is hard for me. Don't laugh. I tend to make a lot of mistakes when I don't look at my knitting for a long time, and for some reason I get ballsy when I'm knitting garter stitch and hence my current WIP has been ripped three times for mistakes."

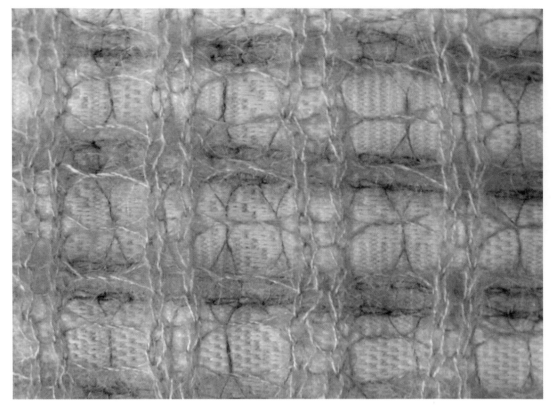

Crisscross laceweight mohair, and you get the plaid they wear in heaven.

Knitted Plaid

Ann ✳ Layers of mohair. I was consumed with the idea of overlapping mohair. I dreamed about it. You can see though the stuff. It weighs almost nothing. It *ought* to overlap, for Pete's sake. I had to find a way to make the most of these qualities.

It turns out that simplicity is the key to overlapping mohair. I tried lace patterns, which tend to clog up when you layer them. And one complex layer obscured the layer under it. The simpler I went, the prettier it looked, until I ended up with a double yarn over pattern that did cool things when I turned the top piece in one direction, and the bottom piece perpendicular to it. It looked like plaid when the two pieces were different colors. And it looked like it would make a simple, gorgeous stole.

The more I messed with it, the more it became clear that it should not have a border, or be seamed all the way around to hold the two layers together. The looser it's worn, the more the colors and pattern arrange themselves in pretty ways. It's a fair amount of knitting, but as with any mohair project, the result is worth the journey.

BELINDA

SIZE
40" x 60" (102cm x 152cm)

After folding the shawl in half, the finished size is 20" x 60" (51cm x 152cm)

MATERIALS
-  **1** super fine
- Rowan Kidsilk Haze, 70% mohair, 30% silk, ¾ oz (25g), 229yd (210m), 2 balls green (color A), 2 balls blue (color B)
- Size 8 (5mm) 14" (35cm) straight needles (circular needles will work, but the cable slows down the knitting quite a bit), or size needed to obtain gauge
- Tapestry needle

GAUGE
14 stitches and 18 rows = 4" (10cm) in stitch pattern after soaking and blocking the swatch

DIFFICULTY
Easy stitch pattern, long rows—you will meditate your way to a new place of serenity, Grasshopper.

≡≡≡ *Tip* ≡≡≡

Blocking Wires: Love Your Gear

If you plan, ever in your life, to make more than one shawl, we encourage you to invest in a set of blocking wires. These thin, metal wires are usually sold in a set of varying lengths and thicknesses. Instead of using dozens of straight pins, you thread a blocking wire through the edge stitches of your finished work, then pin down the wire with three or four straight pins. Pull an entire side of a shawl into shape with a simple tug, instead of moving 40 straight pins and making yourself batty. Blocking wires also work well for blocking sweater pieces, or even large Fair Isle blankets. The flexible ones fit around the curve of a sleeve top, making it easy to shape those unruly curves into symmetry.

Belinda looks great on everybody, but it will make you this young and beautiful only if you actually are this young and beautiful.

Piece One

Using A, cast on 64 stitches using the knitted cast-on method—see page 153.

Row 1 (RS) *ssk, yo twice, k2tog; repeat from * across.

Row 2 (WS) *p1, (p1, k1) into double yo, p1; repeat from * across.

Repeat rows 1 and 2 until you have worked 270 rows (or 135 lace holes, which are easier to count). Bind off very loosely as follows: *k2tog, place the stitch just knitted back onto the left needle; repeat from * across.

Piece Two

Using B, with the RS of Piece One facing, pick up and knit stitches along one long edge of the piece as follows: *Pick up and knit 3 stitches, skip 1 stitch, pick up and knit 4 stitches, skip 1 stitch; repeat from * to last 6 stitches of Piece One, pick up and knit 3 stitches, skip 1 stitch, pick up and knit 2 stitches—208 sts.

Next row (WS) Purl.

Begin stitch pattern as follows:

Row 1 (RS) *ssk, yo twice, k2tog; repeat from * across.

Row 2 (WS) *p1, (p1, k1) into double yo, p1; repeat from * across.

Continue in pattern. Work 90 rows (or 45 lace holes), ending with a completed row 2 of the pattern. Bind off very loosely as follows to make a pretty edge: *k2tog, place the stitch just knitted back onto the left needle; repeat from * across.

Blocking

This wrap will open up dramatically with a good blocking. Soak the wrap in cold water for 15 minutes. Do not wring it. Remove excess moisture by laying the wrap flat on towels and gently rolling it up. (Fold it in half if you don't have a baseball field available for this.) To block, use either a jillion pins or blocking wires. Let the wrap dry for as long as you can stand it—a couple of days is great—then unpin it and marvel at your airy shawl.

Finishing

Fold the shawl along the long joining seam. You can wear it all sorts of ways.

Variation

If you'd like a 6' (183cm) long stole—a superdramatic swath of fluffy beauty—make Piece One 348 rows (or 174 lace holes) long. For Piece Two, pick up and knit 268 stitches as follows: *Pick up and knit 3 stitches, skip 1 stitch, pick up and knit 4 stitches, skip 1 stitch; repeat from * across to last 6 stitches, pick up and knit 3 stitches, skip 1 stitch, pick up and knit 2 stitches.

Tip

Mary Sue Taylor's Tug Tip

If you're new to Kidsilk Haze, and it's giving you a hard time, take this advice from Mary Sue Taylor, one who has walked the distance on this pattern.

She writes: "After the double yarn over, use your left fingers to pull down on the bottom of the next 2 stitches to open them up a little. Knit 2 together. Tug the bottom of the next 2 stitches, etc."

Have fun choosing your two colors. We chose a strong contrast to highlight the plaid effect.

Coaty Coats

Ann ✳ The sweater quandary continues to plague us. We have written before about this problem—the difficulty of wearing your handknits enough—yet we continue to make sweaters. We try to wear them, but it's just hard to put in enough Hours on Person. As we discussed this new book, and the sort of things we would like to make, and own, we realized that there is a category of handknit that we have never even attempted: the coat.

Ohhhhhhhh, the coat. I wear the same coat every day, all winter long. It's not hard to wear that coat enough; it's hard *not* to wear it all the time. But the coat is a dangerous category of handknit: that sagging, drooping sweater on steroids. A good handknit coat is hard to find—nay, *really* hard to find. We see few of them in the field, because the fact is simple: It's not easy to make knitting look like anything but a sweater.

Not long ago, the truth of the coat problem hit me hard. Hubbo and I were at dinner at our friends' house. We'll call them the Talls. Mrs. Tall is somebody who can wear whatever she damn well pleases. She is tall and slim and great. She asked me what I was up to, and I said, "Coats. I'm thinking a lot about knitted coats." Her eyes lit up, but it wasn't a happy recognition. It was rueful, like she had seen an old boyfriend in a public place. She looked like she might throw up.

"Yes," she said. "I have a knitted coat. It was given to me years ago. I haven't worn it. It has"—she paused, gesturing limply at her neck—"a stand-up collar."

"Oh," I said. "A mandarin collar?"

"Yes. And a knitted belt."

"Right."

"It's really long."

"So sorry."

It was a beautiful late winter night in Nashville, so mild that we came outside after our lamb chops to sit around the Talls' fire pit. Mrs. Tall excused herself for a minute, then returned. "This is the coat," she said, which was as necessary as a naked person saying, "I'm wearing no clothes right now."

What a garment! What a heroically scaled, enormous piece of knitting! It was like a duvet with sleeves. It was gray, and cabled, and knit-purl stitched, and furry and slubbed and tweedy and the sort of thing that, in 1974, would have been called a maxi coat.

"It's really warm," she said. "She made it just for me."

Bless her heart.

This is the sort of situation that coats can cause, particularly a coat that was made as a present. The more I think about it, the more it's clear that coats probably ought not fall into the category of Gift Knitting. A coat is a very personal thing. Everybody has ideas about their coats—long or short, heavy or light, made from animal fluff or petroleum products. And a knitted coat? Dangerous.

I want a knitted coat, and I always have, yet I've never seen one that met my list of requirements. Until now. We called in two women whose design skills are up to the challenge of overcoming the hazards: Mercedes Tarasovich-Clark and Bonne Marie Burns. It turns out that there are ways to avoid these problems, and the good news is that the resulting garments are sturdy, unbelted, and unlikely to be mistaken for a sweater. They are, in a word, coaty.

COLOR FORECASTING: A QUICK TRIP TO LOONYVILLE

A friend of ours who works in the fashion industry (OK, our only friend who works in the fashion industry) told us about color forecasting. Color forecasting is where people in a certain industry—furniture, say, or kitchen design, or women's wear—get together to discuss what colors will be popular two years down the road. We quickly discovered that color forecasting is a big deal. Could we get some insight into where color would be, down the road?

Not really. As we poked around, we mostly found a lot of color forecasting that sounded like poems we wrote in eighth grade. A sampling (all quotes 100 percent authentic):

"The bluish shades of the siesta hour give way to the flashy, arty, flowery colors of a frenzied dance on the sand."

"Able to reconcile extremes, from the monumental to the molecular, from the ostentatious to the austere."

Here's our color forecasting: For every single project in this book, we picked colors that we thought were pretty.

1. THE HEARTBREAK OF SAG.
To be warm, a coat involves a fair amount of fabric. When the fabric is knitted, it is hard to prevent sagging from the weight of a dense piece of knitting.

2. BATHROBE SYNDROME.
A knitted belt wrapped around the midsection of a cardigan is going to take a garment right into the territory known as Bathrobe Gulch. A bathrobe is great, but a bathrobe's a bathrobe, not a coat. You don't want to look like you're heading to a spa treatment, unless you actually are.

2. LOOKS LIKE A REALLY BIG SWEATER.

This is tricky, because sweaters are really beautiful. We are unusually fond of sweaters. But there are sweaters, and there are coats. I have a coat closet, and a sweater shelf, and I'd like to keep it that way.

That Girl

The 1960s meant a lot to me. Not JFK and Camelot, not Haight-Ashbury, not Andy Warhol. I was too young for all that. I'm talking about *television* of the 1960's.

TV of the '60s provided my first window into style. Andy Griffith's girlfriend, Helen Crump, was totally sophisticated. As far as I was concerned, Andy was crazy not to marry her. Cissy Davis, Buffy and Jody's big sister on *Family Affair*, always looked great. But the two women who gave me the most to admire were Marlo Thomas, of *That Girl*, and Elizabeth Montgomery, of *Bewitched*. Those women, who were so funny to me, always looked snappy. I didn't really understand the subtleties of Marlo Thomas's life as an aspiring actress living in New York, but I thought her hairdo was fantastic. When curling irons became popular, I flipped my hair just like hers.

The '60s were a high-water moment for the A-line dress, the A-line skirt, the A-line coat.

By the time I was 10, I had two hobbies: reading and watching TV. In particular, daytime TV during the summer was a source of all sorts of mysteries. Those Midol™ ads with the calendar that ballooned for five days a month. What was that about?

It was Charlie perfume that really captured my imagination. "There's a fragrance that's here to stay/And they call it Charlie!" The ads for Charlie involved a leggy blonde (the gorgeous Shelley Hack, who later became a Charlie's Angel, of course) striding with a lot of sass through the big city, laughing at everything and turning guys' heads. She was having an insane amount of fun. When she hopped on a boat in Paris, the captain gave her a hand, and the party was *on*. When she entered a night club in New York, a handsome guy gave her a spin, which was hilarious to her, and Bobby Short was at the piano, singing her song. All I wanted in the whole world was to be Shelley Hack. After my mother brought home some Charlie perfume, apparently wanting to be Shelley Hack too, I would sneak into her bathroom and have a Charlie moment. Once I tried to apply it the way Shelley Hack did it in the commercial (two full squirts three inches from a bared neck), and I was so Charlied up that I gave myself a headache.

The scent of Charlie is optional; it's the spirit of Charlie that inhabits our Metropole coat. If you wear it on a city street, dog walkers will give you their dogs. Busloads of tourists will take pictures of you, because they will think you are famous. You will find yourself striding into a night club like you own the joint, and the ghost of Bobby Short will look up from the piano, delighted to see you, and he'll sing you a song. Kind of fresh, kind of wow!

METROPOLE

by Mercedes Tarasovich-Clark

Five easy pieces make this coat a snap to knit.

SIZE
S (M, L, XL, XXL)

FINISHED MEASUREMENTS
Bust: 41 (45, 49, 53, 57)" (104 [114, 124.5, 134.5, 145]cm)

Length, shoulder to hem: 26 (27½, 28, 29½, 30)" (66 [70, 71, 75, 76]cm)

MATERIALS

- (5) bulky
- Brown Sheep Lamb's Pride Bulky, 85% wool, 15% mohair, 4 oz (113g), 125 yd (114m), 9 (11, 12, 14, 15) skeins Charcoal Heather (main color—MC), 1 skein each Oatmeal

(A), Wild Oak (B), and Chocolate Souffle (C)

- Size 13 (9mm) 26" (60mm) circular needle, or size needed to obtain gauge
- Tapestry needle
- Stitch holders
- Stitch markers
- Size L-11 (8mm) crochet hook
- Small amount fingering weight yarn or heavy thread to match main color
- Five 1⅛" (2.8cm) buttons

GAUGE
14 stitches and 24 rows = 4" (10cm) in linen stitch

DIFFICULTY
A sweet and easy project, but know that linen stitch is a bit slower to work than stockinette stitch.

PATTERN NOTES
Linen Stitch (worked over an odd number of stitches)

Row 1 (RS) k1 (selvedge stitch), *k1, slip 1 with yarn in front; repeat from * to last stitch, k1.

Row 2 (WS) p1 (selvedge stitch), *slip 1 with yarn in back, p1; repeat from * to last stitch, p1.

Repeat rows 1 and 2 for pattern.

STRIPE PATTERNS
Note: Carry colors not in use along the side edge of the work.

For Sleeves and Fold-Down Collar

2 rows A, 2 rows MC, 2 rows B, 2 rows MC, 2 rows C.

For Funnelneck Collar

2 rows C, 2 rows MC, 2 rows B, 2 rows MC, 2 rows A.

NOTES
Sizing is calculated to allow 4" to 6" (10cm to 15cm) of ease. Choose a size 4" to 6" (10cm to 15cm) larger than your actual bust measurement.

Work decreases at the edge of the work, as part of the selvedge: ssk on the right-hand edges, k2tog on the left-hand edges. It is very helpful to use safety pins or locking stitch markers to keep track of your increase and decrease rows, as it can be difficult to discern individual rows in linen stitch.

Work increases by using kfb just inside of the selvedge stitch.

As stitches are increased and decreased, the linen stitch pattern will not stay consistent on the edge. Remember that stitches knit/purled on the previous row will be slipped on the working row. Use this method to orient yourself as stitch counts change. Keep the first and last stitch of every row in stockinette stitch to establish the selvedge, and make these stitches as firm as possible to prevent flaring.

Back

Using MC and the cable cast-on method (see page 152), cast on 81 (87, 95, 101, 109) stitches.

Work even in linen stitch for 12 rows.

Shape Side Edges

Next row (RS) Decrease 1 stitch at each side edge—79 (85, 93, 99, 107) sts.

Decrease 1 stitch at each side edge every following 8th row 8 times more—63 (69, 77, 83, 91) sts.

Work even in linen stitch pattern as established until the piece measures 17 (18, 18, 19, 19)" (43 [46, 46, 48, 48]cm) from the cast-on edge, ending with a WS row.

Next row (RS) Increase 1 stitch at each side edge—65 (71, 79, 85, 93) sts.

Increase 1 stitch at each side edge every following 6th row 3 times more—71 (77, 85, 91, 99) sts.

Work even until the piece measures 23 (24½, 24½, 26, 26)" (58 [62.5, 62.5, 66, 66]cm) from the cast-on row, ending with a WS row.

Shape Armholes

Bind off 5 (5, 6, 6, 6) stitches at the beginning of the next 2 rows—61 (67, 73, 79, 87) sts.

Decrease 1 stitch at each side edge on every other row 6 (7, 0, 0, 0) times, and on every row 0 (0, 8, 10, 12) times—49 (53, 57, 59, 63) sts.

Work even until the piece measures 8 (8½, 9, 9½, 10)" (20 [21.5, 23, 24, 25.5]cm) from the armhole bind-off edge, ending with a WS row.

Shape Shoulders

Size M only Bind off 3 stitches at the beginning of the next 2 rows, then bind off 4 stitches at the beginning of the next 4 rows—31 sts.

All other sizes Bind off 3 (-, 4, 4, 4) stitches at the beginning of the next 6 rows.

All Sizes Place the remaining 31 (31, 33, 35, 39) stitches on a holder for the back neck.

Left Front

Using MC and the cable cast-on method, cast on 45 (48, 52, 55, 59) stitches.

Work even in linen stitch for 12 rows.

Shape Side Edge

Next row (RS) Decrease 1 stitch at the beginning of the row, work in pattern across—44 (47, 51, 54, 58) sts.

Decrease in this way, at the side edge only, on every 8th row 8 times more—36 (39, 43, 46, 50) sts.

Work even in linen stitch pattern as established until the piece measures 17 (18, 18, 19, 19)" (43 [46, 46, 48, 48]cm) from the cast-on edge, ending with a WS row.

Next row (RS) Increase 1 stitch at the beginning of the row—37 (40, 44, 47, 51) sts.

Increase 1 stitch at the side edge only

in this way on every following 6th row 3 times more—40 (43, 47, 50, 54) sts.

Work even until the piece measures 23 (24½, 24½, 26, 26)" (58 [62.5, 62.5, 66, 66]cm) from the cast-on row, ending with a WS row.

Shape Armhole

Next row (RS) Bind off 5 (5, 6, 6, 6) stitches, work in pattern across—35 (38, 41, 44, 48) sts.

Decrease 1 stitch at the armhole edge on every RS row 6 (7, 0, 0, 0) times, and on every row 0 (0, 8, 10, 12) times—29 (31, 33, 34, 36) sts.

Work even until the piece measures 7 (7½, 8, 8½, 9)" (18 [19, 20, 21.5, 23]cm) from the armhole bind-off, ending with a RS row.

Shape Neck and Shoulders

Next row (WS) Work 14 (14, 15, 16, 18) stitches in pattern, place these stitches on a holder for the neck, then continue in pattern to the end of the row—15 (17, 18, 18, 18) sts. Decrease 1 stitch at the neck edge only on every other RS row 6 times, AT THE SAME TIME, when the piece measures 8 (8½, 9, 9½, 10)" (20 [21.5, 23, 24, 25.5]cm) from the armhole bind-off edge, ending with a WS row, shape the shoulders as follows:

Size M only Bind off 3 stitches at the beginning of this RS row, then 4 stitches at the beginning of each of the next 2 RS rows.

All other sizes Bind off 3 (-, 4, 4, 4) stitches at the beginning of the next 3 RS rows.

Mark for Button Placement

Mark button placement beginning 4½" (11.5cm) from the top neck edge; below that, mark placement for 3 additional buttons spaced 6½" (16.5cm) apart. The fifth button will be incorporated into the collar.

The stripes take only a little yarn, so raid your Lamb's Pride leftovers. (Please don't embarrass yourself by pretending you don't have any.)

Right Front

Note As you work the Right Front, work buttonholes on the center front edge to match the button markers on the Left Front as follows:

Row 1 (RS) Work 3 stitches in pattern, bind off the next 3 stitches, and then work in pattern to end of row.

Row 2 (WS) Work in pattern to the 3 bound-off stitches on the previous row, cast on 3 stitches, then work last 3 stitches of the row.

Using MC and the cable cast-on method, cast on 45 (48, 52, 55, 59) stitches.

Work even in linen stitch for 12 rows.

Shape Side Edge

Next row (RS) Work in pattern across to last 2 stitches, decrease 1 stitch—44 (47, 51, 54, 58) sts.

Decrease in this way, at the side edge only, on every 8th row 8 times more—36 (39, 43, 46, 50) sts.

Work even in linen stitch pattern as established until the piece measures 17 (18, 18, 19, 19)" (43 [46, 46, 48, 48]cm) from the cast-on edge, ending with a WS row.

Next row (RS) Work in pattern across to last stitches, increase 1 stitch—37 (40, 44, 47, 51) sts.

Work an increase at the side edge only in this way on every following 6th row 3 times more—40 (43, 47, 50, 54) sts.

Work even until the piece measures 23 (24½, 24½, 26, 26)" (58 [62.5, 62.5, 66, 66]cm) from the cast-on row, ending with a RS row.

Shape Armhole

Next row (WS) Bind off 5 (5, 6, 6, 6) stitches, work in pattern across—35 (38, 41, 44, 48) sts.

Decrease 1 stitch at the armhole edge on every RS row 6 (7, 0, 0, 0) times, and on every row 0 (0, 8, 10, 12) times—29 (31, 33, 34, 36) sts.

Work even until the piece measures 7 (7½, 8, 8½, 9)" (18 [19, 20, 21.5, 23]cm) from the armhole bind-off, ending with a WS row.

Shape Neck and Shoulders

Next row (RS) On the next row, work 14 (14, 15, 16, 18) stitches in pattern, place these stitches on a holder for the neck, then continue in pattern to the end of the row—15 (17, 18, 18, 18) sts.

Next row (WS) Work even in pattern.

Next row (RS) Decrease 1 stitch at the neck edge only on every other RS row 6 times, AT THE SAME TIME, when the piece measures 8 (8½, 9, 9½, 10)" (20 [21.5, 23, 24, 25.5]cm) from the armhole bind-off edge, ending with a RS row, shape the shoulders as follows:

Size M only Bind off 3 stitches at the beginning of this row, then 4 stitches at the beginning of each of the next 2 WS rows.

All other sizes Bind off 3 (-, 4, 4, 4) stitches at the beginning of the next 3 WS rows.

Sleeve (make 2)

Using MC and the cable cast-on, cast on 39 (43, 45, 49, 53) stitches.

With RS facing, work even in linen stitch for 8 rows.

Using A, begin the stripe pattern, AT THE SAME TIME, decrease 1 stitch at each edge every 12th row twice—35 (39, 41, 45, 49) sts.

Work even until the piece measures 6 (6½, 7, 7, 7)" (15 [16.5, 18, 18, 18]cm) from the cast-on edge, ending with a WS row.

Increase row (RS) Increase one stitch at each side edge—37 (41, 43, 47, 51) sts.

Repeat the Increase Row every 6th row 10 times more—57 (61, 63, 67, 71) sts.

Work even until the piece measures 17 (18, 18½, 18½, 19)" (43 [46, 47, 47, 48]cm) from the cast-on edge, ending with a WS row.

Shape Sleeve Cap

Bind off 4 (4, 4, 5, 5) stitches at the beginning of the next 2 rows—49 (53, 55, 57, 61) sts.

Decrease 1 stitch at each side edge on every RS row 14 (14, 14, 15, 16) times—21 (25, 27, 27, 29) sts.

Work even until the piece measures 5½ (6, 6½, 7, 8)" (14 [15, 16.5, 18, 20]cm) from the armhole bind-off.

Bind off the remaining stitches.

Collar

Note Choose from two collar options: a funnelneck collar or a fold-down collar.

Sew shoulder seams.

With RS facing, place 14 (14, 15, 16, 18) stitches from the right front neck holder, 31 (31, 33, 35, 39) stitches from the back neck holder, and 14 (14, 15, 16, 18) stitches from the left front neck holder onto the needle.

Next row Join MC at the right front edge, work in pattern across the right front

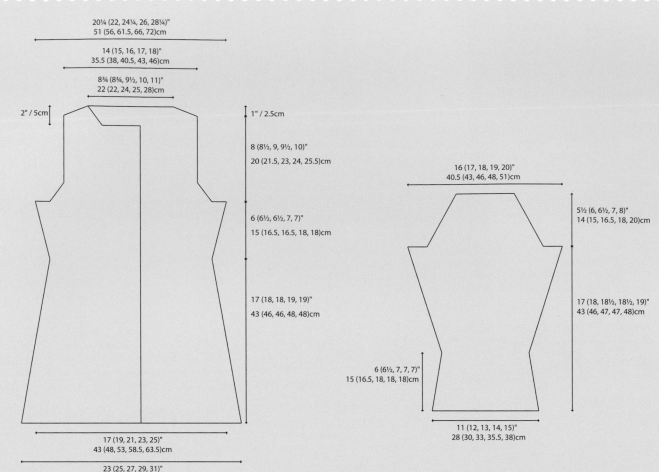

8¾ (8¾, 9½, 10, 11)"
22 (22, 24, 25, 28)cm

14 (15, 16, 17, 18)"
35.5 (38, 40.5, 43, 46)cm

20¼ (22, 24¼, 26, 28¼)"
51 (56, 61.5, 66, 72)cm

2" / 5cm

1" / 2.5cm

8 (8½, 9, 9½, 10)"
20 (21.5, 23, 24, 25.5)cm

6 (6½, 6½, 7, 7)"
15 (16.5, 16.5, 18, 18)cm

17 (18, 18, 19, 19)"
43 (46, 46, 48, 48)cm

17 (19, 21, 23, 25)"
43 (48, 53, 58.5, 63.5)cm

23 (25, 27, 29, 31)"
58.5 (63.5, 68.5, 73.5, 79)cm

16 (17, 18, 19, 20)"
40.5 (43, 46, 48, 51)cm

5½ (6, 6½, 7, 8)"
14 (15, 16.5, 18, 20)cm

17 (18, 18½, 18½, 19)"
43 (46, 47, 47, 48)cm

6 (6½, 7, 7, 7)"
15 (16.5, 18, 18, 18)cm

11 (12, 13, 14, 15)"
28 (30, 33, 35.5, 38)cm

neck stitches, pick up and knit 6 stitches along the shaped right front neck edge, work in pattern across the back neck stitches, pick up and knit 6 stitches along the shaped left front neck edge, work in pattern across the left front stitches—71 (71, 75, 79, 87) sts.

For Funnelneck Collar

Work even for 5 more rows.

With RS of collar facing and using C, work the collar stripe pattern, AT THE SAME TIME, when the piece measures approximately 6½" (16.5cm) from the topmost buttonhole, work the fifth buttonhole as follows:

Row 1 (WS) Work to last 6 stitches in pattern, bind off the next 3 stitches, then work in pattern to end of row.
Row 2 (RS) Work in pattern to the 3

bound-off stitches on the previous row, cast on 3 stitches, then work in pattern to the end of the row.

Using MC, work 4 rows of MC after the last color. A full repeat of the stripe pattern has been worked. Bind off.

For Fold-Down Collar

After following pick-up instructions, work the next row as a RS stripe pattern row to reverse the stripe pattern to the "inside" of the collar. Reversing the stripe pattern will make it show on the RS of the coat when folded down.

Work even for 3 more rows.

With inside of collar facing and using A, work the collar stripe pattern. AT THE SAME TIME, when the piece measures approximately 6½" (16.5cm) from the topmost buttonhole

work the fifth buttonhole as follows:

Row 1 (RS) Work to last 6 stitches in pattern, bind off the next 3 stitches, then work in pattern to end of row.
Row 2 (WS) Work in pattern to the 3 bound-off stitches on the previous row, cast on 3 stitches, then work in pattern to the end of the row.

Using MC, work 4 rows of MC after the last color. A full repeat of the stripe pattern has been worked. Bind off.

Finishing

Sew the sleeve and side seams. Weave in ends. With crochet hook and MC, work 1 row of single crochet along the front edges, keeping the crochet gauge firm to prevent the front edges from flaring. Sew the buttons in place where marked, using thinner yarn or thread. Block to final measurements.

A Coat for Every Fabulous Day

Bonne Marie Burns's chicknits.net was one of the first knitting blogs we discovered, back when knitting had just hit us like dengue fever. Her designs are always classic, always beautiful—pieces that flatter all sorts of women. She has a knack for matching the right yarn with the perfect garment. Every Chic Knits design includes dressmaker details, and tailoring that is rare to find in handknit designs. So you can see why we might (instantly) think of Bonne Marie in our quest for the great knitted coat.

#032

Our favorite thing in the whole wide world is a simple stitch pattern used to great effect. Knits and purls combine to give texture to this classic silhouette.

YANK

By Bonne Marie Burns

Nobody knows exactly how the peacoat got its name. Could it have been from the Dutch or Frisian word *pij*, a sturdy fabric from the 1700s? Could we be Googling a bit too much? Most people agree that the peacoat doesn't have much to do with peas, but we think a peacoat is a snappy, kicky little number to have at the ready.

We like it in pea green, but you are obviously free to make it in the original navy, or orange, or the brightest red you can find. This is a coat you can wear all the time, whether you're crossing the Chesapeake in your sloop or navigating the aisles at the grocery store.

SIZE
S (M, L, XL)

FINISHED MEASUREMENTS
Bust: 34 (38, 42, 46)" (86.5 [96.5, 107, 117]cm)

Length: 29 (30, 30, 31)" (73.5 [76, 76, 79]cm)

MATERIALS
- (4) medium/worsted
- 10 (10, 11, 12) skeins Cascade Pastaza, 50% llama, 50% wool, 3½ oz (100g), 132 yd (120m), in pea green
- Size 8 (5mm) needles, or size needed to obtain gauge
- Size 9 (5.5mm) needles, or size needed to obtain gauge
- Safety pins or unlocking stitch markers
- Eight 1⅛" (3cm) buttons
- 1 coat hook and eye
- Tapestry needle

GAUGE
16 stitches and 22 rows = 4" (10cm) over texture pattern using larger needles

DIFFICULTY
Plenty to keep you engaged as you navigate this double-breasted peacoat. But nothing to make you jump overboard.

Back

With smaller needles, cast on 70 (78, 85, 94) stitches.

Next row (WS) p1, knit to last stitch, p1.

Texture Pattern

Row 1 (RS) k1 (2, 1, 1); *p2, k1; repeat from * across to last 0 (1, 0, 0) stitches; k0 (1, 0, 0).
Row 2 (WS) Purl.

Repeat the last 2 rows once more, then change to the larger needles.

Continue in texture pattern as established for 32 (36, 36, 38) rows.

Side Shaping

Note To maintain the texture pattern throughout, make decreases as indicated below.

Decrease Row (RS) k1, k2tog (or p2tog as needed to maintain texture pattern); work in texture pattern as established to last 3 stitches, ssk (or ssp as needed to maintain texture pattern), k1—68 (76, 83, 92) sts.

Continue as established, repeating Decrease Row every 8 rows 4 times more—60 (68, 75, 84) sts.

Work 5 rows even.

Increase Row (RS) k1, m1, work in texture pattern to last stitch, m1, k1—62 (70, 77, 86) sts.

Work the increased stitches into texture pattern, repeating Increase Row every 8 rows 4 times more—70 (78, 85, 94) sts.

Work even until the piece measures 19¾ (20, 20, 20½)" (50 [50.5, 50.5, 52]cm), ending with a WS row.

Armhole Shaping

Bind off 4 (4, 4, 5) stitches at the beginning of the next 2 rows—62 (70, 77, 84) sts.

Decrease Row (RS) k2, k2tog (or p2tog), work in texture pattern to last 4 stitches, ssk (or ssp), k2—60 (68, 75, 82) sts.

Repeat the Decrease Row every 2 rows 3 (3, 5, 5) times more—54 (62, 65, 72) sts.

Work even until the piece measures 28 (29, 29, 30)" (71 [73.5, 73.5, 76]cm) from the beginning, ending with a WS row.

Bind off 5 (6, 6, 7) stitches at the beginning of the next 6 (6, 4, 6) rows, then 0 (0, 7, 0) stitches at the beginning of the next 2 rows—24 (26, 27, 30) sts.

Bind off the remaining stitches.

Left Front

With smaller needles, cast on 26 (30, 34, 38) stitches.

Row 1 (WS) p1, knit to last stitch, p1.

Texture Pattern

Row 1 (RS) k2 (1, 1, 2), p0 (1, 0, 0), k0 (1, 0, 0); *p2, k1; repeat from * across.
Row 2 (WS) Purl.

Repeat the last 2 rows once more, then change to the larger needles.

Continue in texture pattern for 32 (36, 36, 38) rows.

Side Shaping

Decrease Row (RS) k1, k2tog (or p2tog), work in texture pattern as established—25 (29, 33, 37) sts.

Continue in texture pattern as established and repeat Decrease Row every 8 rows 4 times more—21 (25, 29, 33) sts.

Work 5 rows even.

Increase Row (RS) k1, m1, work across in texture pattern as established—22 (26, 30, 34) sts.

Work the increased stitches into texture pattern and repeat Increase Row every 8 rows 4 times more—26 (30, 34, 38) sts.

Work even until the Left Front measures

Aw c'mon, when's the last time you made something with a back belt detail?

19¾ (20, 20, 20½)" (50 [51, 51, 52]cm), ending with a WS row.

Armhole Shaping

Bind off 4 (4, 4, 5) stitches at the beginning of next row—22 (26, 30, 33) sts. Work 1 row even.

Decrease Row (RS) k2, k2tog (or p2tog), work across in texture pattern as established—21 (25, 29, 32) sts.

Repeat Decrease Row on every other row 3 (3, 5, 5) times more—18 (22, 24, 27) sts.

Continue in texture pattern as established until the Left Front measures 26 (27, 27, 27½)" (66 [68.5, 68.5, 70]cm) from the cast-on edge, ending with a WS row.

Neckline Shaping

Decrease Row (RS) Work in texture pattern to last 4 stitches, ssk, k2—17 (21, 23, 26) sts.

Decrease 1 stitch (ssk on RS; ssp on WS) at neck edge only on every row 2 (3, 4, 5) times—15 (18, 19, 21) sts.

Work even until the Left Front measures 28 (29, 29, 30)" (71 [73.5, 73.5, 76]cm), ending with a WS row.

Bind off 5 (6, 6, 7) stitches at the armhole edge on the next 2 RS rows, then 5 (6, 7, 7) stitches on the next RS row.

Right Front

Work as for the Left Front until Side Shaping.

Side Shaping

Decrease Row (RS) Work in texture pattern to last 3 stitches, ssk (or ssp), k1—25 (29, 33, 37) sts.

Continue in texture pattern as established and repeat Decrease Row every 8 rows 4 times more—21 (25, 29, 33) sts.

Work 5 rows even.

Increase Row (RS) Work in pattern to last stitch, m1, k1—22 (26, 30, 34) sts.

Work the increased stitches into the texture pattern and repeat Increase Row every 8 rows 4 times more—26 (30, 34, 38) sts.

Work even until the Right Front measures 19¾ (20, 20, 20½)" (50 [51, 51, 52]cm), ending with a RS row.

Armhole Shaping

Bind off 4 (4, 4, 5) stitches at the beginning of the next row—22 (26, 30, 33) sts.

Decrease Row (RS) Work across in texture pattern as established to last 3 stitches, ssk (or ssp), k1—21 (25, 29, 32) sts.

Repeat the decrease row on every other row 3 (3, 5, 5) times more—18 (22, 24, 27) sts.

Continue in texture pattern as established until the Right Front measures 26 (27, 27, 27½)" (66 [68.5, 68.5, 70]cm) from the cast-on edge, ending with a WS row.

Neckline Shaping

Decrease Row (RS) k2, k2tog, work in pattern to end—17 (21, 23, 26) sts.

Decrease 1 stitch (k2tog on RS; p2tog on WS) at the neck edge only on every row 2 (3, 4, 5) times—15 (18, 19, 21) sts.

Work even until the Right Front measures 28 (29, 29, 30)" (71 [73.5, 73.5, 76]cm), ending with a RS row.

Bind off 5 (6, 6, 7) stitches at the armhole edge on the next 2 WS rows, then 5 (6, 7, 7) stitches on the next WS row.

Sleeve (make 2)

With smaller needles, cast on 40 (43, 43, 46) stitches.

Next Row (WS) p1, knit across to last st, p1.

Texture Pattern

Row 1 (RS) k1, *p2, k1; repeat from * across.
Row 2 (WS) Purl.

Repeat these 2 rows once then change to the larger needles.

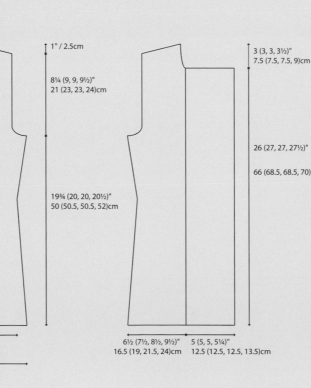

6 (6½, 6¾, 7½)"
15 (16.5, 17, 19)cm

1" / 2.5cm

8¼ (9, 9, 9½)"
21 (23, 23, 24)cm

3 (3, 3, 3½)"
7.5 (7.5, 7.5, 9)cm

26 (27, 27, 27½)"
66 (68.5, 68.5, 70)cm

19¾ (20, 20, 20½)"
50 (50.5, 50.5, 52)cm

15 (17, 18¾, 21)"
38 (43, 47.5, 53)cm

17 (19, 21, 23)"
43 (48, 53, 58)cm

6½ (7½, 8½, 9½)"
16.5 (19, 21.5, 24)cm

5 (5, 5, 5¼)"
12.5 (12.5, 12.5, 13.5)cm

Increase Row (RS) k1, m1, work in texture pattern to last stitch, m1, k1—42 (45, 45, 48) sts.

Work the increased stitches into texture pattern, repeating Increase Row every 8 rows 6 (6, 6, 4) times, then every 10 rows 4 (4, 4, 6) times—62 (65, 65, 68) sts.

Work even until the sleeve measures 18 (19, 19, 19½)" (45.5 [48, 48, 49.5]cm), ending with a WS row.

Bind off 4 (4, 4, 5) stitches at the beginning of the next 2 rows—54 (57, 57, 58) sts.

Decrease Row (RS) k1, k2tog (or p2tog); work across to last 3 stitches; ssk (or ssp); k1—52 (55, 55, 56) sts.

Repeat the Decrease Row on each of the next 2 (2, 2, 0) rows—48 (51, 51, 56) sts. Then decrease on every RS row 11 (5, 5, 5) times—26 (41, 41, 46) sts. Decrease every other RS row 0 (1, 1, 1) times—26 (39, 39, 44) sts—and every RS row 0 (5, 5, 7) times—26 (29, 29, 30) sts.

Bind off 2 stitches at the beginning of the next 2 rows, then bind off 3 stitches at the beginning of the next 2 rows—16 (19, 19, 20) sts.

Bind off the remaining stitches.

Finishing

Left Front Band

With RS facing and using the smaller needles, pick up and knit 110 (114, 114, 118) stitches along the Left Front edge.

Next row (WS) p1, *p2, k2; repeat from * across to last stitch, k1.

Next row Slip 1 stitch purlwise, *p2, k2; repeat from * across to last stitch, k1.

Repeat the last row until the Left Front Band measures 5 (5, 5, 5¼)" (12.5 [12.5, 12.5, 13.5]cm), ending with a RS row. Bind off all stitches knitwise.

Right Front Band

Work as for the Left Front Band until it measures 3½ (3½, 3½, 3¾)" (9 [9, 9, 9.5]cm) ending with a WS row.

Mark positions for 3 buttonholes, with the first buttonhole 6½ (7, 7, 7½)" (16.5 [18, 18, 19]cm) from the neck edge; then 2 more buttonholes below that one, each 4½ (4¾, 4¾, 5)" (11.5 [12, 12, 12.5]cm) apart. Count the number of ribs between all to check for even spacing, and position the buttonhole to span 2 knit stitches or 2 purl stitches. Check for fit: One buttonhole should hit at mid-chest; one at the waist; and the last at jeans pocket-top level. Adjust placement if necessary.

Buttonhole Row (RS) Work in pattern for 6½ (7, 7, 7½)" (16.5 [18, 18, 19]cm); *Work 2-stitch buttonhole: With yarn in front, slip next stitch. Yarn back; slip second stitch. Drop yarn. Pass the first slipped stitch over the second slipped stitch. Slip another stitch and pass the previous slipped stitch over it. Pass the last slipped stitch back to the left needle. Turn work. With yarn in back, cable cast on 2 stitches. Cast on 1 more stitch, but bring yarn to the front between this extra stitch and the last buttonhole stitch before placing the extra stitch on the left needle. Turn work. Slip a stitch from the left needle, pass the extra stitch over the slipped stitch and tighten the extra stitch firmly. Repeat from * every 4½ (4¾, 4¾, 5)" (11.5 [12, 12, 12.5]cm) or as marked twice more.

Work even until the Right Front Band measures 5 (5, 5, 5¼)" (12.5 [12.5, 12.5, 13.5]cm), ending with a RS row.

Bind off all stitches knitwise.

Collar

With larger needles, cast on 76 (80, 80, 84) stitches. Change to smaller needles.

Next row (WS) p3, *k2, p2; repeat from * across to last stitch, p1.

Row 1 (RS) Slip 1 stitch purlwise, *k2, p2; repeat from * across to last 3 stitches, k3.
Row 2 (WS) Slip 1 stitch purlwise, *p2, k2; repeat from * across to last 3 stitches, p3.

Repeat the last 2 rows until the Collar measures 2¾ (3, 3, 3¼)" (7 [7.5, 7.5, 8]cm), ending with a WS row.

Decrease Row (RS) k2, ssk, work in pattern to last 4 stitches, k2tog, k2.

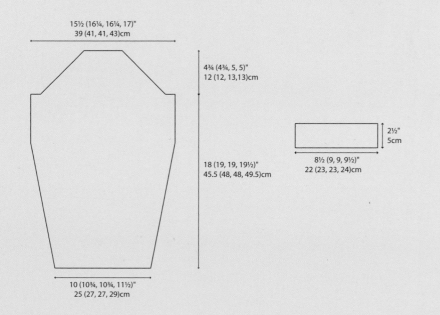

15½ (16¼, 16¼, 17)"
39 (41, 41, 43)cm

4¾ (4¾, 5, 5)"
12 (12, 13,13)cm

18 (19, 19, 19½)"
45.5 (48, 48, 49.5)cm

10 (10¾, 10¾, 11½)"
25 (27, 27, 29)cm

8½ (9, 9, 9½)"
22 (23, 23, 24)cm

2½"
5cm

The subtle, heathered yarn makes the coat visually rich.

With larger needles, cast on 10 stitches.

Row 1 (WS) p1, knit across to last stitch, p1.

Row 2 (RS) Slip 1 purlwise, k1, (p2, k2) twice.

Row 3 (WS) Slip 1 purlwise, purl to the end.

Repeat rows 2 and 3 until the piece measures 8½ (9, 9, 9½)" (21.5 [23, 23, 24]cm) from the cast-on edge, ending with a RS row.

Bind off all stitches knitwise.

Assembly

Block all pieces. Steam the Front Bands and Collar so the ribbing lies flat. Seam the shoulders and sides.

Sew 3 buttons on each Band, positioning the center of each button 1" (2.5cm) from the pick-up edge of the band, with 3 on the Right Front, adjacent to the buttonholes, and 3 on the Left Front. Attach the hook and eye fastener with the hook flush with the Left Front edge at the waistline and the eye at the pick-up edge on the wrong side of the Right Front at the waistline.

Sew the sleeve seams and attach to body.

Attach Collar

Mark the center points of the Front Bands at the neckline edge. Using a yarn needle slip stitch the Collar to the Body, with the WS of the Collar facing the RS of the Body as follows: starting at Right Front, match the first angled edge to the Right Front band area; then the bound-off edge of the Collar to the Body neckline; then the second angled edge to the Left Front band area.

Sew one button on each end of the Belt, 1" (2.5cm) from each short edge. Position the Belt at the center Back at waist level and sew in place.

Weave in ends.

Next row and all WS rows Work stitches as they appear (knit the knit stitches, purl the purl stitches) across.

Repeat Decrease Row on every RS row 3 times more—74 (78, 78, 82) sts.

Next row (WS) p2, p2tog, work in pattern to last 4 stitches, ssp, p2—72 (76, 76, 80) sts.

Next row (RS) k2, ssk, work in pattern to last 4 stitches, k2tog, k2—70 (74, 74, 78) sts.

Next row (WS) p2, p2tog, work in pattern to last 4 stitches, ssp, p2—68 (72, 72, 76) sts.

Bind off all stitches knitwise.

The Independent Knitter, or Where Have You Gone, Elizabeth Zimmermann?

Kay ✳ My fellow knitters, brothers and sisters, gather round. I have something to say that you need to hear. I am fond of telling people, particularly people with advanced degrees, that it takes serious IQ to be a knitter. That there are no stupid knitters. Knitting, even fairly straightforward, bone-simple knitting, presents intellectual problems. Knitting forgives imperfection, but it does not forgive imprecision. Make a mistake in your knitting, and it'll be there, staring at you coolly, every time you look at it. So knitters routinely solve the problems of knitting by thinking them through, and by understanding what they're doing. Over long rows, they ponder the deep mysteries of the relationship between the Right Side and the Wrong Side. An eight-year-old child who knows how to knit can look at the Wrong Side and tell you what stitches were made on the Right Side, where the increases and decreases are, and what kind. If you have an eight-year-old child who knows how to knit, do not worry about this kid's SATs.

Smart as we are, you would think that knitters would relish figuring things out for themselves. And some do. Some famously do. Look at Elizabeth Zimmermann, who constantly set herself problems and puzzles and solved them all, showing us her work and encouraging us to do the same. Look at Lucy Neatby, who had the audacity to think of a new way to bind off. But most knitters, particularly experienced knitters, want a pattern to tell them exactly how to do every stitch, like a driver who gets so dependent on the GPS voice that she doesn't remember how to get to the grocery store anymore.

I remember, as a sophomore knitter, working my way through my third or fourth Rowan pattern. A Rowan pattern does not leave a lot to chance. But as I gained skill, I was learning surprising facts, such as (get this): Did you know that "knit 2 together," the Mother Decrease, is not the only way to decrease one stitch? People! This blew my mind! As soon as I learned that you could make a decrease lean to the right *or* you could make it lean to the left, something weird happened in a perfectionist, prissy corner of my psyche. I wanted to decrease the *right* way. I was mad when a pattern just said, "decrease one stitch." I was incensed! Which way was I supposed to decrease? Which decrease would optimize the theoretical perfection of this garment? And why were they holding out on me?

It hasn't always been this way. Not that long ago, knitting patterns were pretty sketchy. This sort of thing: "Cast on a goodly amount of stitches in worsted sheepsdown. Work fancy pier-glass pattern dec armscye BO in patt and make up." Knitters learned the basic recipe, then, by necessity, they used their powerful brains to adjust the pattern to fit the body it needed to fit, and to think of stitch patterns to improve the garment, or to entertain themselves as they sat on the rocks knitting. That's how they knit in the Old Days. On rocks. Wearing black dresses. (I was born too late, I tell you.) All the cool little tricks, artistic embellishments (like cables and Fair Isle), and architectural innovations (like turned heels on socks, and steeks) came straight out of the brains of early knitters, who may well have been illiterate.

But they were whip smart.

So the message of this sermonette is this: As a knitter, your handiest tool is not the Chibi needle case—it's your head. The next time a pattern doesn't spell out a detail, ask yourself: What are the alternatives? Usually there will be only one or two. Try one way, then the other. Which way makes the most sense? And if you can't tell the difference between the two ways? Then it doesn't matter. Knit to the next problem.

When in Doubt, Knit It Upside Down

Kay ✳ Ann Buechner is our friend who is most likely to knit patterns upside down just to see what they look like. She discovered that the Bleeding Hearts lace pattern from Barbara Walker's *Third Treasury of Knitting Patterns*, when oriented upside down, looks like leaves.

The main purpose of this vaguely Victorian reticule is to give you an excuse to buy a pair of the cool handles that are for sale at what the English call haberdasheries and we Americans, in our plodding way, call "shops that sell buttons and bag hardware."

A lacy handbag is the tops in self-decoration. It is strictly for fun. Fun and a cell phone.

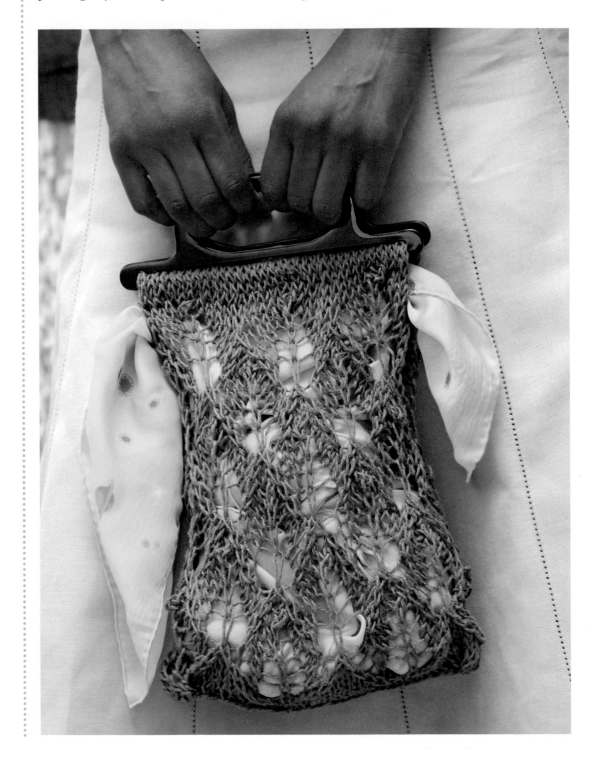

LEAFY RETICULE

by Ann Hahn Buechner

SIZE
9" (23cm) wide and 10" (25cm) high

MATERIALS
-  light/DK
- 1 skein Lanaknits allhemp6, 100% hemp, 3½ oz (100g), 165 yd (150m), in avocado
- Size 10 (6mm) 20" (50cm) circular needle
- Stitch marker
- Tapestry needle
- 7½" (19cm) handles (Lucite Purse Handles from Lacis.com), or knit a garter stitch strap as for the Monteagle Bag (page 131)

GAUGE
14 stitches and 20 rows = 4" (10cm) in stockinette stitch

DIFFICULTY
A tasty first lace project.

NOTE
Because of the stretchiness of this pattern stitch, the gauge is a fluid thing. It is not necessary to get the exact gauge if you like the fabric of your lace. The bag will grow if filled with hefty items.

Bag Body

Loosely cast on 72 stitches and join in the round, taking care not to twist the stitches. Place a marker for the beginning of the round.

Rounds 1–3 Knit.
Round 4 (yo, ssk, k7, k2tog, yo, k1) 6 times.
Round 5 (yo, k1, ssk, k5, k2tog, k1, yo, k1) 6 times.
Round 6 (yo, k2, ssk, k3, k2tog, k2, yo, k1) 6 times.
Round 7 (yo, k3, ssk, k1, k2tog, k3, yo, k1) 6 times.
Round 8 (yo, k4, slip 2 stitches together as if to knit, k1, pass both slipped

stitches together over the knit stitch, k4, yo, k1) 6 times.
Round 9 (k3, k2tog, yo, k1, yo, ssk, k4) 6 times.
Round 10 (k2, k2tog, k1, yo, k1, yo, k1, ssk, k3) 6 times.
Round 11 (k1, k2tog, k2, yo, k1, yo, k2, ssk, k2) 6 times.
Round 12 (k2tog, k3, yo, k1, yo, k3, ssk, k1) 6 times.
Round 13 Remove the marker, slip the first stitch of the round to the right needle, and place the marker, (k4, yo, k1, yo, k4, slip 2 stitches together as if to knit, k1, pass both slipped stitches together over the knit stitch) 6 times.

Repeat rounds 4–13 twice more.

Next round Knit.

Top Edges

On the next round, k36 and turn, putting the remaining stitches on a holder. Beginning with a WS (purl) row, work 5 rows of stockinette stitch. Bind off on the next row. Rejoin the yarn and work the remaining 36 stitches in the same way.

Finishing

Sew the bottom seam. Attach the handles with a dense whip stitch. Fill the bag with something heavy and hang it up to stretch out the stitches so the pattern will show.

Can you believe this tangly, beautiful stitch is the result of the basic food groups of knitting: knit, purl, ssk, yo, k2tog?

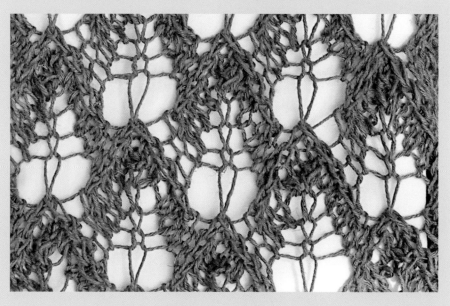

Once you've felted Flapotis, the stitches blur, and the whole thing looks like crushed velvet. This continues to amaze us.

A Glimpse of Something Special

Kay ✳ This scarf was inspired by an elegant woman in a coffee shop, whose silk wrap had a velvet trim that fluttered as she took off her coat. An idea for a flappy scarf leapt into my brain and refused to leave until I knitted it up.

The name is an affectionate homage to Kate Gilbert's celebrated Clapotis wrap. I would bet the farm (if I had one) that Clapotis is the undisputed number-one most-knitted pattern ever published on knitty.com, the free online knitting magazine. (If you haven't made it at least once, I worry for you. Are you feeling OK?) I am under no illusions that our *petit* Flapotis shares its namesake's *je ne sais quoi*, but it is loaded with *joie de vivre. Mes amies*, we must never underestimate the allure of a neck swaddled in crushed velvet flaps.

FLAPOTIS

SIZE
Approximately 80" x 7" (204cm x 18cm) before felting

MATERIALS
- ▣ medium/worsted
- 7 balls Muench Touch Me, 72% Viscose, 28% wool, 1¾ oz (50g), 61 yd (55m), shown in light gray, cornflower blue, redwood, and wine
- Size 7 (4.5mm) needles, or size needed to obtain gauge
- Tapestry needle
- Zippered pillow cover for felting

GAUGE
18 stitches and 19 rows = 4" (10cm) in stockinette stitch before felting

DIFFICULTY
You have to pay attention to the flaps, but the pattern is easily memorized and makes excellent TV or travel knitting. Any wonky bits melt away when you gently felt the piece after knitting.

Flaps
Cast on 7 stitches.

First Flap

Row 1 k1, *p1, k1; repeat from * across.

This row establishes the seed stitch pattern.

Repeat this row 11 times more. Cut the yarn, leaving the stitches on the needle.

Second Flap

Cast 7 stitches onto the needle that is holding the first flap. Repeat instructions for First Flap to make a second flap, leaving the stitches on the needle; do not cut the yarn.

Join Flaps

With RS of the completed flaps facing, work 7 stitches of Second Flap in seed stitch as established. Using the knitted cast-on method (page 152), cast on 1

stitch, then work the 7 stitches of First Flap in seed stitch—15 sts.

Body
Row 1 With WS facing and using the knitted cast-on method, cast on 8 stitches. With WS still facing, work 11 stitches in seed stitch, p9, work 3 stitches in seed stitch.

Row 2 With RS facing and using the knitted cast-on method, cast on 8 stitches. With RS still facing, work

Insouciant, nonchalant floppiness.

11 stitches in seed stitch, k9, work 11 stitches in seed stitch.

Row 3 (WS) Work 11 stitches in seed stitch, p9, work 11 stitches in seed stitch.

Row 4 (RS) Work 11 stitches in seed stitch, k9, work 11 stitches in seed stitch.

Rows 5–12 Repeat rows 3 and 4 four times more.

Row 13 (WS) Bind off 8 stitches in seed stitch, p1, k1, p9, work 11 stitches in seed stitch—23 sts.

Row 14 (RS) Bind off 8 stitches in seed stitch, p1, k1, p9 (note: you really do purl 9 here, because at this point you are changing from stockinette stitch to reverse stockinette stitch for the next flap section), work 3 stitches in seed stitch—15 sts.

Row 15 With WS facing and using the knitted cast-on method, cast on 8 stitches. With WS still facing, work 11 stitches in seed stitch, k9, work 3 stitches in seed stitch.

Row 16 With RS facing and using the knitted cast-on method, cast on 8 stitches. With RS still facing, work 11 stitches in seed stitch, p9, work 11 stitches in seed stitch.

Row 17 (WS) Work 11 stitches in seed stitch, k9, work 11 stitches in seed stitch.

Row 18 (RS) Work 11 stitches in seed stitch, p9, work 11 stitches in seed stitch.

Rows 19–24 Repeat rows 17 and 18 four times more.

Row 25 (WS) Bind off 8 stitches in seed stitch, p1, k1, k9, work 11 stitches in seed stitch.

Row 26 (RS) Bind off 8 stitches in seed stitch, p1, k1, k9 (note: once again you are changing stitch pattern, this time from reverse stockinette to stockinette stitch), work 3 stitches in seed stitch.

Repeat rows 1–26 until you have 28 flaps along each vertical edge, then repeat rows 1–13 once more—23 sts.

End Flaps

Next row (RS) Bind off 8 stitches in seed stitch. Work 7 stitches in seed stitch. Turn work, leaving remaining stitches on a holder and working these 7 stitches only.

Work 11 rows in seed stitch. Bind off in seed stitch.

Rejoin yarn to remaining stitches. With RS facing, bind off 1 stitch, work remaining 7 stitches in seed stitch.

If we had Touch-o-vision, you could feel the softness of this scarf.

Work 11 rows in seed stitch. Bind off in seed stitch.

Weave in ends.

Finishing

You have finished knitting the scarf, but the scarf is not yet finished. Touch Me is a special yarn. Its hidden core of wool is covered in a fuzzy chenille made of rayon (a man-made fiber cooked up from wood pulp) and microfiber. While

Touch Me is lovely straight off the ball, the knitted fabric achieves a whole new level of lushness when you take the extra step of gently felting it. After a warm wash, a short turn in the dryer, and an overnight rest on a flat surface, your scarf will have a beautiful crushed-velvet appearance, a zingy drape, and nuanced color. Follow these simple instructions for a stunning effect:

Place the scarf in a zippered pillow cover to protect it. Wash it in a washing machine on the gentle cycle with a warm temperature setting. Use a small amount of your regular detergent, and place a few lint-free items such as T-shirts in the load. Run the complete wash program, including the spin cycle. Place the scarf, still in its zippered case, in the dryer, and run it on a warm (not the hottest, for "cotton" or "sturdy" fabrics) setting for approximately 30 minutes. Remove the scarf from the dryer when it is still damp. Spread the scarf on a blocking board or other flat surface. With your fingers, press the edges of all the flaps to straighten them. (This is tedious but deeply satisfying.) Allow the scarf to air dry. You will notice that the scarf has decreased quite a bit in length, but not much in width. In the washing process, the wool core of the yarn shrinks, but the rayon microfiber wrapped around the outside of the yarn does not shrink, so it has to squish up. This is what creates the scarf's shimmering surface.

If you substitute another yarn for Touch Me, do not follow this felting procedure. You may also want to knit your scarf a bit shorter, since you will not need to allow for shrinkage. Flapotis would look divine in a self-striping yarn such as Noro Silk Garden.

Now tell me this doesn't look better than a sweatshirt. Seriously, y'all.

Your First Top-Down Knitting Project

Kay ✳ If there's a chill in the air, and I'm particularly low on ideas, I will wear a baggy sweatshirt. You know what I'm talking about. You probably have one. It may or may not have the name of a professional sports team on it. The government should require a license to wear something that looks so bad on most women: the thick fabric, the band at the bottom that pulls the hem in and makes even a slim-waisted woman look like a baked potato, the crew neck that does not flatter one single attribute of the female form. We should vow that we will never wear them again. Not even if the Red Sox [insert your team here] win the World Series [insert championship event here] again. Wear a hat. A pin. A giant foam finger. Anything but a sweatshirt.

During an existential crisis about my sweatshirts, I remembered that I am a knitter. As a knitter, I know how to do decreases and increases that shape a garment and flatter the form. It occurred to me that instead of fleecy abominations, I should have a stack of easy-going, everyday sweaters. These sweaters should be fun to knit, and they should really, really fit. The easiest way to ensure that a sweater will really, really fit is to knit it from the top down.

EASE IS NOT EASY

In this pattern, we give you the finished measurements of the sweater, provided you knit to the specified gauge. How do you know which size to knit? You start with your own chest measurement, taking the tape measure at the level of your underarm. Then, unless you want a skin-tight fit like Miss Pamela Anderson, you will want to add some ease. Standard ease is to add 2" (5cm) to actual measurements, for a not loose, not snug, comfy fit. Four inches (10cm) gives a sporty, casual amount of ease, and you want to add another inch if you are going to be wearing the sweater over another garment.

Some people, and we're not naming names, will go to their graves without ever measuring themselves. They just don't want to. The feeling of a tape measure under the armpits gives them bad bridesmaid flashbacks. Here's a trick if you don't want to take your measurements: take a sweater out of your closet that fits the way you would like your new sweater to fit. Lay it flat, without stretching, and measure it carefully. This measurement has the ease built right in. Consult the sizing on the pattern, and knit the size that comes closest.

How to Overcome Gravity and Look Great, Too!

Like most knitters, I knit my first sweaters in pieces. Each piece started at the bottom edge—be it a sleeve, a front, or a back—or hell, be it a collar. The rule was: start at the bottom, make all the pieces, sew them together, and (this is the scary part) try it on. You discover whether the garment actually fits only after you have knit the whole thing and sewn it up—when it's too late to fix anything without a lot of ripping and cussing.

It never occurred to me to question why we knit sweaters this way. The pattern said to make it this way, so I did. I was often disappointed, even when my measurements of my gauge, myself, and the flat pieces were right. Usually, the culprit was gravity. A sleeve would be exactly the same length as my shoulder-to-wrist measurement when laying flat, but it grew a lot when it was hanging from the shoulder seam and lengthening from its own weight. Gravity's effects could be compounded if the shoulders of the sweater were even an inch too wide—because that inch would hang over onto my arm, lengthening the sleeve even further.

I know some smart knitters, and a few of them kept nudging me gently toward trying top-down knitting. One such pal, a cool customer not prone to hyperbole, told me that now that she knew top-down, she would never knit another sweater from the bottom up again. I absorbed that statement with the appropriate awe. I read Elizabeth Zimmermann and Barbara Walker's wise words on knitting from the top. But I kept falling in love with sweaters in magazines, and I kept casting them on at the bottom edge. Next time I'll figure out how to knit this thing top-down, I told myself. Next time. How hard can it be?

It takes a cute pattern to make me cast on. If the picture is cute, I don't care if I have to learn how to cast on under water; all I want to know is, where are my goggles?

In the end, it was cuteness that finally got me to knit something top down. Something very small. Something called a One-Skein Wonder, designed by Stefanie Japel, who is something of a top-down prodigy. Stefanie understands top-down knitting on a very deep level. The One-Skein Wonder, designed for women, is a teeny raglan shrug that starts at the neck and ends before exiting the armpit. It's not a great look for a matronly physique (such as mine), but I had this idea that an even teenier version was just the thing to knit, in a couple of hours, for all the little girls in my life. It's so simple, yet because it's three-dimensional (the opposite of how I had come to understand sweater construction) it's mind-blowing. Along the way, you find little moments of surprise that suddenly make sense when you try it on.

Just Try It On, Will Ya?

When you are knitting top-down, you can try your sweater on *any time you want to*. By trying it on, you can make amazing discoveries—maybe you're skinnier between the bust and the waist shaping than you were giving yourself credit for. You can adjust the fit on the spot, often without ripping. You can simply say, whoopsy, it's a little big under the maracas, I should decrease a few stitches away over the next inch of knitting. It is so refreshing to try on a sleeve, allow gravity to do its worst, observe that the sleeve is only a quarter inch away from being the right length, and bind the thing off. It's a feeling of competence. It's a feeling of not wasting your time knitting a sweater that has some minor fit flaw that you say you don't mind, but you do mind, or that you say you are going to fix, but you're not going to fix because you're already knitting the next thing.

If you are interested in top-down knitting, the indispensable authority is Barbara Walker. *Knitting from the Top* is one of Barbara Walker's many gifts to knitters. She figured it out, and she wrote it down, in great detail and with impeccable clarity. My only beef with *Knitting from the Top* is that it is truly design-your-own. At every point of every type of sweater, there is a choice to make: what neckline, what collar, what bands, what stitch pattern, what what what. There are many options to consider, and each choice is then followed by a measurement and a calculation. I'm impatient with that. I want to start with a pattern that makes a lot of the choices for me. I don't mind having the choices made for me, and neither should you—because you can always change those choices. As you knit your first top-down pattern, the lights will go on, and they will keep going on. You will see, from doing, how you could change something, make it longer or shorter, higher in the front or lower in the back. But you can start with a pattern. There's nothing wrong with that.

So consider the Daily Sweater pattern a top-down primer. You will learn a lot about top-down knitting, just from doing it. And even if you knit the rest of your sweaters bottom-up, knowing top-down gives you insight into what works and what doesn't when it comes to knitting to fit.

Color Me Beeyootiful: A Scientific Exploration of Color Theory

Ann's Color Wheel

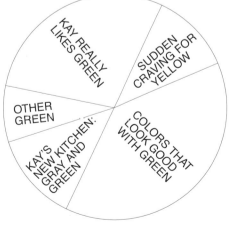

Kay's Color Wheel

THE DAILY SWEATER

At first glance, this is a plain-vanilla top-down raglan. What makes this sweater different are the details that give a flattering fit. For example, the ribbed edging at the neck, hem, and cuffs doesn't behave like a ribbed edging—it doesn't pull in at the hips and make your belly pooch out. To achieve this, the ribbing is knit over many more stitches than the body of the sweater. The other major improvement is in the armhole shaping. A typical raglan increases two stitches at each of the four raglan seams until the bottom of the armhole is reached. This is easy to work, but results in unsightly flaps of extra fabric under the arm. By cleverly distributing the raglan increases, the Daily Sweater marks the first time that knitting will actually improve the appearance of your triceps muscles.

SIZE
XS (S, M, L, XL, XXL)

FINISHED CHEST MEASUREMENT
38 (40, 45, 50, 54, 58)" [96 (101, 114, 127, 137, 147)cm]

MATERIALS
- (4) medium/worsted

8 (8, 9, 10, 11, 12) balls Rowan Calmer, 75% cotton, 25% acrylic/microfiber, 1³/₄ oz (50g), 175 yd (160m) in kiwi

- Size 5 (3.75mm) 24" (60cm) circular needles
- Size 7 (4.5mm) 24" (60cm) circular needles, or size needed to obtain gauge
- Stitch markers
- Stitch holders
- Tapestry needle

GAUGE
21 stitches and 30 rows = 4" (10cm) over stockinette stitch using size 7 (4.5mm) needles

We know that you *always* make a gauge swatch before starting a new project

(ahem). It's fabulous that you're so meticulous, because Calmer plays tricks on those other knitters, those reckless fools who don't pay attention to gauge. The yarn's slight stretch makes for a flattering fabric, but it also causes gauge to vary widely from one knitter to another. So check your gauge, like you always do (wink).

DIFFICULTY
Embrace the round-by-round table and this is a snap.

NOTES
LT (left twist): Knit into the back of the second stitch, but do not transfer to the right needle. Knit the first and second stitches together through the back loops and transfer both stitches to the right needle.

RT (right twist): k2tog, but do not transfer to the right needle. Knit the first stitch again and transfer both stitches to the right needle.

These twists form mini cables that are worked on every 4th row of the raglan seams (rounds 1, 5, 9, etc).

m1 right: Using the left needle, pick up the strand between the stitches from the back and knit into the front of the lifted strand to twist it and form a new stitch.

m1 left: Using the left needle, pick up the strand between the stitches from the front and knit into the back of the lifted strand to twist it and form a new stitch.

Sweater

Neckband ribbing

Using size 5 (3.75mm) needle, cast on 138 (138, 146, 146, 156, 158) stitches. (This seems like a lot of stitches to cast on for the neck, but this prevents the ribbing from pulling in tightly. You will decrease the number of stitches after knitting the neckband.) Place a marker and join, taking care not to twist the stitches. The marker indicates the back raglan "seam" of the left armhole.

Round 1 *k1, p1; repeat from * to end.

Rounds 2–7 Repeat round 1.

Round 8 Change to size 7 (4.5mm) needles, *k2tog, k1; repeat from * to last 0 (0, 2, 2, 0, 2) stitches, k 0 (0, 2, 2, 0, 2)—92 (92, 98, 98, 104, 106) sts.

Body and sleeve tops

Round 1 k31 (31, 33, 33, 35, 35) for back, p1, LT, p1, k7 (7, 8, 8, 9, 10) for right sleeve, p1, RT, p1, k8 (8, 9, 9, 10, 10), p15 for first row of front purl triangle, k8 (8, 9, 9, 10, 10) for the front, p1, LT, p1, k7 (7, 8, 8, 9, 10) for left sleeve, p1, RT, p1.

Round 2 k31 (31, 33, 33, 35, 35), p1, k2, p1, k7 (7, 8, 8, 9, 10), p1, k2, p1, k9 (9, 10, 10, 11, 11), p13, k9 (9, 10, 10, 11, 11), p1, k2, p1, k7 (7, 8, 8, 9, 10), p1, k2, p1.

Note On the next round, increases are made on body stitches only, not on sleeve stitches.

Round 3 k31 (31, 33, 33, 35, 35), m1 right, p1, k2, p1, k7 (7, 8, 8, 9, 10), p1, k2, p1, m1 left, k10 (10, 11, 11, 12, 12), p11, k10 (10, 11, 11, 12, 12), m1 right, p1, k2, p1, k7 (7, 8, 8, 9, 10), p1, k2, p1, m1 left—96 (96, 102, 102, 108, 110) sts.

Note On the next round, increases are made on sleeve stitches only, not on body stitches.

Round 4 k33 (33, 35, 35, 37, 37), p1, k2, p1, m1 left, k7 (7, 8, 8, 9, 10), m1 right, p1, k2, p1, k12 (12, 13, 13, 14, 14), p9, k12 (12, 13, 13, 14, 14), p1, k2, p1, m1 left, k7 (7, 8, 8, 9, 10), m1 right, p1, k2, p1—100 (100, 106, 106, 112, 114) sts.

Continue to work the chart for the front purl texture panel and, AT THE SAME TIME, work increases and twists as indicated on the table for your size.

Divide for Sleeves and Body

After working all of the rounds on the table for your size, across the back stitches to the 4 stitches of the right back raglan, knit the next purl stitch, knit the first cable stitch, slip the next 67 (67, 72, 76, 77, 84) stitches—1 cable stitch, 1 purl stitch,

HOW TO USE THE HANDY TABLES

1. Stay calm. We know they look like the Periodic Table of Elements, but these tables are easy to follow. Check off each box as you complete the round.

2. Each box represents a round of knitting (top left number).

3. Start with box 5. You have already followed the written instructions for the first four rounds, which set the increases and cable twists.

4. "T" = you twist the cables. "B" = you increase in the body sections.

"S" = you increase in the sleeve sections.

"WE" = work even, no increases or twists.

5. The numbers in the bottom right of each box are the most helpful part: the stitch count you should have in *each* body/sleeve section after working that round.

1 T	2 WE	3 B 33/7	4 S 33/9	5 TBS 35/9	6 WE
7 BS 37/11	8 WE	9 TBS 39/13	10 WE	11 BS 41/15	12 WE
13 TBS 43/17	14 WE	15 BS 45/19	16 WE	17 TBS 47/21	18 WE
19 BS 49/23	20 WE	21 TBS 51/25	22 WE	23 BS 53/27	24 WE
25 TBS 55/29	26 WE	27 BS 57/31	28 WE	29 TBS 59/33	30 WE
31 BS 61/35	32 WE	33 TBS 63/37	34 WE	35 BS 65/39	36 WE
37 TBS 67/41	38 WE	39 BS 69/43	40 WE	41 TBS 71/45	42 WE
43 BS 73/47	44 WE	45 TBS 75/49	46 WE	47 BS 77/51	48 WE
49 TBS 79/53	50 WE	51 BS 81/55	52 WE	53 TBS 83/57	54 WE
55 BS 85/59	56 WE	57 TBS 87/61	58 WE	59 BS 89/63	60 B 91/63
61 B 93/63					

Daily Sweater, X-Small

1 T	2 WE	3 B	4 S 33/9	5 TB 35/9	6 S 35/11
7 B 37/11	8 S 37/13	9 TB 39/13	10 S 39/15	11 B 41/15	12 S 41/17
13 TB 43/17	14 S 43/19	15 B 45/19	16 S 45/21	17 TB 47/21	18 S 47/23
19 B 49/23	20 S 49/25	21 TB 51/25	22 S 51/27	23 B 53/27	24 S 53/29
25 TB 55/29	26 S 55/31	27 B 57/31	28 S 57/33	29 TB 59/33	30 S 59/35
31 B 61/35	32 S 61/37	33 TB 63/37	34 BS 65/39	35 WE	36 BS 67/41
37 TB 69/41	38 S 69/43	39 B 71/45	40 BS 73/45	41 T 73/45	42 BS 75/47
43 B 77/47	44 S 77/49	45 TB 79/49	46 BS 81/51	47 WE	48 BS 83/53
49 TB 85/53	50 S 85/55	51 B 87/55	52 BS 89/57	53 T 89/57	54 BS 91/59
55 B 93/59	56 S 93/61	57 TB 95/61	58 BS 97/63	59 WE	60 B 99/63

Daily Sweater, Small

1 T	2 WE	3 B 35/8	4 S 35/10	5 TB 37/10	6 BS 39/12
7 WE	8 BS 41/14	9 TB 43/14	10 BS 45/16	11 WE	12 BS 47/18
13 TB 49/18	14 BS 51/20	15 WE	16 BS 53/22	17 TB 55/22	18 BS 57/24
19 WE	20 BS 59/26	21 TB 61/26	22 BS 63/28	23 WE	24 BS 65/30
25 TB 67/30	26 BS 69/32	27 WE	28 BS 71/34	29 TB 73/34	30 BS 75/36
31 WE	32 BS 77/38	33 TB 79/38	34 BS 81/40	35 WE	36 BS 83/42
37 TB 85/42	38 BS 87/44	39 WE	40 BS 89/46	41 TB 91/46	42 BS 93/48
43 WE	44 BS 95/50	45 T	46 BS 97/52	47 WE	48 BS 99/54
49 T	50 BS 101/56	51 B 103/56	52 BS 103/58	53 T	54 BS 105/60
55 WE	56 BS 107/62	57 T	58 BS 109/64	59 WE	60 BS 111/68
61 T	62 B 113/68				

Daily Sweater, Medium

1 T	2 WE	3 B 37/9	4 S 37/11	5 TB 39/11	6 S 39/13
7 B 41/13	8 B 43/15	9 TS 43/15	10 B 45/15	11 BS 47/17	12 WE
13 TB 49/17	14 BS 51/19	15 WE	16 BS 53/21	17 TB 55/21	18 WE
19 BS 57/23	20 B 59/23	21 TS 59/25	22 B 61/25	23 B 63/25	24 S 63/27
25 TB 65/27	26 BS 67/29	27 WE	28 B 69/29	29 TBS 71/31	30 WE
31 BS 73/33	32 B 75/33	33 T 75/33	34 BS 77/35	35 B 79/35	36 S 79/37
37 TB 81/37	38 BS 83/39	39 WE	40 BS 85/41	41 TB 87/41	42 S 87/43
43 B 89/43	44 BS 91/45	45 T 91/45	46 BS 93/47	47 B 95/47	48 S 95/49
49 TB 97/49	50 BS 99/51	51 WE	52 BS 101/53	53 TB 103/53	54 S 103/55
55 B 105/55	56 BS 107/57	57 T 107/57	58 BS 109/59	59 B 111/59	60 S 111/61
61 TB 113/61	62 BS 115/63	63 WE	64 BS 117/65	65 TB 119/65	66 BS 121/67
67 B 123/67	68 BS 125/69	69 TB 127/69	70 BS 129/71	71 B 131/71	72 BS 133/73

Daily Sweater, X-Large

1 T	2 WE	3 B 37/9	4 S 37/11	5 TB 39/11	6 S 39/13
7 B 41/13	8 B 43/13	9 TS 43/15	10 B 45/15	11 BS 47/17	12 WE
13 TB 49/17	14 BS 51/19	15 WE	16 BS 53/21	17 TB 55/21	18 WE
19 BS 57/23	20 B 59/23	21 TS 59/25	22 B 61/25	23 B 63/25	24 S 63/27
25 TB 65/27	26 BS 67/29	27 WE	28 B 69/29	29 TBS 71/31	30 WE
31 BS 73/33	32 B 75/33	33 T 75/33	34 BS 77/35	35 B 79/35	36 S 79/37
37 TB 81/37	38 BS 83/39	39 WE	40 BS 85/41	41 TB 87/41	42 S 87/43
43 B 89/43	44 BS 91/45	45 T 91/45	46 BS 93/47	47 B 95/47	48 S 95/49
49 TB 97/49	50 BS 99/51	51 WE	52 BS 101/53	53 TB 103/53	54 S 103/55
55 B 105/55	56 BS 107/57	57 T 107/57	58 BS 109/59	59 B 111/59	60 S 111/61
61 TB 113/61	62 BS 115/63	63 WE	64 BS 117/65	65 TB 119/65	66 BS 121/67
67 B 123/67	68 BS 125/69	69 TB 127/69	70 BS 129/71	71 B 131/71	72 BS 133/73

Daily Sweater, X-Large

1 T	2 WE	3 B 37/10	4 S 37/12	5 TB 39/12	6 S 39/14
7 B 41/14	8 B 43/14	9 TS 43/16	10 B 45/16	11 BS 47/18	12 WE
13 TB 49/20	14 BS 51/22	15 WE	16 BS 53/24	17 TB 55/24	18 WE
19 BS 57/26	20 B 59/26	21 TS 59/28	22 B 61/28	23 BS 63/30	24 WE
25 TBS 65/32	26 B 67/32	27 S 67/34	28 B 69/34	29 TBS 71/36	30 WE
31 BS 73/38	32 B 75/38	33 TS 75/40	34 B 77/40	35 BS 79/42	36 WE
37 TBS 81/44	38 B 83/44	39 S 83/46	40 B 85/46	41 TBS 87/48	42 WE
43 BS 89/50	44 B 91/50	45 TS 91/52	46 B 93/52	47 BS 95/54	48 WE
49 TBS 97/56	50 B 99/56	51 S 99/58	52 B 101/58	53 TBS 103/60	54 B 105/60
55 BS 107/62	56 B 109/62	57 BS 111/64	58 B 113/64	59 BS 115/66	60 B 117/66
61 TBS 119/68	62 B 121/68	63 BS 123/70	64 B 125/70	65 TBS 127/72	66 B 129/72
67 BS 131/74	68 B 133/74	69 TBS 135/76	70 B 137/76	71 BS 139/78	72 B 141/78

Daily Sweater, XX-Large

63 (63, 68, 72, 73, 80) sleeve stitches, 1 purl stitch, 1 cable stitch—onto a stitch holder for sleeve, cast on 3 (3, 3, 5, 5, 5) stitches for underarm marking the middle cast-on stitch, knit 97 (103, 117, 127, 137, 149) front stitches—1 cable stitch, 1 purl stitch, 93 (99, 113, 123, 133, 145) front stitches, 1 purl stitch, 1 cable stitch—slip next 67 (67, 72, 76, 77, 84) stitches to a stitch holder for left sleeve, cast on 3 (3, 3, 5, 5, 5) stitches for underarm, mark middle stitch of these cast-on stitches as the new beginning of the round. The body now has 200 (212, 240, 264, 284, 308) stitches, and there are 67 (67, 72, 76, 77, 84) stitches on each holder for each sleeve.

Work in rounds on the body stitches, working the middle stitch of the 3 or 5 cast-on stitches of each underarm as a purl stitch throughout to create a fake side seam. Work even until the body measures 14 (14½, 14½, 15, 15½, 16)" (35.5 [37, 37, 38, 39, 41]cm) from the underarm cast-on, or 2½" (6cm) shorter than you would like your sweater to be.

Side slits and lower edge ribbing of back

Change to size 5 (3.75mm) needle, bind off the purl stitch at the beginning of round, then *k1, m1, k2, m1; repeat from * across to the stitch before the next purl stitch "seam," k1, turn.

Note You are no longer working in the round.

Next row (WS) *p1, k1; repeat from * to end.

Work back and forth in k1, p1 ribbing

as established until the ribbing measures 2½" (6cm). Bind off in rib.

Rejoin yarn at remaining purl stitch (right side seam) and bind off purl stitch. Increase and work k1, p1 ribbing as for the back.

Sleeve (make 2)

With RS facing, slip the held stitches for one sleeve onto the size 7 (4.5mm) circular needle. Rejoin yarn, knit across these stitches, cast on 3 (3, 3, 5, 5, 5) stitches for underarm, marking the middle cast-on stitch of these for the purl-stitch fake seam and as the new beginning of the round, and join into a round—70 (70, 75, 81, 82, 89) sts. Work 3 rounds even, purling the marked stitch.

Decrease round p1, k2, k2tog, knit to last 4 stitches of round, ssk, k2.

Work 10 (10, 8, 8, 7, 7) rounds even. Repeat the last 11 (11, 9, 9, 8, 8) rounds until there are 48 (48, 51, 51, 51, 57) stitches, work even until the length of sleeve is 2½" (6cm) shorter than your preferred sleeve length when you try your sweater on (as you can do now).

Change to size 5 (3.75mm) needles, *k1, m1, k2, m1; repeat from * to end of round. Work in k1, p1 rib for 2½" (6cm). Bind off.

Repeat for the other sleeve.

Finishing

You may have noticed by now that you have a finished sweater in your lap. Sew the underarms, weave in the ends, give it a light steam, and put it on. Daily.

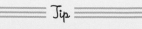
Tip

Whizz Even

I love Briton Nigel Slater's cookbooks. For the food, to be sure, but also for the zingy, ultra-clear way he writes a recipe. Where others would instruct the hapless homemaker to place ingredients in a food processor and "process for 30 seconds to a smooth paste," Nigel boils it down to one word: whizz. What more do you need to know? Your garlic and oil is in the food processor. What are you waiting for? Whizz, already!

Wouldn't it be great if knitting patterns had instructions like "whizz"? Surely we can do better than "work even." Maybe not. "Work even" says a lot in two short words. But when you get to the part of a sweater that repeats and repeats and repeats, wouldn't it be great if the pattern told you, simply, "Clickety-click"?

After you've divided the body and sleeves of the Daily Sweater, it is time, at last, to clickety-click.

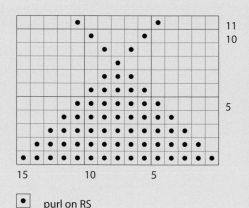

● purl on RS

The secret of flattering raglans: a wider "seam" line that slims the shoulders.

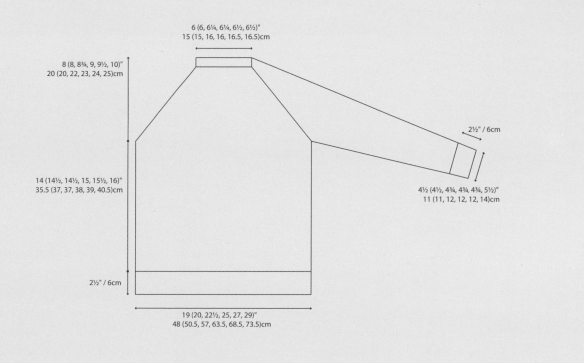

6 (6, 6¼, 6¼, 6½, 6½)"
15 (15, 16, 16, 16.5, 16.5)cm

8 (8, 8¾, 9, 9½, 10)"
20 (20, 22, 23, 24, 25)cm

2½" / 6cm

14 (14½, 14½, 15, 15½, 16)"
35.5 (37, 37, 38, 39, 40.5)cm

4½ (4½, 4¾, 4¾, 4¾, 5½)"
11 (11, 12, 12, 12, 14)cm

2½" / 6cm

19 (20, 22½, 25, 27, 29)"
48 (50.5, 57, 63.5, 68.5, 73.5)cm

How to Make Cables: A Seminar Disguised as a Pair of Sock Patterns

Ann ✳ Socks. Oh, socks.

Until very recently, you would have found me over at sockpeoplearenuts.com, spouting no end of vitriol about the folly of making socks by hand in an age where you can buy them by the bale for not much money. I try not to judge others, particularly when it comes to knitting. But there was something about sock-making that really bugged me.

Kooky sock knitters. Sitting there with those skinny needles, going on and on about how this yarn or that is the greatest sock yarn ever made, taking pictures of their feet, carrying on as if making a sock were the most natural thing on earth. *Don't you people know how crazy it is to spend your sweet, precious knitting time on socks?*

Life had turned into an endless infomercial where

I was a card-carrying Anti-Sockist. You couldn't pay me to make a sock. Put me in Antarctica with an Eddie Bauer tent and a case of Koigu, and I'm making mittens for my feet, but I am not making a sock.

I remember vividly the first time I had a twinge about sock-making. It was at a knitting party in Chicago, a few days after Christmas, at my sister-in-law Mary Neal's loft.

It was one of those evenings where knitting brought us all together, a group of women who mostly didn't know each other until they arrived at Mary Neal's. After admiring Erica's artichoke dip and loading up on eggnog, we all settled into our knitting. "What're you making?" I'd ask.

"Oh, a sock."

"You know, a sock."

I nodded, and for the first time, I felt like I was missing out on something. Everybody seemed so pleased to be working on their socks. Such a cheerful attitude everybody had toward their socks. They made it sound so simple. So unpretentious.

Suddenly, everywhere I looked, I saw sockmakers. They clearly led happier lives, had better memory, and probably never let trans fats into their kitchens. Life had turned into an endless infomercial where the product was socks, and I couldn't change the channel.

I was a goner. It happened the way people describe a car accident or falling in love—"I don't know what happened." I was in a yarn shop in Overland Park, Kansas, feeling sturdy, when without a word I slid two balls of Trekking XXL sock yarn across the counter and said, "What do I do now?"

I made only one kind of sock, Cat Bordhi's Simple Sock from *Socks Soar on Two Circular Needles*, which is a k2, p2 ribbed sock. Ribbed socks fit well. I was like Cézanne about the ribbed sock. Each sock was tidier than the one before, if identical in design, and I came to love k2, p2 ribbing, which until then had been something I hated to work. The secret, I found, was to go from the knit stitch to the purl stitch with a very careful tug. The tug was what kept that column of knit stitches from ballooning out in an unseemly way.

See? Socks were solving all sorts of problems for me.

As I made these many ribbed socks, I imagined the endless possibilities that a ribbed sock presents. What if the ribs didn't maintain their parallel journeys? What if they started to . . . wander?

I discussed the nature of the ribbed sock with Anna Bell, a Londoner whose designs I've admired online for some time. When I described the idea of the wayward rib, she nodded. She knew what I was talking about. She had an idea.

When her pattern arrived, it was exactly what we had discussed—k2, p2 ribs that tend to wander. Yet it was utterly different from the sock I had in mind. Her ribs don't simply wander; they meander and twist and tangle and waver *and* wander. I was struck with how very differently one idea can be interpreted by two people. Her socks are a total puzzle, and they are great fun to knit. And, before I converted to the One True Faith and discovered the joy of socks, they would have looked like something only a genius could make.

The following two patterns make a tidy little seminar, How to Make Cables Without Really Trying. You will learn seven different cable stitches. Watch as you knit, and you will quickly see what happens when stitches twist over and under each other. Once you've mastered the twisty trails of wandering ribs, you will learn how to make cables without a cable needle. Liberation! Freedom!

the product was socks, and I couldn't change the channel.

ERRANT SOCKS

By Anna Bell

SIZE
Foot circumference 8–9" (20–22.5cm)

MATERIALS
- **1** super fine
- 2 skeins Louet Gems Pearl Merino, 100% extrafine merino, 1³/₄ oz (50g), 185 yd (169m), in Ginger
- Size 1.5 (2.5mm) circular needle 32" (80cm) long for magic loop technique, or two 24" (60cm) circular needles, or size needed to obtain gauge
- 2 cable needles
- Spare needle or stitch holder
- Tapestry needle

GAUGE
32 stitches and 48 rows = 4" (10cm) in stockinette stitch

DIFFICULTY
A real adventure for the intermediate sock knitter.

PATTERN NOTES
For a quick refresher on knitting with two circular needles, see page 116.

This sock is knit from the toe up using your choice of a figure 8, Turkish, or Magic Cast-On (from knitty.com); gusset increases; and a rounded short-row heel with flap.

Sock

Toe

Using the figure 8, Turkish, or Magic Cast-On method, cast on 16 stitches. Divide between two circular needles or two halves of magic loop—8 sts each.

Increase Round 1 (k1, m1, k6, m1, k1) twice—4 sts increased.
Increase Round 2 (k1, m1, k8, m1, k1) twice.
Increase Round 3 (k1, m1, k10, m1, k1) twice.
Increase Round 4 (k1, m1, k12, m1, k1) twice—32 sts.

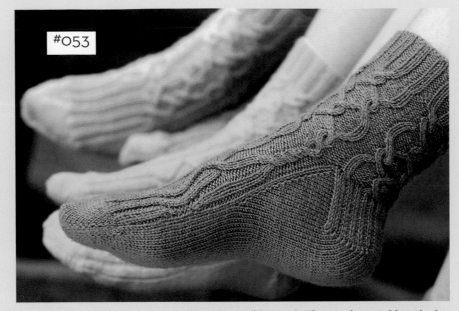

These socks are a fantastic way to learn how cables work. The wandering ribbing looks intricate, but it's actually quite straightforward.

Round 5 Knit all stitches.

Working increases as established (moving over 1 stitch on each Increase Round), alternate 1 Increase Round and 1 round worked even until you have 64 stitches.

Foot

Next Round p1, (k2, p2) 7 times, k2, p1, k32—the first 32 stitches form the instep; the remaining 32 stitches form the sole.

Repeat this round until the piece measures 5½" (14cm) less than the length of the foot. Then begin working from row 1 of Chart 1 across instep stitches (all sole stitches are worked in knit only). When 12 rows of Chart 1 are complete, begin Gusset shaping.

Gusset

Round 1 Work row 13 of Chart 1 across instep stitches; on sole stitches, k1, m1, knit to last stitch, m1, k1—2 sts increased.
Round 2 Work row 14 of Chart 1 across instep stitches; knit all sole stitches.

Repeat these 2 rounds, following Chart 1 for instep stitches, until row 41 of Chart 1 has been completed—94 sts.

Work row 42 of Chart 1 across the instep stitches, place the 32 instep stitches just worked on a spare needle or stitch holder. Heel will be worked back and forth (not in the round) over the remaining (sole) stitches.

Heel

Row 1 (RS) k47, w&t.
Row 2 (WS) p32, w&t.
Row 3 (RS) k31, w&t.
Row 4 (WS) p30, w&t.

Continue as established, working one fewer stitch between w&ts, until you end with a WS row: p14, w&t.

Next row (RS) k14, knit the next 9 stitches, picking up each wrap and knitting it through the back loop together with the stitch it wrapped. Pick up next wrap and sssk (wrap, stitch it wrapped, and the next stitch). Turn work.

Next row (WS) Slip 1, p23; purl the next 9 stitches, picking up each wrap and purling it together with the stitch it wrapped. Pick up next wrap and p3tog (wrap, stitch it wrapped, and the next stitch). Turn work.

Next row (RS) (slip 1, k1) 16 times, slip 1, ssk. Turn work.

Next row (WS) slip 1, p32, p2tog. Turn work.

Repeat these 2 rows until all stitches have been worked—34 sts on this needle.

Leg

Next Round k34 Heel stitches; pick up and knit 1 stitch between the Gusset and the front leg stitches, purl into it, and add this new stitch to the front leg stitches; work from stitch 3 of Chart 2 across the front leg stitches; pick up and knit the loop between the Gusset and the front leg stitches, purl into it, and add this new stitch to the front leg stitches—68 sts.

Continue Chart 2 across the back leg stitches.

Work Chart 2 across the front and back leg stitches until 48 rounds (2 repeats) of Chart 2 are complete.

Next Round p2tog, (k2, p2) 7 times, k2, p2tog, p2tog, (k2, p2) 7 times, k2, p2tog—64 sts.

Next Round p1, *k2, p2; repeat from * to last 3 stitches, k2, p1.

Repeat the last round until the ribbing measures 2" (5cm). Work sewn bind-off (see page 154).

Finishing

Weave in ends. Make a second sock, which will go faster than the first one, now that you've got the hang of it!

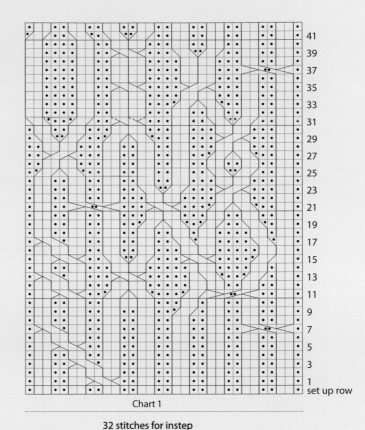

Chart 1

32 stitches for instep

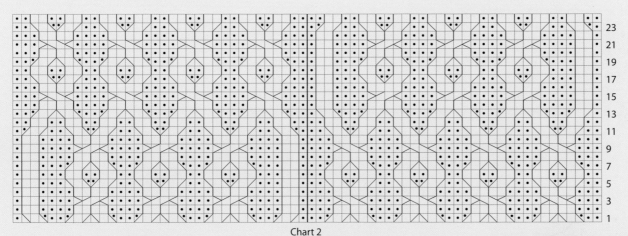

Chart 2

34 stitches   34 stitches

·	purl

slip the next 2 stitches to cable needle and hold at front of work, k2, k2 from cable needle

slip the next 2 stitches to cable needle and hold at back of work, k2, k2 from cable needle

slip the next stitch to cable needle and hold at back of work, k2, p1 from cable needle

slip the next 2 stitches to cable needle and hold at front of work, p1, k2 from cable needle

slip the next 2 stitches to cable needle and hold at front of the work, p2, k2 from cable needle

slip the next 2 stitches to cable needle #1 and hold at front of the work. Slip the next 2 stitches to cable needle #2 and hold at back of the work. k2. p2 from cable needle #2, k2 from cable needle #1

slip the next 4 stitches to cable needle and hold at the back of work. k2, slip last 2 stitches from cable needle to left needle, p2. k2 from cable needle

 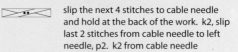

The First Amendment as Expressed by Socks

After making the Errant Socks, I discovered that the pattern had taught me how cables work. Anna uses such a variety in close proximity that her socks really are a tutorial in the fine art of twisting stitches here and there. I went cable crazy—obsessed in the same delirious way that I'd jumped into making socks in the first place. I figured out how to work cables without a needle, and that liberation from a cable needle meant I could achieve the rhythm of knitting that I really crave.

I started to imagine how simple a pattern like this could be. How few cable stitches would it require to create the maximum amount of chaos?

Four. With four little stitches, you can make your ribs lean, list, spiral, and twist. You can make almost all the sock in perfectly normal k2, p2 ribbing, then go completely nuts for a bit. Or you can end up braiding the ribs together. Once you've made the Errant Socks, this next pattern will let you really cut loose.

STEPHEN COLBERT SOCKS

We name these for Stephen Colbert, the host of *The Colbert Report*. Why? Because we think he is not only a great American, he is the *greatest* American.

SIZE
Foot circumference 8–9" (20–22.5cm)

MATERIALS
- (1) super fine
- 2 skeins Koigu KPM fingering weight, 100% merino wool, 1³⁄₄ oz (50g), 175 yd (150m), in #2151 light blue or any beloved sock yarn in a solid or semi-solid color. Variegated yarn will hide a lot of the texture in this pattern, so we can't really recommend it.
- Two size 1 (2.25mm) 24" (60cm) circular needles, or size needed to obtain gauge
- Tapestry needle

GAUGE
32 stitches and 45 rows = 4" (10cm)

DIFFICULTY
These socks are for Americans, not American'ts. Intermediate good times.

NOTES
For a quick refresher on knitting with two circular needles, see page 116.

Socks are worked from the top down.

These four stitches will send your 2 x 2 ribs wandering all over the place. Work these stitches without a cable needle, using only the nimble fingers you were born with.

1. To make a rib shift a stitch to the left. Slip 3 stitches purlwise to the right needle—2 knit stitches followed by a purl stitch. Insert the left needle into the front of the 2 knit stitches, pinch the base of the 3 stitches, remove the right needle, catch the purl stitch in back of the knit stitches, place the purl stitch on the left needle, p1, k2.

2. To make a rib shift a stitch to the right. Slip 3 stitches purlwise to the right needle—a purl stitch followed by 2 knit stitches. Insert the left needle into the back of the purl stitch, pinch the base of the 3 stitches, remove the right needle, catch the 2 knit stitches in front of the purl stitch, place 2 knit stitches on the left needle, k2, p1.

3. To make two ribs cross, with the right rib going over the left. Slip 4 stitches purlwise to the right needle. Insert the left needle into the front of the first 2 stitches you slipped to the right needle, pinch the base of the 4 slipped stitches, remove the right needle from the 4 stitches, move the freed 2 stitches behind the 2 stitches still on the left needle, and place them on the left needle, k4.

4. To make two ribs cross, with the left rib going over the right. Slip 4 stitches purlwise to the right needle. Insert the left needle into the back of the first 2 stitches you slipped to the right needle, pinch the base of the 4 slipped stitches, remove the right needle from the 4 stitches, move the freed 2 stitches in front of the 2 stitches still on the left needle, and place them on the left needle, k4.

Sock

Using size 1 (2.25mm) circular needle, cast on 64 stitches. Divide the stitches between 2 circular needles—32 sts on each needle. Join the stitches to begin knitting in the round, taking care not to twist the stitches.

Next round *k2, p2; repeat from * to end of the round.

From here, this sock's destiny is in your hands. Knit a few rounds of k2, p2 to get started, then begin messing with your ribs. Use the four stitch options shown above to move your ribs to the right or left. Once the ribs bump into each other, use the crossing stitches to send one rib in front of another.

Work the leg until it measures 6 ½" (16.5cm).

Heel Flap

Work the Heel Flap on the 32 stitches of one circular needle, back and forth. The other needle with its 32 stitches waits politely.

Next row (RS) *slip 1, k1; repeat from * to end.
Next row (WS) slip 1, purl to end.
Repeat these 2 rows 15 times more, ending with a WS row—32 sts.

Turn the Heel

Row 1 (RS) k19, k2tog, k1, turn.
Row 2 (WS) slip 1, p7, ssp, p1, turn.
Row 3 (RS) slip 1, k8, k2tog, k1, turn.
Row 4 (WS) slip 1, p9, ssp, p1, turn.

Row 5 (RS) slip 1, k10, k2tog, k1, turn.
Row 6 (WS) slip 1, p11, ssp, p1, turn.
Row 7 (RS) slip 1, k12, k2tog, k1, turn.
Row 8 (WS) slip 1, p13, ssp, k1, turn.
Row 9 (RS) slip 1, k14, k2tog, k1, turn.
Row 10 (WS) slip 1, p15, ssp, k1, turn.
Row 11 (RS) slip 1, k16, k2tog, k1, turn.
Row 12 (WS) slip 1, p17, ssp, k1, turn.
Row 13 (RS) k20.

Pick up the Gusset Stitches

Pick up and knit 16 stitches up the side of the Heel Flap, m1 between the Heel Flap and the beginning of the instep—37 sts on Circular 1.

Transfer the far 10 Heel Turn stitches from Circular 1 to Circular 2—27 sts on Circular 1.

The next 16 stitches continue your wandering ribs on Circular 1—43 sts on Circular 1.

Using Circular 2, continue your wandering ribs over the next 16 stitches, m1 between the end of the instep and the Heel Flap, pick up and knit 16 stitches down the side of the Heel Flap, knit the 10 stitches you just moved from the other needle—43 sts on Circular 2.

Next Round k10, k15 tbl, k2tog, k32 wandering rib stitches, ssk, k15 tbl, k10—84 sts.

Gusset

Round 1 k24, k2tog, k32 in wandering rib pattern, ssk, k24.
Round 2 and all even-numbered rounds Knit the round, but on the 32 instep stitches, continue messing around with the wandering ribs.
Round 3 k23, k2tog, k32 in wandering rib, ssk, k23.
Round 5 and all odd-numbered rounds Continue decreases as set in Rounds 1 and 3, knitting 1 fewer stitch before the k2tog and after the ssk until you have 32 stitches on each needle.

Foot

Work stalwartly onward toward the toe. Always knit the 32 sole stitches, and continue creating your wandering rib pattern on the other 32 stitches. When you are 2" (5cm) shy of the foot length you are seeking, it's time to work the toe.

Toe

Round 1 On each needle, k13, k2tog, k2, ssk, k13.
Round 2 and all even-numbered rounds Knit all stitches.
Round 3 On each needle, k12, k2tog, k2, ssk, k12.
Round 5 and all odd-numbered rounds Continue knitting one fewer stitch before and after the decreases.

When you have 12 stitches on each needle, stop decreasing. Knit 1 round, then 6 stitches more, then redistribute the stitches so that there are 12 stitches on the top of the sock and 12 on the sole.

Finishing

Slip the stitch on each end of each needle over the adjacent stitch (10 stitches on each needle). Graft the toe together using Kitchener stitch. Weave in ends. Make a second sock with a completely different set of wanderings.

A Mystery Sweater

Ann ✳ One of the first knitting books I ever bought was *Knitting Ganseys* by Beth Brown-Reinsel. I was tentative enough a knitter that I leaned toward single-color knitting—texture was about all the excitement I could stand in those early days, and gansey knitting seemed perfect.

The book includes a bit of history about these traditional fisherman's sweaters, along with some photographs of British women knitting in a superfocused way. Knitting was serious stuff; it meant income, not amusement. A fisherman's gansey was the Gore Tex® of its day, and if the sweater you made wasn't dense and snug fitting, the fisherman wearing it was going to be cold.

As I read more knitting history, this detail jumped out at me: The lore says that a fisherman's initials were added to a sweater in case a shipwrecked fisherman ever washed up on shore. Wow. Beth's book includes an alphabet chart so that modern-day gansey makers can continue the tradition, though for less dramatic reasons. It got me thinking about knitting and words. Knitted words.

My sister-in-law, Mary Neal Meador, thinks about knitted words, too. She is the sort of knitter I aspire to be: fearless, patternless. She doesn't knit all the time, which makes her work all the more admirable—and maddening to the rest of us. She gets in the mood, and before long she has cooked up a jacket that is made almost entirely with short rows. From a pattern that resides inside her head. Gah! How did she do that?

She likes the traditional materials and techniques of knitting. The dense fabric of traditional ganseys is something she has returned to in several of her designs. (If there is one person in the world who admires a scratchy wool more than me, it's Mary Neal.) But her sweaters tend to look utterly modern.

One day, I sent her a link to a shawl I'd seen on the Internet: a delicate Victorian lace shawl with a psalm knitted into it. From a distance, it wasn't clear what was going on in the weblike, white fabric, but the closer you looked, the more the words came into focus. Secret words. We started chewing on the idea of secrets words. Gansey. Dense fabric. Dark, the way old ganseys were dark. Secret words.

I heard not another word from Mary Neal until weeks later, when a package landed at my house. I could not imagine how she had created secret words, so I was dying to see what she had done. Swatting away children and leaving the pasta water boiling, I squirreled away in my little office to have a moment with Mary Neal's creation.

As I pulled the sweater out of its wrapping, I immediately loved the yarn, a deep hyacinth purple wool, sturdy and dense. Heavy. I held it up, and I was shocked to discover:

Utterly feminine. The silhouette was not anything a hardworking fisherman in the North Atlantic would wear. It has elements of the gansey, but it would never, ever be mistaken for a gansey. It was the unganseyest gansey I'd ever seen. It was *pretty*.

With words on it. At the top. Lots of words, not knitted into the fabric but chain stitched in the same yarn as the background along horizontal lines, like a child writing in a school tablet.

Secret words. What did she write?

From Martin Luther King Jr.: "The means we use must be as pure as the ends we seek." And Gandhi: "You must be the change you want to see in the world." What does it say on the back? A quote from Margaret Mead: "Never doubt that a small group of citizens can change the world. Indeed, it is the only thing that ever has." Give this sweater a Nobel Prize!

MARGARET *by Mary Neal Meador*

SIZE
XS (S, M, L, XL)

FINISHED GARMENT SIZE
32½ (35, 38, 45, 51½)" (82.5 [89, 96.5, 114, 131]cm)

to fit bust 30 (33, 36, 40-42, 44-46)" (76 [84, 91, 102-107, 112-117]cm)

Note: As sized, this garment has a trim, tailored fit, not meant to be worn over bulky clothing.

MATERIALS
- 🧶 medium/worsted
- 7 (7, 8, 9, 10) skeins of Harrisville New England Knitters Highland, 100% wool, 200 yd (183m), 3½ oz (100g), in hyacinth
- Size 5 (3.75mm) needles, or size needed to obtain gauge
- Size 5 (3.75mm) 32" (80cm) circular needle (or longer for larger sizes)
- Size 5 (3.75mm) 16" (40cm) circular needle
- Crochet hook and scrap yarn
- Stitch holders
- Tapestry needle
- 10 (10, 10, 11, 11) ½" (13mm) buttons

GAUGE
18 stitches and 26 rows = 4" (10cm) in stockinette stitch

DIFFICULTY
With some experience and an intrepid attitude, you will find this sweater a juicy voyage.

NOTES
12-Row Write-On Lines (WOL) Pattern

Row 1 (RS) Knit.

Row 2 (WS) Purl.

Repeat these 2 rows 4 times more. Knit 2 rows.

K2, P2 Rib

Row 1 *k2, p2; repeat from * to end.

Row 2 Knit the knit stitches and purl the purl stitches as they appear.

m1 for the Expanding Rib pattern: pick up and knit the loop BELOW the first knit stitch of the rib.

Back

Provisionally cast on 60 (64, 70, 82, 96) stitches (see page 153). Knit 1 row. This set-up row is Row 0.

Work the 12-Row WOL Pattern, increasing 1 stitch at each end of the 5th and every following 6th row until there are 72 (76, 82, 98, 112) stitches. Work even until a total of 42 (42, 42, 54, 54) rows have been worked.

Shape Armholes

Continuing to work the 12-Row WOL Pattern, bind off 3 stitches at the beginning of the next 2 rows; 1 (1, 2, 3, 3) stitches at the beginning of the next 2 rows, and 1 stitch at the beginning of the next 0 (0, 0, 4, 8) rows—64 (68, 72, 82, 92) sts.

Work even until you have completed 6 (6, 6, 7, 7) 12-Row WOL Patterns— 72 (72, 72, 84, 84) rows total from provisional cast-on.

Shape Shoulders

Row 73 (73, 73, 85, 85) (RS) k54 (58, 62, 72, 82), w&t.
Row 74 (74, 74, 86, 86) (WS) p44 (48, 52, 62, 72), w&t.
Row 75 (75, 75, 87, 87) k34 (38, 42, 52, 62), w&t.
Row 76 (76, 76, 88, 88) p24 (28, 32, 42, 52), w&t.
Row 77 (77, 77, 89, 89) Knit to end, picking up and knitting the 2 wraps together with the wrapped stitches.
Row 78 (78, 78, 90, 90) Purl, picking up and purling the other 2 wraps together with the wrapped stitches.

Work 6 more rows in stockinette stitch for a total of 84 (84, 84, 96, 96) rows.

Put all stitches on a holder.

Left Front

Provisionally cast on 29 (33, 36, 42, 50) stitches. Knit 1 row. This set-up row is Row 0.

Work the 12-Row WOL Pattern. Make 1 stitch at the beginning of the 5th and every following 6th row until there are 35 (39, 42, 50, 58) stitches. Work even until you have completed a total of 42 (42, 42, 54, 54) rows.

Shape Armhole

Continuing to work in 12-Row WOL Pattern, bind off 3 stitches at the beginning of the next RS row. Bind off 2 (2, 2, 3, 3) stitches at the beginning of the following RS row; 1 stitch at the beginning of the next 1 (1, 1, 2, 3) RS row(s)—29 (33, 36, 42, 49) sts.

Work even in 12-Row WOL Pattern until there are 67 (67, 67, 79, 79) rows.

Shape Neck

Row 68 (68, 68, 80, 80) (WS) Bind off 4 (4, 5, 5, 6) stitches, work to end.
Row 69 (69, 69, 81, 81) (RS) Knit.
Row 70 (70, 70, 82, 82) (WS) Bind off 1 (2, 2, 3, 3) stitches, work to end.
Row 71 (71, 71, 83, 83) (RS) Knit.
Row 72 (72, 72, 84, 84) (WS) Bind off 1 (2, 2, 3, 3) stitches. Knit to end to complete a WOL Pattern.
Row 73 (73, 73, 85, 85) (RS) Knit.
Row 74 (74, 74, 86, 86) (WS) Bind off 0 (0, 0, 1, 2) stitches, work to end.
Row 75 (75, 75, 87, 87) (RS) Knit.

Shape Shoulder

Row 76 (76, 76, 88, 88) (WS) p18 (20, 22, 25, 30), w&t.
Row 77 (77, 77, 89, 89) Knit.

This very special sweater lets you carry with you whatever words you want to keep close to your heart: names of the ones you love, birthdays, your favorite naughty limerick. Let it all out. This is no time for a haiku.

Row 78 (78, 78, 90, 90) p13 (15, 17, 20, 25), w&t.

Row 79 (79, 79, 91, 91) Knit.

Row 80 (80, 80, 92, 92) Purl, picking up and purling the wraps together with the wrapped stitches.

Work 4 more rows to complete the WOL Pattern.

Put the remaining 23 (25, 27, 30, 35) stitches on a holder.

Right Front

Provisionally cast on 29 (33, 36, 42, 50) stitches. Knit 1 row. This set-up row is Row 0.

Work in 12-Row WOL Pattern. Make 1 stitch at the end of the 5th and every following 6th row until there are 35 (39, 42, 50, 58) stitches. Work even until you have completed a total of 42 (42, 42, 54, 54) rows.

Shape Armhole

Continuing to work in 12-Row WOL Pattern, bind off 3 stitches at the beginning of the next WS row; 2 (2, 2, 3, 3) stitches at the beginning of the following WS row; 1 stitch at beginning of the next 1 (1, 1, 2, 3) WS row(s)—29 (33, 36, 42, 49) sts.

Work even in 12-Row WOL Pattern until there are 66 (66, 66, 78, 78) rows.

Shape Neck

Row 67 (67, 67, 79, 79) (RS) Bind off 4 (4, 5, 5, 6) stitches, work to end.

Row 68 (68, 68, 80, 80) (WS) Purl.

Row 69 (69, 69, 81, 81) (WS) Bind off 1 (2, 2, 3, 3) stitches, work to end.

Row 70 (70, 70, 82, 82) (RS) Purl.

Row 71 (71, 71, 83, 83) (WS) Bind off 1 (2, 2, 3, 3) stitches, work to end.

Row 72 (72, 72, 84, 84) (RS) Knit to end to complete a WOL Pattern.

Row 73 (73, 73, 85, 85) (WS) Bind off 0 (0, 0, 1, 2) stitches, work to end.

Row 74 (74, 74, 86, 86) (RS) Purl.

Shape Shoulder

Row 75 (75, 75, 87, 87) (RS) k18 (20, 22, 25, 30), w&t.

Row 76 (76, 76, 88, 88) Purl.

Row 77 (77, 77, 89, 89) k13 (15, 17, 20, 25), w&t.

Row 78 (78, 78, 90, 90) Purl.

Row 79 (79, 79, 91, 91) Knit, picking up and knitting the wraps together with the wrapped stitches.

Work 5 more rows to complete the WOL Pattern.

Put the remaining 23 (25, 27, 30, 35) stitches on a holder.

Skirt

Undo the provisional cast-on at the waist and put the right front, the back, then the left front stitches onto the long circular needle—118 (130, 142, 166, 196) sts. To set up the Expanding Rib pattern, knit 4, then purl into the front and back of the next stitch to increase 1. This establishes a k4, p2 rib. Follow the instructions below to adjust at the beginning and/or end of the first row, according to size.

For size XS only

First row (RS) *k4, pfb, repeat from* to last 3 stitches. k1, kfb, k1—142.

For size S

First row (RS) *k4, pfb, repeat from* to last 5 stitches. k1, k2tog, k2—154.

For size M

First row (RS) k1, kfb, k1, pfb, *k4, pfb, repeat from* to last 3 stitches. k1—172.

For sizes L, XL

First row (RS) k2, k2tog, k1, pfb, *k4, pfb, repeat from* to last 5 stitches, k1, k2tog, k2—196 (232).

All sizes

Continue in k4, p2 rib for 11 more rows.

Next row (RS) *m1, k4, p2; repeat from *

across, end m1, k4. This establishes a k5, p2 rib. Continue in k5, p2 rib for 13 rows.

Next RS row *m1, k5, p2; repeat from * to last 5 stitches, end m1, k5. This establishes a k6, p2 rib. Continue in k6, p2 rib for 14 rows.

Next WS row *p6, m1, k2; repeat from * to the last 6 stitches, end p6. This establishes a k6, p3 rib. Continue in k6, p3 rib for 15 rows.

Next RS row * m1, k6, p3; repeat from * across to last 6 stitches, end m1, k6. This establishes a k7, p3 rib. Continue in k7, p3 rib for 17 rows.

Next RS row * m1, k7, p3; repeat from * across to last 7 stitches, end m1, k7. This establishes a k8, p3 rib. Continue in k8, p3 rib for 18 rows.

Next WS row *p8, m1, k3; repeat from * across to last 8 stitches, end p8. This establishes a k8, p4 rib. Continue in k8, p4 rib for 19 rows.

Bind off loosely, or if you want a longer skirt, continue increasing in this manner until skirt is the desired length.

Sleeve (make 2)

To achieve an exact sleeve length, put a tape measure right up into your armpit, put your arm down by your side, and measure to your preferred sleeve length on the inside of your wrist. Subtract 2" (5cm). Call this measurement "S."

Using circular needles, cast on 44 (44, 44, 50, 50) stitches. Using another ball of yarn, do the same again. Work both sleeves simultaneously.

Row 1 (WS) p2 *k4, p2; repeat from * to end of row.

While continuing the ribbed pattern as set in row 1, increase 1 stitch at the beginning and end of every 9th (8th, 7th, 7th, 6th) row 11 (12, 14, 14, 17) times—66 (68, 72, 78, 84) sts. Work even in ribbed pattern until the sleeve reaches "S" length.

Sleeve Cap

Bind off 5 (4, 4, 4, 5) stitches at the beginning of the next 2 rows.

Bind off 2 (2, 2, 1, 1) stitches at the beginning of the next 22 (24, 26, 10, 10) rows.

Bind off 0 (0, 0, 2, 2) stitches at the beginning of the next 0 (0, 0, 24, 26) rows—12 sts.

Saddle

For size XS, S, M, L:

Row 1 (RS) k2, p2, k4, p2, k2.

Row 2 (WS) p2, k2, p4, k2, p2.

For size XL:

Row 1 (RS) p1, k4, p2, k4, p1.

Row 2 (WS) k1, p4, k2, p4, k1.

Continue in ribbed pattern for 31 (33, 36, 40, 46) more rows. Put the 12 stitches onto a holder.

Attach Sleeves

With RS facing and a straight needle, pick up and knit 23 (25, 27, 30, 35) stitches from the Right Front shoulder stitch holder. Knit 1 row. Set aside.

Using the shorter circular needle, pick up and knit 3 stitches for every 4 rows along the right side of one Sleeve Saddle—23 (25, 27, 30, 35) sts.

Using the three-needle bind-off method (page 154), attach the Front to the Sleeve Saddle, with the bound-off seam on the outside of the garment.

Using this same procedure, work your way around the bodice, knitting up stitches from the Saddle, and picking up the same number of stitches from the back right and left Shoulders and Left Front.

To finish sewing the Sleeve onto the bodice, you can simply sew them together neatly. Or you can knit up an equal number of stitches from the Armhole and the Sleeve Cap and use a three-needle bind-off. Sew the side and Sleeve seams using mattress stitch (page 153).

Neck Band

With RS facing, starting at the Right Front neck, pick up and knit 20 (20, 21, 22, 24) stitches from the neck shaping; the 12 stitches from the right Saddle; 18 (18, 18, 22, 22) stitches from the Back neck; 12 stitches from the left Saddle; and 20 (20, 21, 22, 24) stitches from the Left Front—82 (82, 84, 92, 94) sts.

Work in k2, p2 rib for 6 rows. Bind off loosely.

Button Band

With your longest circular needle and the right side of the Left Front facing, pick up and knit 3 stitches for every 4 rows from the neckband edge to the lower edge of the skirt. For XS, S, and M, pick up 63 stitches from the bodice. For L and XL, pick up 72 stitches from the bodice. For the skirt as written, pick up 87 (87, 87, 86, 86) stitches. For longer or shorter skirt, adjust, being sure to have a number of stitches divisible by 4 with 2 extra

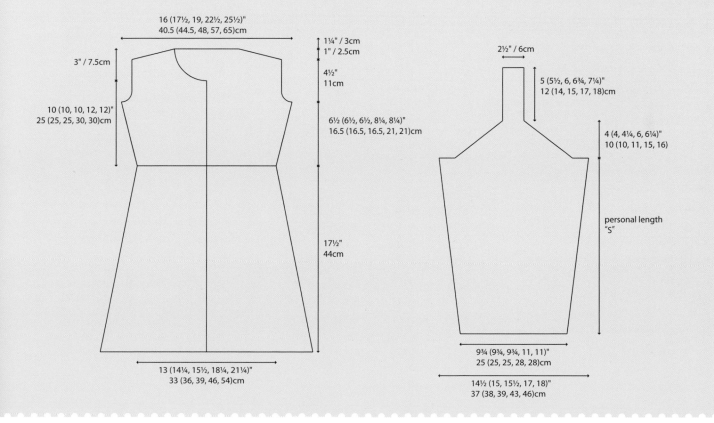

16 (17½, 19, 22½, 25½)"
40.5 (44.5, 48, 57, 65)cm

3" / 7.5cm

10 (10, 10, 12, 12)"
25 (25, 25, 30, 30)cm

1¼" / 3cm
1" / 2.5cm

4½"
11cm

6½ (6½, 6½, 8¼, 8¼)"
16.5 (16.5, 16.5, 21, 21)cm

17½"
44cm

13 (14¼, 15½, 18¼, 21¼)"
33 (36, 39, 46, 54)cm

2½" / 6cm

5 (5½, 6, 6¾, 7¼)"
12 (14, 15, 17, 18)cm

4 (4, 4¼, 6, 6¼)"
10 (10, 11, 15, 16)

personal length
"S"

9¾ (9¾, 9¾, 11, 11)"
25 (25, 25, 28, 28)cm

14½ (15, 15½, 17, 18)"
37 (38, 39, 43, 46)cm

stitches. Work in a loose k2, p2 rib for 6 rows. Bind off loosely.

Buttonhole Band

With RS of the Right Front facing, pick up and knit 3 stitches for every 4 rows, having an equal number of stitches as the Left Front, from the lower edge of the right side to the top edge of the neckband. Work in a loose p2, k2 ribbing for 2 rows. Using stitch markers or pieces of contrasting yarn, mark the locations for buttonholes every 16 stitches or so, beginning at the third stitch from the top. Adjust button spacing if desired.

Next row (WS) p2, *(slip 1, k1, psso), continue in ribbing pattern to next marker; repeat from * to end of row.

Next row Work in a loose k2, p2 rib, working yo over the psso of the previous row.

Continue in k2, p2 rib for 3 more rows.

Bind off loosely.

Embroidery

Pick an inspirational text of about 20 to 25 words for the back, plus about 15 to 20 words for the front. Using your best handwriting or a font from your computer, sketch it out on paper, seeing how you can make the words fit. Be sure to spell check! Once you have determined your layout, use a soft lead pencil for a light-colored garment, or white tailor's chalk for a dark-coloredgarment, and mark it out. Use a chain stitch to embroider your personal message.

Chain stitch

Use a tapestry needle and yarn. With the needle at the back, come up to the front, and go back through the same hole, leaving a loop. Come up to the front at the next position along your line, *through the loop*, snug it up, and go back through the same hole, leaving a loop. Repeat.

Finishing

Wash to remove markup. Pin out flat to dry. Blocking is particularly important for this garment, since the skirt needs to be set with the ribs as open as possible in order to achieve the proper flare. Sew the buttons in place on the left front button band.

Personal Style: A Look Back   From the Gardiner/Shayne Costume Institute:

  *Ann*

1. GYMSUIT, SIXTH GRADE.
One piece, polyester, maroon with white pinstripes. Snaps at the shoulder. There comes a time when a child is too old for a onesie.

2. EIGHTH GRADE CHEERLEADING UNIFORM.
One piece, polyester, maroon jumper with light blue inverted pleats. The waistline on this fit-and-flare garment hit me about three inches under my armpits.

3. PI KAPPA ALPHA SEMI-FORMAL, 1982.
A Princess Diana look, only more floral and with more ruffles.

4. THE DRESS, 1995–2001.
Beige unironed linen, ankle length. Because it wasn't technically a maternity dress, I concluded that I could wear this dress long after my children were born. Borrowed by a friend who was going to a costume party as a medieval beggar.

5. THE HAIRCUT, 1996.
After giving birth to my first child. It was like a bob. But not really.

6. THE T-SHIRT, 2002–PRESENT.
Continues to be worn despite vocal coauthor comments that it "doesn't do a thing for me."

Kay

1. FIRST PAIR OF GLASSES.
My mom felt sorry for me needing glasses, which she was sure would be the ruin of my social life (I was eight), so she promised I could pick out any pair I wanted. "White goes with everything, Mommy!"

2. 1976.
Autumn. A rare college date night. I hadn't seen David Eck since fifth grade, when he mesmerized me with his ability to kill flies by slamming his music book shut on them. For this fern bar outing, I wore denim gauchos and brown suede boots. My hairdo was the love child of Dorothy Hamill and Farrah Fawcett, and my eyelids (visible through gold-rimmed specs that were intended to invoke John Lennon but stopped in the neighborhood of John Denver) were touched by the delicate albeit metallic blue of butterfly wings. Didn't see David again. Decided it was for the best.

3. FAMOLARE SANDALS OF 1980,
Worn with a Susy Wong-ish dress and nylons. Because nothing is hotter than rubber-soled sandals with nylons.

4. EARLY '80S. CANDIES.
Worn while maintaining, above the ankles, my Hillary Rodham Clinton ("The Little Rock Years") Shetland-V-neck-over-collared-shirt look.

5. FIRST DAY AT THE LAW FIRM, SUMMER OF 1983, WASHINGTON, D.C.
One other summer associate was starting that day, also a foxy young woman aspiring to Beltway chic. We wore identical navy blue cotton twill suits and silk foulards tied in a bow under the chin. At the cocktail party in our honor, the senior partner welcomed us with a humorous speech in which he mentioned our resemblance to airline stewardesses. "Where are your wings?" I laughed gaily, choking on feminist rage.

Chapter Two

The Fairest Isle
OF ALL

Ann ✳ I can't believe I'm doing this.

It's time to talk about Fair Isle knitting. Hold on! Don't turn the page. Please?
You may think you would never, in a million years or at least the next decade,
consider knitting in the Fair Isle way. Frankly, I don't blame you.

Fair Isle is cool. It's not like any other kind of knitting. I now understand the impulse that certain ministers have when confronted with people who are skeptics, or Episcopalians, or otherwise not interested in hearing about soul-savin' salvation. I'm kind of evangelical about this: If I wave my arms around enough, if I quote enough texts at you, maybe I can convert you. No? Stay with me for a minute.

Your doubts about Fair Isle likely include the following issues:

1. Knitting with two hands.
2. Using tiny needles.
3. Keeping track of 12 different shades of yarn.
4. Following a fussy and complicated stitch pattern.
5. Cutting up your knitting to make an armhole.
6. The terrifying possibility of ending up with a boxy, loud sweater after spending 200 hours of your life working on it.
7. Never finishing.

This chapter will answer each and every one of those doubts. One promise: you won't end up with a boxy, loud sweater because there are no sweater patterns in this chapter. You will, however, gain the skills to make anything in the Fair Isle way, including the boxy, loud sweater of your dreams.

The road to salvation may not lie in learning to knit with two hands, but you will likely have a religious experience of some kind once you crank a round of the stuff in less than 30 minutes. This may be the first you've read about Fair Isle, but we hope it isn't the last.

A Journey (In My Head) to Fair Isle

Right up front, I want to make it clear that I have never been to Fair Isle—the real island, in Scotland, above the *northern* part of Scotland, in the North Atlantic. For a very long time, I didn't even quite know where it was. In my suburb-bound imagination, I envisioned an island filled with women—a no-man zone—busily making colorful sweaters. I had it in my head that they all lived in stone cottages with thatched roofs, sort of like in the movie *Rob Roy* where Jessica Lange wanders in and out of her lochside cottage, waiting for Liam Neeson to come home from his adventures in manliness. Hell, I kind of imagined that I *was* Jessica Lange, seeing as how she favored a loose-fitting, dun-colored, burlappy style of dress that I already owned (see page 59).

The island of Fair Isle was as remote to me as the prospect of knitting something in the Fair Isle way. It was impossibly distant, a sort of knitting so complicated and alien that I figured I would never go there. It would be one of those hard things, like water-skiing or rotating my tires, that I would never do.

It was Alice Starmore of the Isle of Lewis who did the deed, who got me to knit with both hands. If you take a look at her books, which are mostly out of print as I write, you are likely to be struck by what you see. Hers are not the sweaters that come to mind when I hear the words *Fair Isle*. A traditional Fair Isle sweater is a very clever garment, but the traditional color schemes tend to be quite dramatic: mustard yellow and brick red. Brown and bright blue. According to Fair Isleologist Ann Feitelson, the colors came from the dyes that were readily available. Back in the day, there was no such thing as a hundred shades of two-ply Shetland yarn.

But these Alice Starmore sweaters—amazing! Starmore draws on the coastal landscapes of her native island off the west coast of Scotland and uses rich, heathered yarns combined in subtle shifting progression and stark contrast. Lovely. I couldn't resist trying one.

Years later, I'm still not finished. I may never finish. It is a demanding project: size 3 (3.25mm) needles, a gauge of almost 8 stitches to the inch, and a tricky pattern chart. If I had approached the project with a bit of experience under my belt, I would have been better equipped to stick with it. If I'd had some simple, gratifying projects on which to cut my teeth, I'd have had more confidence. My experience with this project made me wish I'd had an easy introduction to Fair Isle knitting.

DAVE WHEELER OF FAIR ISLE

An Easy Introduction to Fair Isle Knitting with Simple, Gratifying Projects

My humbling efforts have left me convinced that Fair Isle is one of the few things in life that really is worth the effort. Keeping my marriage on the blacktop, going to the bathroom, eating Famous Amos chocolate chip cookies—Fair Isle knitting is right up there, one of those things I will never regret doing.

Once I had Alice Starmore's sweater dancing in my head—once I got the bug—I had to figure out how to knit in the Fair Isle way. The basic challenge of Fair Isle is to work two colors of yarn in the same row. My fear of knitting two yarns at once rivaled my fear of panty hose. I started where I always start, with June Hemmons Hiatt's *Principles of Knitting*. She writes that for anyone doing Fair Isle only on an occasional basis, it is simple to do two-color knitting by slipping the stitch for the color you're not currently knitting, then coming back on the next round and knitting the slipped stitch with the second color. This seemed brilliant, because it meant I had only one color of yarn working at any time. This slip stitch thing sounded great.

Unfortunately, a little experimentation showed me that slipping half my stitches on every round basically meant that I was knitting each row two times: forever scootching stitches along the needle. Scootching all day long. Sometimes I'd finish a round and forget that I had the second color round to do. So sometimes I'd have all these giant slipped stitches which should have been knitted. And I kept creating hairballs of tangled yarns. It was a mess.

It became clear, after talking with some experienced Fair Islers, that the way to do Fair Isle was to bite the bullet and use both hands. I heard the same thing, over and over: Using two hands means the yarns do not tangle. It's easier to get a rhythm going. Do not tangle. Get a rhythm. All I have wanted, for my whole entire life, was not to tangle, and to get a rhythm. (It should be noted that the Shetland knitters, and some supercoordinated civilians elsewhere, work Fair Isle by holding both colors in one hand. My attempts at this left me shaky, tearful, and certain that I would never make it as a knitter in the North Atlantic.)

The two-handed Fair Isle was successful, after a period of staring at my left hand, urging it to participate, yet feeling like somebody else's hand had been stuck on the end of my arm. It was counterintuitive at first, but then, so was learning to type. After a few hours of lumpy knitting, I got a bit of a groove going, and once I got up the nerve to start my Alice Starmore pattern (during spring break at the Polynesian Beach Resort at Walt Disney World), I was thrilled when the pattern started to emerge.

I have felt cleverer only upon giving birth to a child. It was as exhilarating as riding a bicycle with a fresh pair of tires. It's like standing on the cliff at Rock City, dropping a quarter into the giant binoculars, and discovering that yes, in fact, you can see seven states.

I taught myself, and now, if you'll bear with me, I'll teach you.

MASON-DIXON RULE NUMBER 34: *Bad weather, good knitting.*

SHETLAND WOOL

The traditional yarn of Fair Isle knitting is a perfect match for the technique. Shetland wool is a scratchy, hairy wool that comes from sheep who have grown accustomed to a place where coping with weather is a full-time occupation. The nature of the wool makes it well suited to colorwork: It makes a halo, a blending of shades that makes colorwork quite unusual. And its velcrolike cling means that you can cut steeks that will stick together without ever sewing them up. This is hard to believe, but it is true.

It really is perfectly suited to making a distinctive sort of fabric. For a distinctive climate. Which is cold. When you are finished with the projects in this book, you will crave time with this fingering-weight, original yarn.

Workin' It: How to Knit Fair Isle

air Isle is nothing but knit stitches, which you already know how to do. The only difference here is that you are working these stitches using two different colors within one row. The main challenge is knowing how to hold the yarns so they don't tangle. The following method is one of several possible techniques. It's the one that works best for us. Take it slow, and soon your fingers will know what to do.

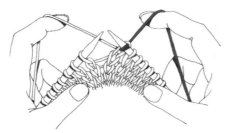

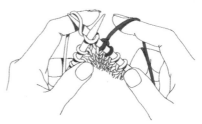

Hold the needles loosely in your hands.

Your right hand works Color A; your left hand works Color B.

Drape Color A across the top of your right index finger, front to back.

Drape Color B across the top of your left index finger, front to back.

Your thumbs and other fingers hold the needles in place.

(Relax! Aim for nonchalance.)

To knit Color A, insert the right needle knitwise into the next stitch.

Using your right index finger, knit Color A. (See? It's easy!)

To knit Color B, insert the right needle knitwise into the next stitch.

Using your left index finger, pull Color B so that it is somewhat snug—not loose, not too tight.

Move the tip of the right needle to the right of Color B, then move it behind Color B.

Color B is now over the right needle, going from front to back. With the right needle, pull Color B through to complete a knit stitch.

That's it. That's all there is to knitting two colors with two hands in one row.

As you work the stitch pattern, you will start to see horizontal lines of yarn across the back of your work. These strands need to be not too loose, not too tight. When you begin using a new color of yarn, slightly spread apart the stitches on your right needle as you bring the new color behind them. This will create a bit of slack in the new color.

After you do the above method for a while, you will develop a rhythm, halting at first, but more fluid as you practice. The hand that you normally don't use for knitting is the one that will need practice. Stay cool, and remember that it is in fact connected to your body and will soon respond to your brain's commands.

The more consistent you make your motions, the more consistent your stitches will be. Try to make the same motion with each stitch.

Eventually you will start to develop your own distinctive way of working the two yarns. You will figure out your own super-secret shortcut technique, and you will be cranking out Fair Isle.

Weaving a Long Strand: Easier Than Landing a 747

The goal here is to eliminate long strands of yarn on the back side of your Fair Isle knitting. If your strand is longer than an inch's worth of stitches, the strand will be too long and may snag. Two little maneuvers, to be used depending on which color yarn you want to secure, will keep the strands tidy on the back of your work.

Summary:

When you knit with A, weave B behind it. When you knit with B, weave A behind it. As you work through a Fair Isle pattern, you will recognize when a strand is getting too long and needs to be woven.

Here's how we'll do this:

In one of the great terrible movies of all time, *Aiport 1975,* the actress Karen Black plays a flight attendant whose 747 is hit by another plane, killing the pilots. It falls to her to bring home the jet, which is loaded with passengers including Helen Reddy portraying a singing nun. It's a dicey situation, sort of like learning to weave a long strand behind your Fair Isle knitting.

I'm going to talk you down. You are Karen Black, and I'm Charlton Heston, up here in air traffic control. Together, we are going to land this plane. By the end of it, we may fall in love and meet on the tarmac.

Weaving Color B behind Color A

You do this maneuver when you are knitting more than an inch's worth of Color A stitches. Halfway through that batch of Color A stitches, you need to catch the unused Color B on the back of your work.

Insert the right needle knitwise into the next stitch.

Slip the right needle under Color B.

Color A stays out of the way.

Wrap Color A around the right needle as if to knit.

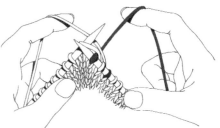

Lift Color B over Color A, off the needle.

Finish knitting Color A.

Result: Color B is woven behind Color A. Tidy, clean, piece of cake!

Weaving Color A behind Color B

You do this maneuver when you are knitting more than an inch's worth of Color B stitches. Halfway through that batch of Color B stitches, you need to catch the unused Color A on the back of your work.

Insert the right needle knitwise into the stitch on the left needle.

Wrap Color A around the right needle as if to knit.

Wrap Color B around the right needle as if to knit.

Lift Color A over Color B, then off the needle.

Finish knitting Color B.

Result: Color A (the color not in use) is woven behind Color B (the color in use).

You're done. The jet is on the tarmac. You're a hero! Roll credits!

Sharp scissors are a must when performing this bit of surgery. Using your child's blunt-nosed scissors—the ones he was using to chop up shoeboxes last week—will result in heartbreak, a chewed-up steek, and unwarranted crabbiness toward your beloved offspring.

After cutting a steek, it's common to trim it down to reduce bulk. Once you start whacking at your knitting, it's hard to stop.

The Steek: Part of Nature's Plan

A steek allows you to cut your knitting apart. It's the knitterly equivalent of a controlled burn in a forest. It sounds terrible—*you're setting the forest on fire on purpose?* But it's actually very efficient, a part of nature, and in the end, a means to a result that would not otherwise be possible.

A steek is a column of extra stitches that gives you a place to cut open a tube of knitting. It is useful when you are knitting Fair Isle, because Fair Isle is most sensibly knit in the round, not flat. Anybody who has ever worked Fair Isle flat will tell you of the dark moment of the soul that comes when working the back side of a piece and the stitch pattern goes haywire. There are few reasons a person might knit Fair Isle flat, and we are not going to go into them here. Assume, for our purposes, that all Fair Isle is knitted in the round. Anything else just ain't right. Ain't nacherul.

There are times when the tube of stuff knitted in the round needs to be interrupted. Two common examples:

An armhole. You can't have sleeves on a sweater unless you have armholes.

The opening for a cardigan. If you fail to include an opening in your cardigan, it's a pullover, plain and simple.

We are not making Fair Isle garments in this book, but we are making blankets and rugs that involve multicolor knitting. A steek makes it easy to work fast, in the round. And the steek cutting is exhilarating in the extreme.

Imagine that you have a piece of paper, and you curl it into a tube so that the edges touch, exactly at the edge and not overlapping.

That edge-touching part is what a steek is all about. Where the edges meet is where you will be cutting your steek.

The steeks we are making have ten stitches. The center of the steek is where the action takes place. This is where you start a new color, where you leave off an old color. You never have to weave in ends, because cutting the steek means that those ends will be eliminated during the exciting chopping.

Our hope is that you will give a steek a try, because there is nothing else like it in the knitting world. It allows you to make beautiful, colorful handknits that look fantastically complex but which, in fact, are not.

A Quick Swatch for Practicing Your Fair Isle

R eally. Fair Isle is best worked on the right side only, in the round. To make a quick swatch for practicing your skills without casting on 100 stitches on a circular needle and knitting in the round, here's a little recipe:

Using a circular needle, cast on 20 stitches using an aran weight or heavier yarn.

Row 1: Work a row of Fair Isle using Color A and Color B, alternating colors. Turn your work.

Row 2: Purl Color A. Slide the stitches to the other end of the needle.

Row 3: Purl Color B. This returns both yarns to a RS row so that you can practice your Fair Isle on a RS row.

Repeat these 3 rows.

The traditionalist's way to swatch Fair Isle is to knit a row, cut the yarns, then begin a knit row anew with new ends. When you get to the stage that you are swatching for gauge, this method is the way to go. But for messing around with your technique, the quick swatch is less fiddly, and you don't have to cut yarns all the time.

THE SIMPLE JOY OF CUTTING A STEEK

Step 1: Aim, rilly! When beginning to cut a steek, remember, this is no time to show off your scherenschnitte skills. You're not cutting paper dolls, OK? This is not scrapbooking. Simply cut a straight line, right in there between the center two stitches. You're turning your tube of knitting into a flat piece.

Step 2: Relax! See? It's just a straight line. Just be sure to hold the steek in the air as you cut, to avoid the unpleasant possibility of snipping into nearby knitting that is not the steek. We have never had a problem with this. But we get a little queasy thinking about you having a problem with it.

Step 3: Get ready for the big reveal! Once you've cut the whole steek, you will notice that other than a big slice up the middle of your knitting, nothing much else has happened. Stitches have not suddenly and shockingly unraveled. They're just sitting there, waiting for you to tidy them up.

Step 4: Observe! All of sudden, your knitting looks huge, looking twice as big as before. It's finally a blanket! Or rug! We try to act blasé whenever we cut a steek, but really—it's the knitting equivalent of bungee jumping. Congradualizations! From here, you move on to creating a binding to seal up the raw edges.

One secret of the Kiki Mariko Rug is that it will work with pretty much any collection of colors. We think this would be cool in neutrals, in a series of subtle jewel colors, or even neons.

Gobsmacking color, Mariko style.

Kiki, Mariko, and the Power of Destiny

Big yarn. Simple chart. Felting. This is a good place to start your own personal Fair Isle journey. There is something rewarding about knitting a five-foot-long tube of bulky yarn. It's fast work. It's a way to dip into Fair Isle knitting in the most forgiving way possible. And it means that you could, in a pinch, knit a really fuzzy strapless ball gown.

This rug requires only that you hold one color consistently in the right hand, and the other in the left. Because this rug is felted, you won't need to worry about how tightly you are pulling the strands across the back. Once you wash this rug, it's going to transform itself utterly, leaving you with a chewy, dense mat that will make getting out of bed a warm and pleasant experience.

This rug does involve cutting a steek. However, you will cut the steek only *after* you have felted the tube of knitting. It's a foolproof steek: The stitches cannot unravel, because they are *stuck together*. If you can cut a straight line, you can do this.

The stitch pattern is cool—I first saw it used in a vest by our friend in Portland, Mariko Fujinaka. She used small needles and tons of shades, resulting in a riot of color. Mariko modestly pointed me to the website where she'd first seen the stitch pattern. My own trip to lusciousgracious.com connected me with Kiki Hall, a lusciously gracious knitter living in Arizona-for-heaven's-sake, whose open-ended attitude toward knitting is a tonic. After adapting the stitch pattern and using giant yarn, I knew in about a second that this was going to be a great rug, and it needed to bear the name of the women who inspired it.

KIKI MARIKO

FINISHED SIZE
Approximately 34" x 60" (86cm x 152.5cm) before felting; 30" x 40" (76cm x 101.5cm) after felting

MATERIALS
- 🔲 bulky
- Brown Sheep Lamb's Pride Bulky, 85% wool, 15% mohair, 4 oz (112g), 125 yd (114m), 2 skeins in brown (A); 1 skein each in sage green (B), blue (C), purple (D), yellow (E), orange (F), red (G), tan (H)
- Size 15 (10mm) 32" (80cm) circular needle, or size needed to obtain gauge
- Stitch marker
- Scissors
- Tapestry needle

GAUGE
12 stitches and 14 rows = 4" (10cm) before felting

DIFFICULTY
Try it, you'll like it!

Rug

Using A, cast on 118 stitches. Join stitches to begin knitting in the round, taking care not to twist the stitches.

Knit to last 10 stitches of the round. Place a marker at the beginning of the steek.

Begin the Steek

The steek is composed of 1 edge stitch, 8 steek stitches, and a second edge stitch. To set up the proper place for new yarns to be joined, knit 5 using A. Join B and k1 B, k1 A, k1 B, k1 A, k1 A (NOTE: Yes, the last stitch is A.) On the next and subsequent rows, you will create a checkerboard by knitting the 8 center stitches in the opposite of the color of the stitch below it. The edge stitches will vary in color depending on where you are in the pattern.

Using the Fair Isle knitting technique (see page 64 for instructions), begin the Fair Isle chart, starting at the lower right corner and reading the chart from right to left. Repeat the chart pattern a total of 9 times until you reach the stitch marker; then work the 10 steek stitches.

When you start the next round, begin at the right side of the chart, row 2.

To end one color and begin a new one, change yarns in the middle of the steek, between Stitch 4 and 5. Leave 6 inches of tail for the beginning and end of yarn.

Knit the colors as shown in the chart, or in whatever order you choose. Try to use colors in a balanced way to avoid running out of one color. Or buy more yarn if you're loving the way it's going.

Work the chart until you have completed row 32, then begin the chart again. Repeat the chart until the piece measures 60" from the cast-on edge.

End with 1 row of Color A. Bind off all stitches.

Felting

Place the rug in a pillowcase, fold the edge of the pillowcase over several times, and secure it with safety pins.
Use a top-loading machine to wash it in hot water, with detergent. Check the progress of your felting, and periodically shake out the rug to minimize creasing.

When the wash cycle is complete, remove your rug and see how it's looking. We have seen rugs shrink in one direction by a third because the Fair Isle stranding felts dramatically.

Finishing

Using sharp scissors, and working at a large table, cut the steek between stitch 4 and stitch 5. At this point you have a felted, colorful rectangle. You will likely need to manhandle it to get the edges as straight as possible; sometimes there is a bit of flare-out at the corners. Do this while the rug is wet, when the fibers are more responsive to yanking. Let the rug dry for a day or two away from direct sunlight or heat. Either trim off the checkerboard steek, or leave it as a decorative element. Whipstitch the raw edges with Color A, and enjoy your rug.

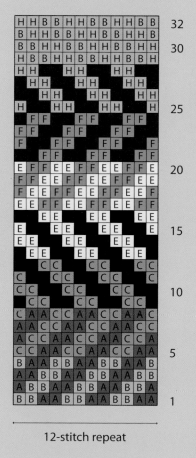

12-stitch repeat

A	color A (brown)
B	color B (green)
C	color C (blue)
■	color D (purple)
E	color E (yellow)
F	color F (orange)
■	color G (red)
H	color H (tan)

Watermelon colors for your sweet little watermelon.

Unapologetically
Untraditional Fair Isle

There are traditionalists for whom Fair Isle is a very particular thing: Shetland yarn, fingering weight, in a lot of colors, knitted on size 3 (3.25mm) needles, in the round, working traditional stitch patterns. I love that stuff, but I'm not wedded to it. I'm not a traditionalist. In fact, I have spent a fair amount of time trying to find ways of using the Fair Isle technique that are anything but traditional.

One chronic puzzle is the problem of choosing colors for a project. Hard! Complicated! Too many choices! May require knowledge of the color wheel!

One of the great recent developments in the evolution of yarn is the availability of multicolor yarns, where you can find a symphony of pleasing colors built right into one skein of yarn. If you work Fair Isle with two different colorways of one of these clever yarns, you can end up with an extremely colorful result with little heartbreak. The Baby Dotty Blanket is designed to make the most of variegated yarns. It is also designed to be a very flexible pattern, easily adapted to whatever gauge yarn you happen to have. As written, it calls for chunky yarn that is worked on size 10 ½ (6.5mm) needles.

A very simple Fair Isle pattern, worked on large needles, means that you will have a finished blanket pretty soon. At left, Noro Silk Garden. Center: Lorna's Laces Shepherd Bulky. Right: Crystal Palace Merino Stripes.

BABY DOTTY

A Fair Isle blanket, worked in the round with a steek. After cutting the steek, a tidy binding seals up the raw edges and creates a finished edge. All will be explained.

FINISHED SIZE
30" x 38" (76cm x 96.5cm)

MATERIALS
- 🔵 bulky
- Crystal Palace Merino Stripes, 90% merino wool, 10% acrylic, 1¾ oz (50g), 115 yd (106m) 6 balls in green (A)
4 balls in pink (B)
- Size 10½ (6.5mm) 26" (60cm) circular needle, or size needed to obtain gauge
- Size 10½ (6.5mm) 40" (100cm) circular needle
- Stitch markers
- Scissors
- Straight pins
- Tapestry needle

GAUGE
16 stitches and 17 rows = 4" (10cm) in stockinette stitch, after washing and blocking

DIFFICULTY
No epidural required.

Blanket

Using A and the shorter needles, cast on 114 stitches.

Working back and forth in stockinette stitch, make the binding as follows:

Row 1 (RS) k2, m1, knit to last 2 stitches, m1, k2.

Row 2 (WS) Purl.

Work these 2 rows twice more— 120 sts.

Next row (RS) Purl 1 row. (This is the folding edge for the hem.) Place a marker

to mark the beginning of the steek. Set up the steek by casting on 5 stitches, place a marker to mark the beginning and end of the blanket, and cast on 5 more stitches— 130 sts.

Join the stitches to begin knitting in the round, taking care not to twist the stitches. Using A, knit 3 rounds.

Next round Knit to last 10 stitches of the round. Slip marker. Begin the steek. (The last 10 stitches of each round will be the steek.) Knit 5 using A, in order to establish the center of the steek, where new yarns will be joined later. Join B and k1 B, k1 A, k1 B, k1 A, k1 A. (Note: Yes, the last stitch is A.) On the next and subsequent rows, you will create a checkerboard by knitting the 8 center stitches in the opposite of the color of the stitch below it.

Begin working the chart, starting at the bottom right corner of the chart and reading from right to left. Knit the first row of the chart a total of 10 times per round. Work the steek at the end of the round.

When you start the next round, begin

at the right side of the chart, Row 2. Continue working chart.

To end one ball of yarn and begin a new one, change yarns in the middle of the steek, between Stitches 4 and 5. Leave 6 inches of tail for the beginning and end of the yarn.

Repeat the 24-row chart a total of 7 times (14 polka dots).

On the last row of the final repeat, knit to the stitch marker and bind off the steek stitches (the last 10 stitches of the round)—120 sts.

From this point on, work back and forth in rows in stockinette stitch.

Next row (RS) Purl 1 row. (This is the folding edge for the binding.)

Next row (WS) Purl 1 row.

Next row (RS) k2, ssk, knit to last 4 stitches of row, k2tog, k2.

Next row (WS) Purl.

Work the last 2 rows 2 times more—114 sts.

Next row (RS) Bind off all stitches.

Cut the steek—see the instructions on page 67.

Fair Isle is the ultimate in non reversible knitting—there is no mistaking the wrong side.

Finishing

At this point, you'll need to handle the blanket with care. It's not going to disintegrate or anything, but you don't want to be waving this thing around. Working at a table is not a bad idea. And not to be naggy or anything, but taking your time with this finishing will help your results. It's not a long process, but pay attention to what you're doing, and your seams will be straight, your binding tidy, and your blanket beautiful.

Make the binding as follows.

With RS facing, using A, and beginning at the right corner of one of the steeked edges, pick up and knit stitches along the inner (uncut) edge of the steek as follows:

*pick up 3 stitches, skip 1 stitch; repeat from * to the end of the row. Turn work.

Using A, purl 1 row.

Next row (RS) k2, ssk, knit to last 4 stitches, k2tog, k2.

Next row Purl.

Work these 2 rows 2 times more.

Bind off all stitches.

Trim the steek down to 2 stitches. Fold the binding over the raw stitches, and use straight pins to hold it in place while you sew. Carefully whipstitch the binding to the back of the blanket, taking care to sew into the back of the blanket, not into the strands, which are not as sturdy.

Repeat this technique for the other steeked edge and the remaining edges.

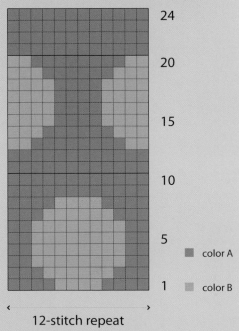

24
20
15
10
5
1

■ color A
■ color B

‹ 12-stitch repeat ›

Tip

Fair Isle Charts: Tips for Success

Part of the fun in Fair Isle knitting is getting the hang of your chart.
• Look for symmetry. Most Fair Isle charts are symmetrical, which means that the second half of a pattern is the same as the first, only backward.
• Look for landmarks in the pattern. Some elements are likely to continue for a number of rounds, which helps you orient yourself in the pattern. A vertical stack of stitches. A long stretch of one color. The steek. Watch for these landmarks.
• Make up little songs. Fair Isle is all about rhythm: 2 2 3 1 2 can be sung to the tune of "Row, Row, Row Your Boat." If you're a Prince fan, "I would die 4 u" also works.
• Use your knitting as your chart. Once you've completed a full repeat of the pattern, you are carrying the chart with you right there in your knitting. You can ditch your chart and refer to the rounds below. Also: you may memorize the pattern without realizing it until you find yourself knitting along, correctly, without looking up. This is an exhilarating moment.

This is knitting for the ages, for the generations. The drape and warmth of this alpaca and wool throw are absolutely delicious.

It Was a Dark and Balmy Night

Ann ✳ After a lifetime of dreaming about England, I finally made it to London, traveling with a full complement of boys and spouse/child wrangler. I managed to cut loose for a few hours on a dark December night to visit my own little Valhalla, Liberty of London on Regent Street. Now, I didn't exactly die a glorious death in battle to get there, but I had crossed the Atlantic in economy class, without a decent book on my iPod or even Ralph Fiennes around.

Amid the throngs of bargain seekers shopping the after-Christmas sale, I found the nest of knitters I sought in the Art Bar Café: the legendary Liberty knitting circle. It seems such a simple thing, to sit and visit for a little while. But it so exemplifies what the world of knitting is all about—connecting, eating scones, and being surrounded by wild wallpaper. A vivid memory.

The wallpaper, especially. The style and over-the-top whimsy of that blue-and-red wallpaper is something I needed to have in my own home, back in middle Tennessee. Short of whipping out my Rowenta and steaming the paper off the walls, I had to figure out a way to capture that wallpaper.

I cooked up this pattern after carefully studying the snapshots of Kay and me looking goofy in our roles as knitting tourists. It's not a literal re-creation of the wallpaper, but when I look at my throw, I know what it's saying to me. It says, "I am a vivid souvenir of your travels, both literal and virtual. And I took a pretty long time to make."

LIBERTY

This throw is worked in the round, using the Fair Isle technique. There's a steek in here—surely the longest steek you'll see this month—and a cool binding for the edges.

FINISHED SIZE
40" x 69" (101.5cm x 175cm)

MATERIALS

- (4) medium/worsted

- Berroco Ultra Alpaca, 50% wool, 50% alpaca, 3½ oz (100g), 215 yd (198m),
  7 skeins in robin's egg blue (A),
  6 skeins in crimson red (B)

- Size 8 (5mm) 24" (60cm) circular needle, or size needed to obtain gauge

- Size 8 (5mm) 48" (120cm) circular needle

- Stitch marker

- Scissors

- Tapestry needle

GAUGE
20 stitches and 23 rows = 4" (10cm) in stockinette stitch

DIFFICULTY
A whole lot of knitting, and a righteous chart. But you'll show off this blanket forever.

Throw

Make the mitered flap for the binding as follows.

Using A, cast on 194 stitches.

Row 1(RS) k2, m1, knit to last 2 stitches, m1, k2.
Row 2 (WS) Purl.

Repeat Rows 1 and 2 twice more—200 sts.

Next row (RS) Purl.

Next row (WS) Purl. (This is the folding edge for the binding. The binding will be stitched to the back side after the throw

is complete.) Place a marker for the beginning of the steek. Set up the steek by casting on 5 stitches, place marker to mark the beginning and end of the blanket, and cast on 5 stitches—210 sts.

Join the round to begin circular knitting, taking care not to twist the stitches. Knit 1 round to last 5 stitches of the round.

Begin the steek

Join B and k1 B, k1 A, k1 B, k1 A, k1 A. (Note: Yes, the last stitch is A.) The steek is composed of 1 edge stitch, 8 steek stitches, and a second edge stitch.

You now have two colors of yarn at work. Begin the pattern chart, starting at the lower right corner of the chart and reading the chart from right to left. Color A is the background, Color B is the pattern. On each round, repeat the chart 4 times, then work the edge stitch, 8 steek stitches at the end of the round, then the second edge stitch. On each round, alternate the blue/red order of the 8 steek stitches to form a checkerboard pattern. The steek's edge stitches will always be A.

Work until you have completed 5 pattern repeats.

the checkerboard pattern. Open up your blanket. Isn't it amazing? Can you believe you just made this thing? *Stop waving it around! You're going to blow out the steek!*

It's time to stabilize the edges.

You're going to make a mitered binding, which seals up the steek in a tidy little covering and creates a dimensional, ropelike edging to the blanket.

(Optional: Before beginning the binding, if you happen to have a sewing machine lying around, you can run one row of machine-stitching up the side alongside the edge stitch, and it wouldn't hurt.)

Using a size 8 (5mm) 48" (120cm) circular needle and yarn A, pick up and knit stitches between the edge stitch and the second stitch along the column of edge stitches as follows: Pick up and knit 3 stitches, skip one, to the end of the row. Turn work.

Next row (WS) Purl.
Next row (RS) k2, ssk, knit to last 4 stitches, k2tog, k2.
Next row (WS) Purl.
Next row (RS) k2, ssk, knit to last 4 stitches, k2tog, k2.
Next row (WS) Purl.
Next row (RS) k2, ssk, knit to last 4 stitches, k2tog, k2.
Next row (WS) Purl.
Next row (RS) Bind off all stitches. Leave a 5' (152.5cm) tail to use in stitching the binding to the back.

Go have a bracing cup of whatever gets you through the day.

Trim the steek down to 2 stitches. Using a tapestry needle, gently stitch the binding to the back of the throw, making sure to stitch into the back side of the stitches, not into the strands, which won't be as sturdy. Repeat this binding for the other side of the blanket. Stitch the end bindings to the back of the throw. Voila!

On the last row of the chart, end the round by binding off the steek stitches (the last 10 stitches of the round).

From this point on, work back and forth in rows in stockinette stitch to make the binding.

Row 1 (RS) Using A, knit.
Row 2 (WS) Knit. This is the folding edge for the binding.
Row 3 (RS) k2, ssk, knit to last 4 stitches, k2tog, k2.

Row 4 (WS) Purl.

Repeat rows 3 and 4 twice more— 194 sts.

Next row (RS) Bind off all stitches.

Finishing

At this point, this project is no longer portable. (You may have noticed this already.) You'll need a nice, wide table to hold the blanket while you perform a bit of surgery and suturing.

Cut the steek between Stitch 4 and 5 of

Take Your Time: How Not to Blow Up When Frustrated

Ann ✳ In thinking about knitting Fair Isle, we have spent a lot of time thinking about our knitting habits. (While knitting, of course.) We are notorious for knitting on the run. We often blast through a project, either because there's a baby or a holiday looming, or because we simply want to be done with it. It's a way to be prolific, but it's not a way to knit anything requiring much focus.

When things get a little too crazy, I go off into a corner and pat a little book I found years ago. *Take Your Time: Finding Balance in a Hurried World* is a short book by the late Eknath Easwaran. This teacher of meditation really would have been a great knitter if we'd only gotten to him soon enough. The calm and joy that he exudes in this book is highly contagious.

His goal is to teach us to slow down, to live intentionally. Listen to what he says about rushing: "When we learn to focus our attention completely in the present, we make an amazing discovery: Problems we thought were huge begin to shrink, and old compulsions we thought we could never break out of fall away. We find we have a breathing space between stimulus and response. We no longer blow up when frustrated, because we are going slow enough to control the situation."

We no longer blow up when frustrated? You mean we can work Fair Isle without blowing up? Gimme some of *that*.

The Road from Here

So here we are, at the end of our journey to the Fairest Isle of All. Let's review all those concerns mentioned at the beginning of the chapter:

✳ **Knitting with two hands.** Piece of cake. See page 64.

✳ **Using tiny needles.** Big needles work for Fair Isle, too. I suspect that before long, you may want to experiment with smaller needles, because very cool stuff starts to happen when you're knitting more stitches per inch. Patterns get more complex, colorwork can include more shades, and the fabric becomes thinner. You might even end up with a Fair Isle sweater. People have been known to use Fair Isle in a sweater.

✳ **Keeping track of 12 different shades of yarn.** This chapter's patterns show that using only two colors of yarn can result in very colorful knitting.

✳ **Following a fussy and complicated stitch pattern.** It's not as fussy and complicated as it appears, once you spend a minute with it. See page 67.

✳ **Cutting up your knitting to make an armhole.** No problem! See page 66.

✳ **The terrifying possibility of ending up with a boxy, loud sweater after spending 200 hours of your life working on it.** Nobody said you had to make a Fair Isle sweater.

✳ **Never finishing.** Our only advice for this is to point out that knitting for a long enough period of time will, in most cases, result in a finished object.

DIANA GABALDON: LIVING THE DREAM

Ann ✳ My elaborate Scottish fantasies began while reading all 5,872 pages of Diana Gabaldon's novels, which involve a lot of Scottish history, the element of time travel, and a ton of romantic intrigue. Our heroine Claire travels through time from 1942 Scotland all the way back to 1743 where (of course) she meets a strapping Scottish dreamboat/cattle rustler named Jamie Fraser. Mistaken identity, forced marriage, burning of witches—we've all been there. The unabridged audio version will take you through months of knitting. The books in the series to date are: *Outlander, Dragonfly in Amber, Voyager, Drums of Autumn, The Fiery Cross,* and *A Breath of Snow and Ashes.*

Chapter Three

Covering
THE SMALL HUMAN

Kay ✳ If you're a knitter, you probably have at least a couple of kids on your knitting radar. Knitters need kids. Kids are small; you can achieve high-volume sweater production stats if you're knitting for smaller bodies. And kids are gullible—they don't think there's anything wrong with rabbit ears on a hat, and in fact the rest of their wardrobe leads them to think dressing like a woodland creature is normal.

You don't have to look that far back in vintage knitting books to conclude that kids bear the brunt of most of the "cute" ideas that we knitters come up with. If you think I'm lying, ask yourself this question: When was the last time you put knitted ears on a garment for an adult? I'm guessing every pom-pom you've ever committed was for someone too young to vote.

If the kid you knit for is teeny, you're reading this complacently. You're smiling to yourself, thinking of how little Johnny shrieks with delight when you tell him that the project you've got on the needles is aimed at him. You're remembering how Dylan just loves when you knit diaphanous wings to go with her handknit fairy outfit. You're living in a dream world. Someday, my friend, you will wake up to the cold, hard facts of life: Kids grow up. Somewhere in the range of 8 to 10, Johnny and Dylan get the idea that what Auntie Knitty is making for them is flat-out the fugliest stuff they have ever seen. They dig in their heels, and their heels are *not* wearing handknit slipper socks.

Dos and Don'ts of Knitting for Children Who Have Reached the Age of Reason

This is when most knitters give up and look for a new, younger victim. Like those folks in *Rosemary's Baby* with the tannis-root milkshakes, they befriend pregnant women, searching for a replacement vehicle for handknits. We think there's a better way. We're not sure you're ready for it, but we'll just lay it on you, cold. If you want to hang onto Johnny and Dylan, you must grit your teeth and KNIT SOMETHING A SELF-RESPECTING KID WOULD NOT BE ASHAMED TO WEAR.

It is forbidden to knit:

1. Animals, whole or in parts. Even if they're really cute. Just cut it out.

2. Fake Heidi braids, and anything inspired by Pippi Longstocking.

3. Anything vintage or ethnic. (Ski sweaters with reindeer violate Rules 1 and 3.)

4. Argyle. Don't ask why. Life is not fair. Kids do not like argyle.

5. Fair Isle. To be safe, just avoid anything ending in "ile." (Crocodile? See what I mean?)

6. Intarsia. Intarsia is a big offender, and not just because it so often portrays our animal friends. Your son likes to surf. I know it makes no sense to you at all, but this does not mean he wants a pullover with a surfboard knitted into it, particularly if his mom made it. I can hear you saying, "But what about knitting a groovy catchphrase, like 'Hang Ten' or 'Cowabunga'—wouldn't that be super?" NO. That would not be super. Stop it RIGHT NOW.

The only way is to:

Look at what kids are actually wearing. The shapes are simple and roomy. The colors are, generally speaking, not pastel, not handpaint, or even space-dye. We know that this is hard to accept. Don't shoot the messenger.

There is only one rule: Knit what kids want to wear. Handknits for even the youngest babes need not be saccharine to be simply adorable.

Besweatering the Unsweaterable

There is real poetry in the gloomy style affected by the kids who spend all their spare time riding skateboards. Their baggy, drab gear shouts, "I don't care how I look, o shallow elder. In my eleven long years on this planet, I have seen it all. I am beyond caring about anything. Except riding this skateboard." If that's true, why are they all wearing the exact same brand of sneakers? They *do* care. The worse they look, the more time and effort they are putting into it. Show me a kid who's wearing what his mom wants him to—now that's a kid who doesn't care.

Most knitters would walk away from the challenge of making a sweater for a kid who aspires to skateboard chic. After years of knitting with denim yarn and exploring its possibilities for looking artfully trashed, I am just cocky enough to try. I'm laying it on the line and proposing a deconstructed denim pullover that I think a big kid will actually wear. (And by wear, I mean, leave the house in.) If I'm so sure of myself, why did I include smaller sizes? Insurance, just insurance.

SK8R

This unisex pullover has an unusual construction that results in a single diagonal seam across the chest. The body is knit in one piece, with a surface pattern formed by lines of twisted stitches. The pattern tells you the exact location of the lines on a sample sweater, but it's a lot more fun to stop and start them randomly. That way you don't have to carry the pattern around with you, and your sweater will be unlike any other.

The inspiration for this raffish look was the loose, busted-out hoodies and pants worn by skateboarders on the streets and office plazas of urban areas. If the kid who will wear your Sk8r is a fan of the Matrix films, or otherwise wants to look like a dark lord from the future, you can take this sweater to new levels of deconstruction. Rub it gently with an emery board to make faded lines parallel to the twisted stitches, or leave the diagonal seam open at the neck for an even looser fit. If your skater is very adventurous and stylish, bear down on the emery board and rub a few holes into the sweater. (If the very idea of blasting holes in a new handknit gives you the wobblies, we apologize. Lie down with a cool compress on your forehead, and forget that we said anything.)

SIZE
4–6 (8–10, 12–14)

FINISHED CHEST SIZE
35 (39, 43)" (89 [99, 109]cm)

MATERIALS
- **④** medium/worsted
- 7 (11, 14) balls Rowan Denim, 100% cotton, 1¾ oz (50g), 102 yd (93m), in dark indigo
- Size 4 (3.5mm) needles
- Size 6 (4mm) needles, or size needed to obtain gauge
- Stitch holders
- Row counter (optional but very helpful)
- Tapestry needle

GAUGE
20 stitches and 28 rows = 4" (10cm) in stockinette stitch using larger needles, before washing

A cool, modern pullover for your growing layabout. Sk8r is pure, indigo fun from start to finish. The denim yarn only improves as it takes more abuse.

20 stitches and 32 rows = 4" (10cm) after washing

DIFFICULTY
The perfect combination of inventive construction and straight-ahead knitting.

NOTES
After knitting, the sweater will shrink approximately 5 to 15 percent, in length only, on the first washing in hot water. The pattern takes this shrinkage into account.

The twisted stitch lines are formed using left and right twists, which are made as follows:

LT (left twist): Knit into the back of the second stitch, but do not transfer to the right needle. Knit the first and second stitches together through the back loops and transfer both stitches to the right needle.

RT (right twist): k2tog, but do not transfer to the right needle. Knit the first stitch again and transfer both stitches to the right needle.

All twisted stitches are worked on RS rows. To make diagonal lines, knit across the row to the stitch you want to be the start point, and work a right twist or a left twist. On subsequent RS rows, work the same twist one stitch to the right (for right-twist stitches) or left (for left-twist stitches) of the twist on the previous RS row. On our samples, the lines start and stop randomly, sometimes intersecting or in parallel.

Body

Using the larger needles, cast on 174 (194, 214) stitches. Work 4 rows in stockinette stitch. Change to smaller needles and work 4 rows in garter stitch. Change back to larger needles.

Row 1 (RS) k86 (96, 106), p1, k85 (95, 105), p1, k1.
Row 2 (WS) p1, k1, p85 (95, 105), k1, p86 (96, 106).

Note The 2 stitches that are purled on RS and knit on WS will be unraveled later to form phony side seams. These stitches

Yeah, we're all wearing the same sweater. That's how we roll.

will be purled on every RS row and knit on every WS row until the armhole shaping begins.

Row 3 and every RS row k2, ssk, work to last stitch of the row working 2 purl stitches as set, m1, k1.
Row 4 and every WS row Purl to the end of the row, working 2 knit stitches as set.

Repeat rows 3 and 4, working twisted stitch lines randomly until 84 (100, 110) rows have been completed.

Armholes

Row 85 (101, 111) Working twisted stitch lines as set, knit across to the purl stitch that marks the location of the right side seam. Drop this stitch off the needle, unravel it to the garter stitch hem, then pick up the dropped stitch again as for the phony seam (page 153). When the stitch is back on the needle, bind off this stitch and the following 2 stitches, work across the Back stitches to the purl stitch that marks the location of the left side seam.

Turn work. Put the stitches for the two front sections onto stitch holders and continue to work the back stitches only as follows: * (WS) Purl the next row, then work 2 rows of stockinette stitch. On the next RS row, k2, ssk, knit to last 4 stitches, k2tog, k2. Repeat from * once more.

Working twisted stitch lines as set, work raglan decreases as follows:

WS rows Purl.
RS rows k2, ssk, knit to last 4 stitches, k2tog, k2.

Repeat the last 2 rows until 34 (38, 42) stitches remain.

Next row (WS) Purl.

Shape Back Neck

Next row (RS) k2, ssk, bind off 26 (30, 34) stitches, k2tog, k2.
Next row (WS) Purl 3 stitches.
Next row (RS) Bind off 1 stitch, k1.
Next row (WS) Bind off remaining 2 stitches.

With RS facing, rejoin yarn to the 3 stitches remaining on the other side of the neck, k1, k2tog.

Next row (WS) Bind off remaining stitches.

Left Side of Front

Slip the stitches for the left side of the front onto the needle. Drop the first stitch, make a phony seam as before, bind off the first 3 stitches when the phony seam is complete. Shape raglan armholes as for the back, while AT THE SAME TIME maintaining the m1 increase at the end of every RS row, until 120 (136, 142) rows have been completed.

Shape Front Neck

Follow the instructions for the size you are knitting.

For size 4–6

Next row (RS) k1, ssk, knit until there are 15 stitches on right needle, turn to work left side of neck.
Next row (WS) Bind off 2 stitches, purl to end of row.
Next row (RS) ssk, knit to end of row.

Repeat these last 2 rows 3 times more. (4 stitches)

Next row (WS) Purl.
Next row (RS) ssk, knit to end of row.
Next row (WS) Bind off 1 stitch, purl to end of row. (2 stitches)

Work even for 2 rows. Bind off remaining stitches.

Slip central 11 stitches to a holder, rejoin yarn to remaining stitches to work right side of neck, knit to the last stitch, m1, k1.

Next row (and all following WS rows) Purl.

Next row (RS) Bind off 2 stitches, knit to last 3 stitches, k2tog, k1. Repeat these last 2 rows 3 times more. (4 stitches)

Next row (RS) k1, k2tog, k1. Bind off 1 stitch at the beginning of the next RS row, purl the next WS row, bind off.

For size 8–10

Next row (RS) k1, ssk, knit until there are 20 stitches on right needle, turn to work left side of neck.

Next row (WS) Bind off 3 stitches, purl to end of row.

Next row (and all following RS rows) k1, ssk, knit to end of row.

Bind off 3 stitches at the beginning of the next WS row, then bind off 2 stitches at the beginning of the next 2 WS rows. Work the next 3 rows decreasing as set at the armhole edge only.

Next row (WS) Bind off 1 stitch at the beginning of the row. Work decreases as set now on armhole edge only until 2

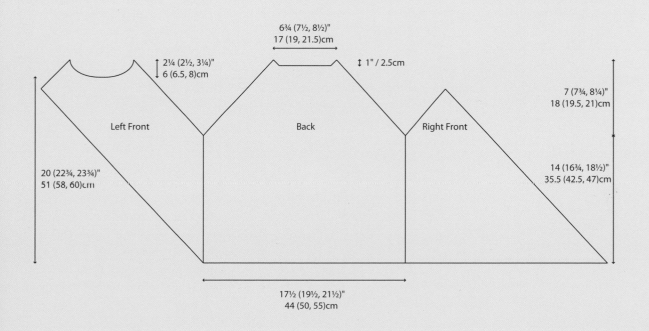

6¾ (7½, 8½)"
17 (19, 21.5)cm

2¼ (2½, 3¼)"
6 (6.5, 8)cm

↕ 1" / 2.5cm

Left Front

Back

Right Front

7 (7¾, 8¼)"
18 (19.5, 21)cm

20 (22¾, 23¾)"
51 (58, 60)cm

14 (16¾, 18½)"
35.5 (42.5, 47)cm

17½ (19½, 21½)"
44 (50, 55)cm

stitches remain, ending with the RS facing. Bind off both stitches.

Slip central 11 stitches to a holder for neckband, rejoin the yarn to the remaining stitches to work the right side of the neck, knit to the last stitch, m1, k1.

Next row (and all following WS rows) Purl.

Next row (RS) Bind off 3 stitches, knit to last 3 stitches, k2tog, k1. This last decrease begins the raglan decreasing for the right side of the neck.

Continuing raglan decreases as set on this last row, bind off 3 stitches at the beginning of the next RS row, then 2 stitches at the beginning of the next 2 RS rows. Work 3 rows decreasing as set at the raglan edge only. (5 stitches)

Bind off 1 stitch at the beginning of the next RS row and work the raglan decrease. (3 stitches)

Next (RS) row k2tog, k1.

Purl 1 row and bind off on the RS.

For size 12–14

Next row (RS) k1, ssk, knit until there are 22 stitches on the right needle, turn to work the left side of the neck.

Next row (WS) Bind off 3 stitches, purl to end of row. Continuing the raglan decreases on RS as set, bind off 3 stitches at the beginning of the next WS row, then 2 stitches at the beginning of the next 2 WS rows. Work 3 rows, decreasing at raglan edge as set, but keeping neck edge straight.

Next row (WS) Bind off 1 stitch, purl to end of row. Decrease now only at raglan edge as set, until 2 stitches remain. Bind off.

Slip the central 12 stitches to a holder for the neckband, rejoin yarn to the remaining stitches to work the right side of the neck, knit to the last stitch, m1, k1.

Next row (and all following WS rows) Purl.

Next row (RS) Bind off 3 stitches at the beginning of the row, knit to the last 3 stitches, k2tog, k1. This last decrease begins the raglan decreasing for the right side of the neck.

Continuing raglan decreases as set on the last row, bind off 3 stitches at the beginning of the next RS row, then 2 stitches at the beginning of the next 2 RS rows. Work 3 rows decreasing as set at the raglan edge only. Bind off 1 stitch at the beginning of the next RS row and work the raglan decrease. Decrease now at raglan edge as set until 2 stitches remain. Bind off.

Right Side of Front

With WS facing, slip the stitches for the right side of the front onto the needle and rejoin the yarn. Shape raglan armholes as for the back, while AT THE SAME TIME maintaining the ssk decrease at the beginning of every RS row, until one stitch remains. Bind off.

Sleeves (make 2)

Note One sleeve is plain stockinette stitch. The other sleeve has twisted stitch lines worked randomly.

Using larger needles, cast on 36 (44, 52) stitches. Work 4 rows in stockinette stitch. Change to smaller needles and work 4 rows in garter stitch.

Change back to larger needles and work stockinette stitch, either plain or with random twisted stitch lines. AT THE SAME TIME, work an increase row on the 7th (9th, 7th) and every following 6th row as follows: k2, m1, knit to last 2 stitches, m1, k2.

Work until there are 58 (64, 70) stitches, and then work even until 70 (80, 90) rows have been completed.

Shape Raglans

Bind off 2 stitches at the beginning of the next 2 rows.

Knit 1 row. *Purl the next row, then work

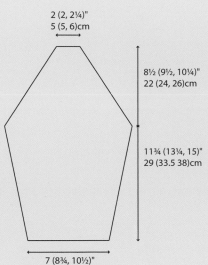

2 (2, 2¼)"
5 (5, 6)cm

8½ (9½, 10¼)"
22 (24, 26)cm

11¾ (13¼, 15)"
29 (33.5 38)cm

7 (8¾, 10½)"
17 (22, 26.5)cm

2 rows of stockinette stitch. On the next RS row, k2, ssk, knit to last 4 stitches, k2tog, k2. Repeat from * once more.

Working in plain stockinette stitch or in random twisted stitch lines as set, work raglan decreases as follows:

WS rows Purl.

RS rows k2, ssk, knit to last 4 stitches, k2tog, k2.

Work even, continuing raglan decreases as set, until 10 (10, 12) stitches remain and 120 (138, 154) rows have been worked. Leave the remaining stitches on a holder to be picked up for the neckband.

Neckband

Using smaller needles, knit across 10 (10, 12) stitches from the right sleeve, pick up and knit 3 stitches down right back neck, 26 (30, 34) stitches across back neck, 3 stitches up left back neck, 10 (10, 12) stitches from the left sleeve, 19 (23, 26) stitches down left front neck, 11 (11, 12) stitches across front neck, and 19 (23, 26) up left front neck—101 (113, 128) sts. Work 8 (10, 10) rows in stockinette stitch. Bind off loosely and evenly.

Finishing

Sew sleeves into armholes using mattress stitch (page 153). Sew front diagonal seam using backstitch (page 152), with "wrong" side of seam showing on the RS of the garment. Leave neckband seam open if added coolness is desired.

Wash the garment in hot water and dry it in the dryer. It will shrink 10 to 15 percent in length. (After the first washing, hot water is not required.) Distress the surface of the pullover according to your whim.

You can arrange your twisted stitch lines in any formation you choose. We love the idea of close parallel lines of twists to suggest patches or diamond shapes.

IT'S NOT A MISTAKE, IT'S A DESIGN FEATURE

Kay ✳ For my entire knitting career, I have scrupulously avoided changing colors in the midst of a seed stitch edging or panel. Why? Because when you knit a stitch on the wrong side (or purl a stitch on the right side), a loop of the old color is pushed to the right side, creating a dotted line of the two colors on the public side of the fabric. Not so neat—or so I thought. In the seed stitch edging on one version of the Jane Austen shrug (see page 94), we violated this bit of conventional wisdom, and that dotted line gives the illusion of beaded piping. The lesson here: doing things "wrong"—disregarding the ordinary conventions—can be a design feature. The eye is charmed by things that are a little bit cockeyed. Think about other rules you can break. Start looking at the wrong side of patterns. Nothing is sacrosanct.

Your mission: Be fierce, look adorable. Use the mighty power of cuteness to fight evil.

A Dress for Your Young Avenger

At a recent meeting of Knitters Seeking Kids to Knit For, a new member, unaware that she was pushing a hot button, pointed out that knitted dress patterns for girls skew strongly toward the smocky, the apronish, and the aggressively ruffled. Could this be the reason girls over the age of three refuse to wear them, she asked? Several members stood up and walked out in silent protest. But she had a point. Ruffles and sashes have a shelf life that expires when girls reach school age.

We call this dress Emma Peel because its snappy A-line shape and hipster skirt remind us of Diana Rigg's intrepid, gorgeous character in the British television series *The Avengers*. It also recalls a style of dress that girls have worn since the 1960s and to the present day. The yarn, Classic Elite Pebbles, has a slight crimp and a touch of acrylic that keeps the dress from drooping. (Mrs. Peel did not droop, ever.)

Does this dress pass the test? Will a girl who can voice her opinion all too well take the bait? When confronted with Emma Peel, our kindergarten-bound model said, spontaneously and with no prompting, payment, or other bribe from us: "I want to wear this for the first day of school."

EMMA PEEL

SIZE
2 (4, 6, 8)

FINISHED CHEST MEASUREMENT
21 (23, 25, 26½)" (53.5 [58.5, 63.5. 67.5]cm)

TOTAL LENGTH FROM TOP OF SHOULDER TO HEM
20¾ (22¼, 23¼, 26)" (53 [56.5, 59, 66]cm)

MATERIALS
- light/DK
- Classic Elite Pebbles, 75% cotton, 25% acrylic, 1¾ oz (50g) balls, 110 yd (100m), 3 (3, 3, 4) in balls pale blue (main color—MC), 2 (2, 2, 3) balls in charcoal gray (contrast color—CC)
- Size 5 (3.75mm) needles, or size needed to obtain gauge
- Stitch holder
- Tapestry needle
- 1 shirt button, ⅜" (1cm)

GAUGE
20 stitches and 28 rows = 4" (10cm) in crossed stockinette stitch

DIFFICULTY
As zippy as driving a Mini.

Back

Using MC, cast on 67 (71, 75, 79) stitches.

Knit 1 row.

Work color-seeded pattern as follows:

Rows 1 (RS) and 2 (WS) Using MC, p1, *k1, p1; repeat from * to end of row.

Row 3 (RS) Using CC, p1, k1, p1, *slip 1 stitch with the yarn in back, p1, k1, p1; repeat from * to end of row.

Row 4 (WS) Using CC, p1, k1, p1, *slip 1 stitch with the yarn in front, p1, k1, p1; repeat from * to end of row.

Repeat Rows 1–4 11 (15, 19, 23) more times, decreasing 1 stitch at the beginning and end of the 13th (17th,

19th, 23rd) row and then on every following 12th (16th, 20th, 24th) row twice—61 (65, 69, 73) sts. Cut the CC yarn.

Waist Stripe

Using MC, knit 1 row.

Next row (WS) k1, *p1, k1; repeat from * to end.

Repeat the previous row 8 (8, 10, 10) more times, ending with a WS row. Cut the MC yarn.

Top

Rows 1 (RS) and 2 (WS) Using CC, work in crossed stockinette stitch as follows: Knit all RS stitches through the back loops, and purl all WS stitches in the usual way.

Shape Top

Decrease Row k2, ssk, knit in pattern to the last 4 stitches, k2tog, k2.

Repeat the decrease row on every following 10th (14th, 18th, 18th) row 3 (3, 2, 3) times—53 (57, 63, 67) sts.

Emma Peel knits up faster than a spy on the run. It's two simple pieces (a front and a back) with trompe l'oeil skirt and belt.

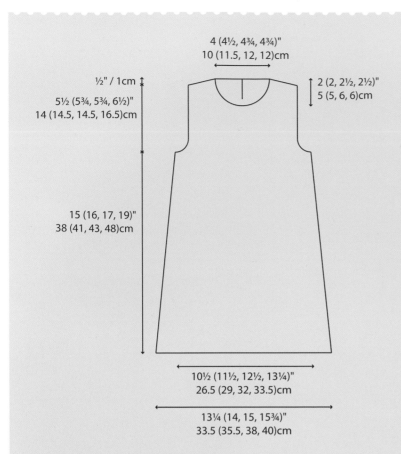

4 (4½, 4¾, 4¾)"
10 (11.5, 12, 12)cm

½" / 1cm

5½ (5¾, 5¾, 6½)"
14 (14.5, 14.5, 16.5)cm

2 (2, 2½, 2½)"
5 (5, 6, 6)cm

15 (16, 17, 19)"
38 (41, 43, 48)cm

10½ (11½, 12½, 13¼)"
26.5 (29, 32, 33.5)cm

13¼ (14, 15, 15¾)"
33.5 (35.5, 38, 40)cm

Work even in crossed stockinette stitch until the piece measures 15 (16, 17, 19)" (38, [40.5, 43, 48.5]cm) from the cast-on edge.

Shape Armholes

Continuing in crossed stockinette stitch, bind off 3 stitches at the beginning of the next 2 rows, then work a decrease row as before on the next 3 (3, 4, 4) RS rows—41 (45, 49, 53) sts.

Work 10 (10, 14, 16) rows in crossed stockinette stitch.

Shape Neck Opening

With RS facing and continuing in crossed stockinette stitch, knit 20 (22, 24, 26) stitches and turn, leaving remaining stitches on a holder.

Work 13 (15, 13, 15) more rows in crossed stockinette stitch, ending with a WS row.

Shape Right Shoulder

Next row (RS) Bind off 5 (6, 6, 7)

stitches, knit to end of row—15 (16, 18, 19) sts.

Next row Purl.
Next row (RS) Bind off 5 (6, 6, 7) stitches, knit to end of row—10 (10, 12, 12) sts.
Next row Purl.
Next row Bind off remaining stitches.

Shape Left Shoulder

Rejoin the yarn to the stitches on the holder.

With RS facing, bind off 1 stitch and knit to end of row—20 (22, 24, 26) sts.

Work 14 (16, 14, 16) rows in crossed stockinette stitch.

Next row (WS) Bind off 5 (6, 6, 7) stitches, purl to end of row—15 (16, 18, 19) sts.

Next row (RS) Knit.

Next row (WS) Bind off 5 (6, 6, 7) stitches, purl to end of row—10 (10, 12, 12) sts.

Next row (RS) Bind off remaining stitches.

Front

Work as for the Back until you reach the neck opening.

Shape Left Front Neck

With RS facing and continuing in crossed stockinette stitch, knit 17 (19, 21, 22) stitches and turn, leaving remaining stitches on a holder.

Next row (WS) Purl.

Next row (RS) Knit.

Next row (WS) Bind off 3 stitches and purl to end of row—14 (16, 18, 19) sts.

Continuing in crossed stockinette stitch, bind off 1 (2, 2, 2) stitches at the neck edge on the next alternate row, 1 (1, 2, 2) stitches at neck edge on the next alternate row, then decrease 1 stitch at the neck edge on each of the next 2 (1, 2, 1) rows— 10 (12, 12, 14) sts. Work even in crossed stockinette stitch until the armhole matches the Back armhole to the start of the shoulder shaping, ending with a WS row.

Shape Left Shoulder

Next row (RS) Bind off 5 (6, 6, 7) stitches, knit to end of row—5 (6, 6, 7) sts.

Next row Purl.

Next row Bind off remaining stitches.

Shape Right Front Neck

With RS facing, rejoin the yarn to the stitches on the holder. Bind off the center 7 (7, 7, 9) stitches and knit to end of row—17, (19, 21, 22) sts.

Next row (WS) Purl.

Next row (RS) Bind off 3 stitches and knit to end of row.

Continuing in crossed stockinette stitch, bind off 1 (2, 2, 2) stitches at the neck edge on the next alternate row, 1 (1, 2, 2) stitches at neck edge on the next alternate row, then decrease 1 stitch at the neck edge on each of the next 2 (1, 2, 1) rows—10 (12, 12, 14) sts. Work even in crossed stockinette stitch until the armhole matches the Back armhole to the start of the shoulder shaping, ending with a RS row.

Next row (WS) Bind off 5 (6, 6, 7) stitches, purl to end of row—5 (6, 6, 7) sts.

Next row (RS) Knit.

Next row (WS) Bind off remaining stitches.

Finishing

Join shoulder seams and side seams using mattress stitch (page 153).

Neck Band

Using CC and beginning at the left edge of the back neck opening, pick up and knit 61 (65, 69, 69) stitches evenly around the neck. Work 2 rows of seed stitch, cut the CC yarn, and change to the MC yarn. Work 2 more rows of seed stitch and bind off in seed stitch.

Using MC, work a cro-Kay edging (page 152) around the armholes and the back neck opening. At the top of one side of the back neck opening, make a button loop by working a crochet chain of 4 stitches. (Simply keep pulling a new loop through the loop just made.) Finish the loop by attaching the last chain stitch to the first one with a slip stitch.

Weave in all ends. Turn the dress inside out and steam lightly, pressing the inside of the seams. Attach button.

Even a crimefighter enjoys a piggyback ride.

Pride and Prejudice for the Modern Girl

A proper girly dress is a necessity in any girl's wardrobe. The most militant tomboy can be soothed into wearing a gown with vaguely historical associations if she gets to be a flower girl in a wedding. There is something about being a flower girl. The bride comes second to the flower girls, and the flower girls know it.

If you are making this dress for a girl who is not slated to be a member of the wedding, it may be necessary to adjust your expectation that the girl will actually wear the dress. Your chances are quite good if the girl is age 6 or under. Seven is a watershed year in which many girls abandon their pink and purple and start trying to look like teenagers, and by eight or nine you are going to get a fight from almost any self-respecting female. Console yourself with the fact that you can probably bribe your girl into wearing the dress once, for a picture, and that the coordinating shrug will look great over her AC/DC T-shirt.

Sorry, but we cannot recommend that you tell a girl that she is going to be in a wedding when in fact she is just going to church.

Most knitted dresses take longer to make than this one, in which the knitting is confined to the empire bodice, and the skirt is a length of fabric that is seamed and gathered, tacked to the inside ruffle of the bodice, and hemmed. This is quite easy, but if you are averse to sewing, take this job to an alterations shop. The bodice is a weekend's worth of knitting or less. It is knitted in one piece, back and forth, with a single seam in back.

JANE AUSTEN DRESS

SIZE
2-3 (4, 6, 8)

FINISHED CHEST MEASUREMENT
22 (24, 26, 28)" (56 [61, 66, 71]cm)

MATERIALS
- 🔵 light/DK
- 2 (2, 3, 3) balls Rowan Cotton Glace, 100% cotton, ¾ oz (25g), 125 yd (114m), in yellow or ecru
- Size 3 (3.25mm) 16" (40cm) and 32" (80cm) circular needles
- Stitch holders
- ¾ (¾, 1, 1) yd or m cotton or linen fabric
- Sewing needle
- Thread
- Button

GAUGE
21 stitches and 31 rows = 4" (10cm) in pattern stitch

DIFFICULTY
A knit so quick you'll still have time for your pianoforte lesson.

PATTERN NOTE
This garment is knit in a single piece, but not in the round. A circular needle is specified to make it easier to hold all the stitches.

Ruffle

Using longer circular needle, cast on 229 (249, 273, 293) stitches. That seems like a lot, but you'll soon decrease by half.

Row 1–11 (1–11, 1–13, 1–13) k1, *p1, k1; repeat from * to end.

Next row (WS) p1, *p2tog; repeat from * to end—115 (125, 137, 147) sts.

Body

Follow the instructions for your size.

For sizes 2–3 (4)

Row 1 (RS) k18 (19), *k2tog, yo, k1tbl*, k14 (16), repeat from * to *, k17 (19),

repeat from * to *, k17 (19), repeat from * to *, k14 (16), repeat from * to *, k20 (21).

Row 2 and all WS rows Purl.

Row 3 k20 (21), *k1tbl, yo, ssk*, k14 (16), repeat from * to *, k17 (19), repeat from * to *, k17 (19), repeat from * to *, k14 (16), repeat from * to *, k18 (19).

Row 4 Repeat Row 2.

These 4 rows establish the stitch pattern.

For size 6

Row 1 (RS) k11, *k2tog, yo, k1tbl, k9*, k2tog, yo, k1tbl, k16, repeat from * to * 4 times, k2tog, yo, k1tbl, k16, repeat * to * twice, end k4.

Row 2 (and all WS rows) Purl.

Row 3 k13, *k1tbl, yo, ssk, k9*, k1tbl, yo, ssk, k16, repeat from * to * 4 times, k1tbl, yo, ssk, k16, repeat from * to * 2 times, end k2.

Row 4 Repeat Row 2.

These 4 rows establish the stitch pattern.

For size 8

Row 1 (RS) k7, *k2tog, yo, k1tbl, k8*, repeat from * to * once more, k2tog, yo, k1tbl, k6 repeat from * to * 6 times, k2tog, yo, k1tbl, k6, repeat from * to * twice, k2tog, yo, k1tbl, k9.

Row 2 (and all WS rows) Purl.

Row 3 k9, *k1tbl, yo, ssk, k8*, repeat

from * to * once more, k1tbl, yo, ssk, k6, repeat from * to * 6 times, k1tbl, yo, ssk, k6, repeat from * to * twice, k1tbl, yo, ssk, k7.

Row 4 Repeat Row 2.

These 4 rows establish the stitch pattern.

For all sizes

Repeat these 4 rows until the work measures 3"(7.5cm) from the top of the ruffle, ending with a WS row.

Divide for Armholes

Next row (RS) Work 28 (30, 34, 35) stitches in pattern for left back, bind off the next 2 stitches, work 54 (60, 64, 72) in pattern for front (there will be 55 [61, 65, 73] stitches in the front section on the right needle), bind off the next 2 stitches, work in pattern to end for right back.

Right Back

With WS facing and working on the first 28 (30, 34, 35) stitches only, work even in pattern until the piece measures 5½ (6½, 7¼, 8)" (14 [16.5, 18.5, 20.5]cm) from the top of the ruffle, ending with a WS row.

Next row (RS) Work in pattern over the first 15 (17, 18, 21) stitches, bind off the remaining stitches. Transfer the first 15 (17, 18, 21) stitches onto a holder for the right shoulder.

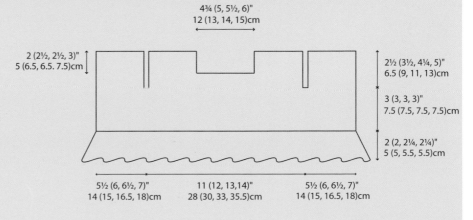

4¾ (5, 5½, 6)"
12 (13, 14, 15)cm

2 (2½, 2½, 3)"
5 (6.5, 6.5. 7.5)cm

2½ (3½, 4¼, 5)"
6.5 (9, 11, 13)cm

3 (3, 3, 3)"
7.5 (7.5, 7.5, 7.5)cm

2 (2, 2¼, 2¼)"
5 (5, 5.5, 5.5)cm

5½ (6, 6½, 7)"
14 (15, 16.5, 18)cm

11 (12, 13,14)"
28 (30, 33, 35.5)cm

5½ (6, 6½, 7)"
14 (15, 16.5, 18)cm

Feed the fantasy! Use the Jane Austen Dress as an opportunity to explain to your girl about the Regency period, who Mr. Darcy was, and how great it is that dowries aren't such a big deal anymore.

Front

With WS facing, rejoin yarn to front. Work even in pattern until the piece is 2 (2½, 2½, 3)" (5 [6.5, 6.5, 7.5]cm) shorter than the right back piece, ending with a WS row.

Shape Neckline

Next row (RS) Work first 15 (17, 18, 21) stitches in pattern, bind off the next 25 (27, 29, 31) stitches, work in pattern to end.

For the right front neck, working on the first 15 (17, 18, 21) stitches only, work in pattern until the piece measures the same as the Right Back. Place the stitches onto a holder for the right shoulder.

With WS facing, rejoin yarn to the left front neck, purl to end. Work in pattern until the left front neck measures the same as the right front neck. Place the stitches onto a holder for the left shoulder.

Left Back

With WS facing, rejoin yarn to the remaining 28 (30, 34, 35) stitches. Work even in pattern until the piece measures 5½ (6½, 7¼, 8)" (14 [16.5, 18.5, 20.5]cm) from the top of the ruffle, ending with a WS row.

Next row (RS) Bind off the first 13 (13, 16, 14) stitches, work across the remaining 15 (17, 18, 21) stitches, and transfer them onto a holder for the left shoulder.

Finishing

Using the three-needle bind-off (page 154), join shoulder seams.

Armhole Trim

Using shorter circular needle with RS of work facing, pick up and knit 35 (43, 51, 59) stitches evenly around armhole.

Next row k1, *p1, k1; repeat from * to end. Bind off in seed stitch.

Neck Trim

Using size 3 (3.25mm) circular needle and beginning at a point 2½" (6cm) down left back piece, pick up and knit 15 stitches to top of left back, 11 (11, 13, 12) stitches across left back neck, 11 (13, 13, 16) stitches down left front neck, 21 (23, 25, 27) stitches across front neck bound-off stitches, 11 (11, 13, 16) stitches up right front neck, 11 (11, 13, 12) stitches across right back neck, and 15 stitches down right back piece—95 (99, 107, 113) sts.

Next row k1, *p1, k1; repeat from * to end. Bind off neatly in seed stitch.

Sew the center back seam from below picked up stitches to bottom of ruffle. Crochet or stitch a loop on the top of left back piece for button closure. Sew on the button. Attach skirt.

Tip

How to make the fabric skirt, or, the only thing I learned in seventh grade home ec class

Examine your fabric. Orient yourself by identifying the two selvedge edges that run on opposite sides of the fabric; these edges will form the back seam of the skirt. With a sewing machine, run two lines of gathering stitches 1" (2cm) from the top edge of the fabric, perpendicular to the selvedges. (If the machine offers a choice of stitch length, choose longer stitches.) Pull gently on the threads to gather the skirt to desired poofiness. (As you can see in the photos, we went for a lo-poof look.) Now fold the fabric in half lengthwise, with the right sides facing, so that the selvedges meet. Sew the back seam using a 1/2" (1cm) seam allowance. Attach the gathered edge of the skirt to the inside of the bodice with hand stitches, just above the ruffle. Hem the skirt to the desired length.

BUSTED

When you get pulled over by the Knitting Police, they don't ask to see your license and registration. They ask to see your swatch.

"Hello Officer, howareyouisn'titabeautifulday?"

"Ma'am. Did you realize you were going 4.5 stitches to the inch in a 5.0 zone?"

"Officer, I was totally getting 5 stitches to the inch! Honest! I counted it and everything!"

"Ma'am. You do realize that that kind of gauge differential can result in a hugely oversized garment?"

"Why yes Officer, of course I realize that. See [rummaging in knitting bag] I have my KnitChek gauge-checker right here with me at all times."

"Ma'am. Did you wash it, ma'am?"

"Did I wash what?"

"The swatch, ma'am. Did you wash. The swatch."

"Er, help me out here—what is the answer you are looking for?"

"Ma'am. Did you block it?"

"I'm sure I did. I always do . . ."

"Ma'am. Are you aware that it's a felony to make a false statement to a police officer?"

[Squirms in seat.]

"Ma'am. I'm going to have to write you up. If, within 10 business days, you present proof that you have ripped that sleeve and started over on a smaller needle, your case will be dismissed. Knit safely, now. Have a nice day."

JANE AUSTEN SHRUG

SIZE

To fit 2 (4, 6, 8) years old

FINISHED MEASUREMENTS

(Across the back, from the midpoint under the armhole to the midpoint under the armhole): 9 (10, 13, 14)" (23 [25.5, 33, 35.5]cm)

MATERIALS

- 🔢 light/DK

- 1 (1, 2, 2) balls Rowan Cotton Glace, 100% cotton, ³⁄₄ oz (25g), 125 yd (114m), blue or brown (main color—MC)

- Optional: Small amount of Cotton Glace in yellow or blue for optional contrast trim (contrast color—CC)

- Size 4 (3.5mm) straight needles and 16" (40 cm) circular needle, or size needed to obtain gauge

- Cable needle

- Stitch holder

- Tapestry needle

GAUGE

22 stitches and 33 rows = 4" (10cm) in stockinette stitch

DIFFICULTY

A short and sweet introduction to top down knitting.

NOTE

This shrug is knit from the top down, beginning at the neck with the front and sleeves formed as you go.

c4b Slip the next 2 stitches to cable needle and hold at back of work, k2, k2 from cable needle.

c4f Slip the next 2 stitches to the cable needle and hold at front of work, k2, k2 from cable needle.

Neck

Using MC, cast on 29 (38, 53, 67) stitches.

Foundation row (RS) k2 (4, 6, 8), *p1, k1, p1, k4, p1, k1, p1*, k5 (10, 21, 31), repeat from * to *, k2 (4, 6, 8).

There's something deconstructed and modern about the way a shrug covers just the shoulders.

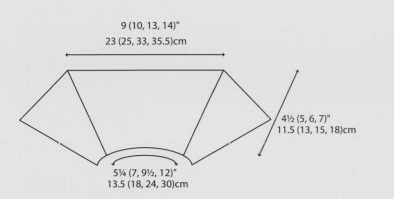

9 (10, 13, 14)"
23 (25, 33, 35.5)cm

4½ (5, 6, 7)"
11.5 (13, 15, 18)cm

5¼ (7, 9½, 12)"
13.5 (18, 24, 30)cm

Row 2 and every WS row p2 (4, 6, 8), *p1, k1, p6, k1, p1*, p5 (10, 21, 31), repeat from * to *, p2 (4, 6, 8). You are keeping continuity of seed stitch and cable "seam" and adding the newly made stitches into the stockinette stitch section.

Row 3 (RS) k4, m1, *p1, k1, p1, c4f, p1, k1, p1* m1, k5 (10, 21, 31), m1, repeat from * to * BUT working c4b instead of c4f, m1, k4.

Row 4 Repeat Row 2, adding the newly made stitches into the stockinette stitch section.

Row 5 Repeat Row 3, but do not work the cable twists, work these stitches in stockinette stitch.

Repeat Rows 2–5 until the raglan "seam" (the seed stitch and cable) measures 4½ (5, 6, 7)" (11.5 [13, 15, 18]cm).

First Sleeve

Work across the stitches to the middle of the first cable, m1, k2, seed stitch 3, turn.

Working on these stitches only, work back and forth in seed stitch for 4 rows, change to CC, work 1 row seed stitch. Bind off. (Alternate: Work 5 rows seed stitch in MC, bind off in seed stitch).

Second Sleeve

Slip center body stitches to a holder until you reach the beginning of the second seed stitch and cable panel. Rejoin yarn, seed stitch 3, k2, m1, work to end of row. Work second sleeve trim to match first.

Body and Neck Trim

With RS facing, rejoin yarn to remaining stitches left on holder, seed stitch across these stitches, pick up and knit 31 (36, 41, 45) stitches up right front, 29 (38, 53, 67) stitches across cast-on stitches around neck, 31 (35, 41, 45) stitches down left front. Depending on how many stitches you had left for the back, you need an even number here to make the seed stitch work properly, so add or lose one if necessary (whichever is the easiest for you). Working in rounds, work 4 rows seed stitch, change to contrast yarn, work 1 round in seed stitch, bind off in seed stitch. Alternate: work 5 rows seed stitch in MC, bind off in seed stitch.

Finishing

Sew up sleeve seams at underarm.

The shoulder "seams" are in a moss and cable pattern that will entertain you for the very short time it takes you to knit the shrug.

It continues to amuse us that a zigzagging strip of seed stitch can become a domelike cap for a baby's head.

Baby Fever: Too Cute Is Never Enough

Excuse us, but the lack of baby knits so far is making us twitchy. When the challenge of dressing the older child becomes overwhelming, we recommend returning to the sweet, quick solace of projects for the child too small to protest. They may flap their chubby arms in distress, but they can't escape the loving application of snurgly, snurfly handknits.

Origami for the Round, Small Head

Heartbreakingly cute. That's not a term we casually throw around. Cute things abound, but it is the rare thing that is so cute you can feel a crack forming in your heart. A baby decked out in an old-fashioned, ear-insulating pilot cap certainly qualifies. Like the wildly popular Heartbreakingly Cute Baby Kimono, which appeared in our first book, this bonnet shows Cristina Shiffman's love for ingenious one-piece construction of three-dimensional garments. Cristina used seed stitch for a sophisticated look, and added I-cord ties to make the cap more comfortable under chubby chins.

This pattern is useful for another reason. I don't know about you, but the hull of the *SS Kay's Stash* is encrusted with single-skein barnacles of Koigu. In the quest for great ways to use this exquisite handpainted merino wool, this pattern is a great destination.

HEARTBREAKINGLY CUTE PILOT CAP *by Cristina Bernardi Shiffman*

SIZE
0–8 (9–24) months

MATERIALS
- (1) super fine
- 1 skein Koigu KPPPM, 100% merino wool, 1¾ oz (50g), 175 yd (160m), in color P609
- Size 3 (3.25mm) single-pointed needles (for body of cap) and double-pointed needles (for I-cord ties)
- Split-ring stitch marker

GAUGE
22 stitches and 42 rows = 4" (10cm) in seed stitch

DIFFICULTY
As easy as loving a baby's big ol' head

NOTE
To simplify the instructions, the pattern is written in sections, but there is no binding off between sections (see illustration). Slip a split-ring marker into the right side of the piece to help remind you which side you're on; move the marker to the first row of each section to help you keep track of rows. Slipping the first stitch of each row purlwise keeps the edges neater.

Cap
Cast on 24 (32) stitches.

Section 1
Row 1 (RS) k2, kfb into next stitch, (k1, p1) across the row (seed stitch) to last 4 stitches, k2tog, k2.

Row 2 (WS) k3, work in seed stitch, purling the knit stitches and knitting the purl stitches to last 3 stitches, k3.

Repeat rows 1–2 until a total of 24 (32) rows have been worked.

Section 2
Row 1 (RS) k2, ssk, work seed stitch across the row to last 3 stitches, kfb into next stitch, k2.

Row 2 (WS) k3, work in seed stitch to last 3 stitches, k3.

Repeat rows 1–2 until a total of 24 (32) rows have been worked.

Section 3
Repeat rows 1–2 of Section 1 until a total of 12 (16) rows have been worked.

Section 4
Repeat rows 1–2 of Section 2 until a total of 12 (16) rows have been worked.

Section 5
Repeat Section 1.

Section 6
Repeat Section 2.

Bind off all stitches.

Referring to the illustration, sew side A to side A, B to B, C to C, and D to D. Weave in ends.

I-Cord Ties
In the illustration, a dot marks the spots where the ties will be placed. Using double-pointed needles, pick up and knit 3 stitches at each marked spot and knit I-cords for 6 to 8" (15–20.5cm). Cut the yarn at the ends, thread through a tapestry needle, and draw it through the 3 stitches, pulling to close. Secure the ends.

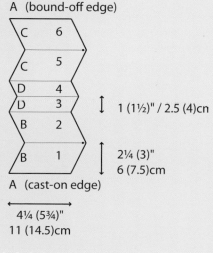

A (bound-off edge)

C	6
C	5
D	4
D	3
B	2
B	1

1 (1½)" / 2.5 (4)cn

2¼ (3)"
6 (7.5)cm

A (cast-on edge)

4¼ (5¾)"
11 (14.5)cm

Blu Jeans! Now More Blu Than Ever!

We love these pants. The original, cuffed jeans version was first published in knitty.com, the online knitting magazine. Babies who wore these pants were mobbed with admirers asking where they got them. We even heard from a Swedish kids boutique that wanted to produce them for sale. They are so irresistible, so comfortable for babies to wear, and so hardwearing and easy-care, that we are on a mission to make Blu baby jeans a staple of the modern baby's wardrobe. It is a crime to put tender baby legs into stiff fabric jeans, when this cuter, stretchier, softer version is there for the knitting. Moms, grans, and aunties of the world: Git going! Make it happen!

Because we can never stop fiddling with an idea, we also cooked up a pattern for unisex baggy shorts. Baby surfers, with their tiny huarache sandals and bushy bushy blond hairdos, need a fringed, cropped version. To make the cropped pants, simply omit the cuff instructions, cast on at the point indicated in the pattern for the cropped version, and otherwise follow the pattern to completion. The instructions for the fringe appear at the end of the pattern.

As with all jeans, you can choose your fit: relaxed, traditional, or slim. The good news is that in short order, your growing baby will end up wearing all three.

BLU

by Cristina Bernardi Shiffman and Kay Gardiner

This pattern calls for denim yarn, which has unique and beautiful properties.

After knitting, the pants will shrink approximately 5 to 15 percent, in length only, on the first washing in hot water. The pattern takes this shrinkage into account. The jeans will also fade gently with washing and wear, showing white flecks just like woven denim fabric.

SIZE:
0–3 (3–6, 6–12, 12–18, 18–24) months

FINISHED MEASUREMENTS (BEFORE SHRINKING)
Waist: 13 (15, 17, 20, 22)" (33 [38, 43, 51, 56]cm)

Inseam Length: 7 (8, 9, 10, 11)" (18 [20, 23, 25, 28]cm)

Side Length: 12 (13, 14½, 16, 18)" (30 [33, 37, 41, 46]cm)

MATERIALS

- 🧶 medium/worsted
- Rowan Denim, 100% cotton, 103 yd (93m), 1¾ oz (50g), 2 (2, 3, 3, 3) skeins in Nashville (dark indigo) (A); 1 (1, 1, 1, 1) skein in Tennessee (light blue) (B)
- 🧶 light/DK
- Small amount of Rowan Handknit Cotton, 100% cotton, 1¾ oz (50g), 93 yd (85m), orange (or desired color) for seams and embroidery
- Size 6 (4mm) straight needles, or size needed to obtain gauge
- Size 11 (8mm) needle for cropped version
- Size D-3 crochet hook (optional)
- Smooth cotton waste yarn
- 18" (45.5cm) length of ¾" (2cm)-wide elastic
- Sewing needle
- Sewing thread
- Optional: Small piece of wool felt for label

Embroidering the details is not a big deal. Freehand it!

- Small amount of blue embroidery floss for label
- Button

GAUGE
20 stitches and 24 rows = 4" (10cm) in stockinette stitch before washing

20 stitches and 28 rows = 4" (10cm) in stockinette stitch after washing

DIFFICULTY
A handful of knitting, a bit of finishing

NOTE ON SUBSTITUTING YARN
Although denim yarn best imitates the look of real blue jeans and makes people laugh with delight, you can substitute any DK-weight yarn with no difficulty. The only adjustment you need to make is to the length of the legs.

The pattern has you knit the legs to a specific measurement, for example, 10" (25.5cm) for the 12–18 month size. If you are using a yarn other than denim, you should subtract 15 percent, in this case 1½" (4cm), from the length. You need not modify any measurements other than leg length. Confession: If it were me doing the knitting, I would not alter the measurements at all, but simply let the baby grow into the slightly longer pants. If there is one thing that we can count on babies to do, it's to grow.

But remember, if you use another yarn, ignore our washing instructions, and follow the care instructions for your yarn. If you wash any other cotton yarn in a hot wash, it is likely to shrink just like denim. If you wash wool pants in hot water, you'll get an adorable pair of hamster pants.

NOTE
Because the selvedges will be visible, slip the first stitch of every row purlwise throughout the pattern.

Right Leg

Cuffed version *Using Color B, cast on 35 (41, 47, 53, 59) stitches.

Work 10 (12, 14, 16, 18) rows in reverse stockinette stitch (purl on RS; knit on WS), ending with a WS row; break yarn.

Cropped version *Using Color A, cast on 35 (41, 47, 53, 59) stitches and start here.

Both versions Using Color A, work 2 rows in stockinette stitch.

Next row (RS) Slip 1, k1, m1, knit to last 2 stitches, m1, k2—37 (43, 49, 55, 61) sts.

Work 3 (3, 5, 5) rows even in stockinette stitch.

Repeat the last 4 (4, 4, 6, 6) rows 7 times more—51 (57, 63, 69, 75) sts.*

Cuffed version Continue in stockinette stitch until the work measures 7 (8, 9, 10, 11)" (18 [20, 23, 25, 28]cm) from the cast-on edge (including cuff), ending with a WS row.

Cropped version Continue in stockinette until the work measures 5½ (6½, 7, 8, 9)" (15[17, 19, 21, 24]cm) from the cast-on edge, ending with a WS row.

Shape Seat

Next row (RS) Bind off 3 stitches, knit to end.
Next row (WS) Bind off 5 stitches, purl to end.
Next row (RS) Slip 1, k2tog, knit to end.
Next row (WS) Bind off 3 stitches, purl to end.
Next row (RS) Slip 1, k2tog, knit to end.
Next row (WS) Slip 1, p2tog, purl to end.

Repeat these last 2 rows once more—35 [41, 47, 53, 59] sts.

Cuffed version** Continue in stockinette stitch and work even until the piece measures 10 (11½, 13, 14½, 16)" (25 [29, 33, 37, 41]cm) from the cast-on edge, ending with a WS row.

Cropped version** Continue in

stockinette stitch and work even until the piece measures 8½ (10, 11, 12½, 14)" (21.5 [25.5, 28, 32, 35.5]cm from the cast-on edge, ending with a WS row.

Phony Seam

Next row (RS) k17 (20, 23, 26, 29); drop the next stitch from the left needle and unravel it down to the first row. With a spare knitting needle and starting at the cast-on edge, pick up the "ladders" of the dropped stitch again, but instead of picking up each ladder individually as you normally would to repair a dropped stitch, pick up 1 ladder, then 2 ladders together, repeating this sequence until you have picked up all the ladders. IMPORTANT: PICK UP AS IF TO KNIT, even on the reverse stockinette stitch of the cuff portion (this creates the illusion of an inside-out seam, as on a real jean cuff). When you have picked up all the way back to the top, place the dropped stitch back on the left needle and knit to the end of the row.

Waistband

Next row (WS) Knit all stitches.

Work 9 (9, 9, 11, 11) rows in stockinette stitch.

Repeat the last 10 (10, 10, 12, 12) rows once more. The first garter ridge marks the lower edge of the waistband; the second garter ridge forms a turning ridge, for folding the waistband over to make an elastic casing.

Place all stitches on a length of waste yarn that is long enough to hold the stitches without bunching. Tie the waste yarn into a firm double knot and trim the ends to 2" (5cm).**

Left Leg

Work as for Right Leg from * to *.

Cuffed version Continue in stockinette stitch until the work measures 7 (8, 9, 10, 11)" (18 [20, 23, 25, 28cm) (including cuff), ending with a RS row.

Cropped version Continue in stockinette

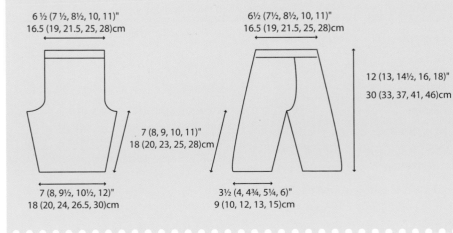

6 ½ (7 ½, 8½, 10, 11)"
16.5 (19, 21.5, 25, 28)cm

7 (8, 9, 10, 11)"
18 (20, 23, 25, 28)cm

7 (8, 9½, 10½, 12)"
18 (20, 24, 26.5, 30)cm

6½ (7½, 8½, 10, 11)"
16.5 (19, 21.5, 25, 28)cm

12 (13, 14½, 16, 18)"
30 (33, 37, 41, 46)cm

3½ (4, 4¾, 5¼, 6)"
9 (10, 12, 13, 15)cm

stitch until the work measures 5.5 (6.5, 7, 8, 9)" (15 [17, 19, 21, 24]cm) from the cast-on edge, ending with a RS row.

Shape Seat

Next row (WS) Bind off 3 stitches, purl to end.
Next row (RS) Bind off 5 stitches, knit to end.
Next row (WS) p1, p2tog, purl to end.
Next row (RS) Bind off 3 stitches, knit to end.
Next row (WS) p1, p2tog, purl to end.
Next row (RS) k1, k2tog, knit to end.

Repeat the last 2 rows once more—35 (41, 47, 53, 59) sts.

Continue as for Right Leg from ** to **.

Finishing

Sew in ends.

If you are using denim yarn, machine wash the pieces in hot water. Tumble dry on the cotton setting. Lightly press to facilitate sewing.

Embroidered Jean Details

Using orange yarn and referring to the photograph as a guide, embroider the fly and the front and back pockets, using backstitch. At the beginning and end of the pocket lines, layer 3 backstitches for the rivets.

Sew on a button, or embroider a faux button, at the top of the fly.

Felt Label (optional)

Cut out and embroider the felt label as desired. Use sewing thread to attach the felt label, or other label of your choice, to the back waistband. Small whipstitches do the job nicely.

Sew the Rise and Inner Legs

Start by joining the rise (the center front and back seams). To orient the edges, lay the left and right pieces flat, right sides up, with both crotch edges meeting in the center. Slightly overlap the left side over the right side at the rise. With orange cotton yarn (or other color of your choice), sew a backstitch seam, starting at the turning ridge of the waistband and working down to the crotch in the front. Now turn the piece over, with the front seam facing down, and sew the back of the rise, working in backstitch, from the turning ridge of the waistband down to the seat. (At this point, the crotch is still open.)

Using mattress stitch (page 153), join the remaining section of the waistband (the short section above the turning ridge, which later will be folded to the inside to form an elastic casing).

Join the Inner Leg Seams

With the front of the jeans facing up, slightly overlap the front leg edges over the back leg edges, and sew the inner seam with backstitch in a single seam from the bottom edge of one leg to the bottom edge of the other leg. This will make a flat, visible inner leg seam that looks like a classic blue jeans seam.

Elastic Waist

Create a loop with the elastic by laying the ends over one another and running a few rows of hand or machine stitches through the overlap to secure. (If possible, try the elastic on the baby to check the fit; it should be secure and flat, but not tight, around the baby's waist. If you can't try it on the baby, make sure the loop of elastic will fit inside the waist of the jeans without either gathering the waist or stretching it out.) Turn the pants inside out and position the elastic inside the waistband. Remove the waste yarn from the live stitches and use matching yarn to sew the live stitches down to the groove of stitches that marks the bottom of the waistband.

Fringe for Cropped Version

Using a size 11 (8mm) needle, pick up and knit stitches one-to-one from the cast on edge of the leg. Using sewing thread, secure the loops with small hand or machine stitches. Snip each loop and trim unevenly. Voila: fringe!

You're done! Put pants on baby and take baby out in public immediately. Collect oohs, aahs, and requests to knit jeans for other babies.

Fern: The Perils of Competitive Knitting

This was the greatest moment in Mr. Zuckerman's life. It is deeply satisfying to win a prize in front of a lot of people. —E. B. White, from Charlotte's Web

Ann ✳ Knitting is not, by its nature, competitive. You knit, and you either finish or you don't. It looks great, or it looks awful. Knitting is either a means to an end or a pleasant way to pass the time. A product or a process. There are no winners or losers in knitting.

Except at the state fair.

My story begins a few years ago, when I had just jumped into the deep swimming hole that is knitting. In the midst of reading every single piece of knitting prose I could find, I discovered the Knitting Guild of America's Master Knitter program. The program provides lists of swatches and projects and reports to make, with difficulty increasing at each level. Level I. Level II. The dreaded Level III, which calls for knitting a hut that can withstand a 50-mph gale.

I was tempted to send off for the instructions for Level I, but I couldn't quite do it. I was uncomfortable with the thought that somebody unknown to me would scrutinize my swatches of knitting. A sympathetic eye, surely—somebody who cared enough about the craft of knitting to volunteer to help complete strangers do their best. Still, these inquiring eyes would be checking to see and would likely notice . . . what? I didn't even know what they would notice, but it was unpleasant to consider the ways in which my knitting might suck. It seemed so objective, so absolute. I didn't see it the way the Knitting Guild of America intended it—the part where they say: "The TKGA Master Knitting Program© is a non-competitive and rewarding achievement program for advanced knitters. Program completion culminates in the presentation of the coveted TKGA Master Knitter title and pin." Participating in this program meant I was either going to be a Master Knitter or not. Pin or no pin. Was I ready to risk the possibility that I might not have what it takes? No *way*.

People at baby showers don't tell you that you sewed on the sleeves wrong. They just smile and say "adorable" no matter what misshapen thing it is that you've given them. Anybody who finishes anything is a winner. That was my story, and I was sticking to it.

A Golden Opportunity

It was the tale of a spider and a pig that changed my thinking about knitting for scrutiny. E. B. White's *Charlotte's Web* has broken my heart many times. As I read the book to small Clif, I cried all over again. Wilbur the pig, the little girl Fern who loves him, and Charlotte the magnificent spider whose eloquent webs save Wilbur's bacon—booooo hoooo! It's perfect, the way the story builds toward the climactic county fair. It is impossible to read *Charlotte's Web* and not feel a fierce need to a) rescue a pig, b) love spiders, and c) enter a county fair.

It was irresistible, this county fair urge. I'd been hit in the head with a funnel cake of purpose. I could be a part of this age-old tradition of harvest celebrations. I could pile the whole family into our truck and sing the lyrics to the *State Fair* song. I wouldn't miss it; I wouldn't even be late. Maybe I didn't have a pig to enter, but I could enter the needlework competition. I could knit something. It would give a little shape to my knitting—a goal, a deadline, an opportunity to try my best and see what would come of it.

State Fair Knitting: The thrill of victory, the agony of . . . somebody else's superior stockinette.

A Piece of Cake

Nobody likes to admit to being competitive. It's not "attractive," as my mother would have said. To my mother, things tended to be either "attractive" (houses, neighbors, the color beige) or "not attractive" (eye shadow on a seventh grader, bragging, calling your sister "Stupid" even when it is obvious that she really is stupid). I wish my mom were here so we could discuss the Southern female imperative of doing it perfectly while not appearing to try, but she died when I was in college, before I noticed how the quest for perfection, in just about every situation, is a great way to drive yourself nuts.

I guess that's the part I inherited from her: never let it show. The fact is, I hate to lose so much that if I'm not pretty sure I'm going to prevail, then I don't even try. It's why I never took calculus: It was likely that I would be bad at it, so why take the class? Isn't that terrible? It's not a very healthy way to go through life, this avoidance of being declared mediocre—and it certainly rules out pretty much any situation in which a pin is awarded: organized sports, sororities, and master knitter programs. Entering the county fair was so gentle a competition, and the stakes were so low, that even I could imagine that it would be fun. Besides, how hard could it be to win a blue ribbon at the Wilson County Fair? *I am a damn fine knitter,* I told myself.

Wilson County is east of Nashville. Their county fair is a gem: baby pageants, lawn mower races, even a speed-crochet contest. It gives a person an impulse to wear gingham and to have a crush on a boy. It feels like 1945. It's just what I wanted to be part of—not too big, and surely not too many knitters. The problem was timing: The Wilson County Fair takes place in mid August. I wouldn't have enough time to make an entry. This unfortunate discovery meant that I was going to have to go straight to the big time: the Tennessee State Fair.

I downloaded the 84-page Tennessee State Fair Creative Arts catalog, which lists every single way a person can win a blue ribbon in the realm of Creative Arts. Department P, Class 9, Lot 4: "Knitting, Children's Sweater." That was the category for me. I had about two months to create an entry, and I couldn't imagine finishing a fabulous adult-sized garment in time.

The yarn I would use was obvious: a batch of tweedy wools in a fingering weight. I imagined a little coat, for a little girl, in the colors of the woods of the Cumberland Plateau outside Nashville. When you walk through the woods in early spring, there's a lovely light that comes because the trees have only just begun to leaf out—a lot of brown down low, shifting to bright green and blue sky above. It's so beautiful in those woods. I had the clear image in my mind of what this coat would be. I'd never been so sure of a project.

The category was "Knitting, Children's Sweater." Did I have what it takes to bring home the bacon?

I swatched and sketched and thought about the coat, and in a few days I was cranking out stripes in six shades of fecund Cumberland Plateau. I've never had such fun. I embroidered fiddleheads along the bottom, remembering how vivid the new ferns are among the leaves in the woods. But I named the coat for the heroine of *Charlotte's Web* as much as for the scrolls of green along the bottom. Fern. That's what I called this coat.

In It to Win It

The day for delivering entries to the Creative Arts Building at the Fairgrounds was hot and flat. Late August in Nashville is not for anybody who craves a cool, misty day. I was excited to bring Fern to meet its destiny. I was also curious to see what the competition would be. From the doorway, it was easy to see one of the entries: a crocheted, five-foot-tall wedding cake.

I walked around the tables filled with entries, trying not to look nosy despite the fact that I was insanely nosy. Shawls, sweaters, socks, scarves. Fair Isle. Intarsia. I was especially interested in children's items—who was I up against? There was a colossal, ivory-colored blanket, perfectly folded: the most serious, hardcore piece of knitting I had ever seen. Was it knitted or crocheted? It didn't matter. It was enormous, and it was there to win. At least it was too big to be a candidate for "Knitting, Children's Sweater." I saw a fair amount of baby stuff, but not much "Knitting, Children's Sweater." It was looking promising. Did I want a true competition, against hundreds of other knitters? Heck no. I wanted to win, however lame it was going to be.

I handed over Fern, on its little hanger, suddenly realizing that it was too weird looking.

The judging was scheduled for a few days after the drop-off, so I waited and entertained myself by seeing the victories that blog friends were scoring in their own state fairs. Most of the other state fairs seemed to have more entries. A couple of brand-new knitters won blue ribbons for their first projects. So great. I learned a lot about batter-fried Oreos, Krystal hamburger-eating competitions, and butter sculptures. Win or lose, I was assured that I could find solace in a deep-fried Twinkie.

The Big Reveal

There was no way I was going alone to see how Fern had weathered the competition. It was just too dorky to go by myself; only a person who had lost all perspective would do a thing like that. I called on a fellow knitter, Angela, to go with me. Angela had a highly developed sense of the absurd. Weeping, swapping ribbons, badmouthing the other entrants—Angela's cool presence would keep me from doing anything unattractive.

As we wandered the Creative Arts Building, we found competition categories to file away for the future: Lego Kit Assembly, Any Other Pie, Ham (judging included "Desirability of aroma as determined by probing"). We glimpsed the five-foot-tall crocheted wedding cake across the hall, a beacon guiding us toward the needlecraft area. I was actually jumpy. Why did I care? Why did it matter? I looked down the row of display cases, seeing colorful examples of knitterly patriotism, fluffy baby things, some ponchos. The first ribbon I noticed was the colossal ivory blanket. Best of Show.

I found Fern.

Posed on a small chair, the sweater looked like the girl inside had just evaporated, leaving behind her handknit. A ribbon was hooked to one of the buttons that I had picked because they looked like a woodland frog's eyes.

Second place. Fern had won a red ribbon. Not terrible, but not TERRIFIC, either. Not RADIANT. It was so anticlimactic, such a thud. Would I have been ecstatic if I'd won a blue ribbon? I don't know, but I was deflated to discover I hadn't. I really thought I had nailed this thing. I was dying to see who had beat me out. Folded into a perfect square beside the chair was a small Fair Isle sweater with a blue ribbon tied to a button. "It looks like it was made by a *machine*," I said to Angela, which was the meanest, sourest, worst thing I could think of to say.

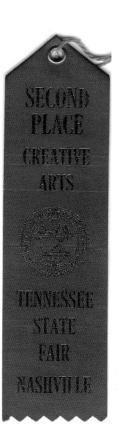

Angela ignored my unattractive comment and chirped: "You won a ribbon!" then took off to chase her small boy across the hall. Alone for a minute, I crouched down to study the blue ribbon winner. Perfect, unwavering stitches. Smooth shoulder seams. Absolutely no wobbly transition between colors. It was a beautiful piece of knitting, and I despised it. I was almost certain it was made from a store-bought pattern—it looked like a Dale of Norway ski sweater! In Tennessee, for heaven's sake! So disrespectful, unlike Fern, which embraced the woods and flora of middle Tennessee. What kind of Tennessean child wears a Norwegian ski sweater? Didn't it matter that my sweater was made from scratch, from my own personal brain, unique? What about originality? Did nobody notice that there were fiddleheads stitched to my sweater? *Fiddleheads*, people.

Of course it didn't matter. It wasn't a design competition; it was a *knitting* competition, and it was obvious in about a second's glance that The Machine's sweater was superior in every way. My sweater, under the fiddleheads and the frog-eye buttons, was flawed in many places. The seed stitch edging was wavy because I hadn't gone down a needle size; the buttonhole bands were attached in what can only be called homemade fashion; the brazillion ends I'd woven in made the inside of the sweater lumpy. The more I studied the perfection of The Machine's work, the more imperfect mine became. I began to realize that my meager sweater was lucky even to be in the same case as The Machine's sweater. As much as I hated to admit it, that blue ribbon sweater looked like the work of . . . a master knitter.

The next day, I discussed the situation with some knitters who were in the know about the situation out there at the Creative Arts Building. They confirmed the fact that yes, The Machine won every year, so skilled that she rarely won anything but blue ribbons. She scared away competition—so dominant, in fact, that the rules were rewritten to make it harder for knitters like The Machine to win a category every year.

Later, after a period during which I tried to be attractive in the face of defeat, I revisited the Master Knitter's website and scanned the list of brave souls who had completed all the Levels. There she was, The Machine, listed right there among the elite group of Master Knitters. Pin owners. The certified. Maybe a person really does need to be a Master Knitter to knit like a master. Maybe a person has to work to improve at something. Maybe she should actually try.

A couple of weeks after the fair ended, a check arrived from the Tennessee State Fair. Seven bucks, the award for second place, "Knitting, Children's Sweater." It was too late for funnel cake, but I decided to mark my experience as best I could. I cashed my check and headed for the nearest Krystal, where I ordered up four cheese Krystals, an order of Vidalia onion rings, and a Diet Coke. As I drove home, a square hamburger in one hand, steering wheel in the other, I remembered that making Fern was the most fun I had ever had as a knitter. The utter joy at coming up with an idea and making it, all by myself, was worth it all: the second placeness of my knitting, my status as one of the many who had lost out to the Master Knitter, the incredible case of heartburn that was soon to come my way.

FERN

This coat is knitted in one piece from the bottom up to the armholes, then the fronts and back are knitted separately in a k3, p1 rib pattern. Set-in sleeves. Seed stitch borders and button bands. Short-row collar.

SIZE
Small (Medium)

FINISHED CHEST CIRCUMFERENCE
26 (28)" (66 [71]cm)

MATERIALS
- (1) super fine
- Jamieson's Spindrift, 100% Shetland wool, ¾ oz (25g), 115 yd (105m), 2 balls in Moss (A), 2 balls in Tundra (B), 2 balls in Bracken (C), 2 balls in Moorgrass (D), 2 balls in Leprechaun (E), 2 balls in Verdigris (F)
- Small amount of Spindrift in chartreuse for embroidery
- Size 2 (2.75mm) 24" (60cm) circular needles
- Size 3 (3.25mm) 24" (60cm) circular needles, or size needed to obtain gauge
- Stitch markers
- Waste yarn
- Stitch holders
- Safety pins
- 8 (9) buttons
- Tapestry needle

GAUGE
26 stitches and 36 rows = 4" (10cm) in stockinette stitch with size 3 (3.25mm) needles

DIFFICULTY
Stay close to the path, and you won't get lost.

NOTES
SKIRT STRIPE PATTERN
Worked in stockinette stitch (knit on RS rows, purl on WS rows). For small size, begin at *; (for medium size, work all rows): 4 rows B, 3C, 4D, 2C, 3B, *3B, 6C, 2D, 3C, 2B, 2C, 2E, 7C, 6B, 3D, 6C, 2B, 2C, 4E, 6C, 7D, 3B, 5C, 6E, 3C, 2F, 2C, 6D, 2B, 2E, 4F.

Yoke Stripe Pattern
Worked in stockinette stitch: 4 rows E, 6D, 3E, 4F, 2D, 2F, 6E, 5D, 2F, 2E, 5D, 6F, 4E. Both sizes: Work final rows in E.

Sleeve Stripe Pattern
Worked in stockinette stitch. For small size, begin at * and end at **. For medium size, work all rows. 4C, 2B, 2C, 2E, 7C, *5B, 3D, 5C, 2B, 2C, 4E, 6C, 6D, 3B, 5C, 6E, 3C, 2F, 2C, 6D, 2B, 2E, 4F, 4E, 7D, 3E, 3D, 3E, 4F, 2D, 2F, 6E, 5D, 2F, 2E, 5D, 5F, 3E**, 4F, 4E.

Body

Skirt

With smaller needles and using color A, cast on 222 (254) stitches.

Row 1 (RS) *k1, p1; repeat from * over first 57 (65) stitches, place a stitch marker, continue in pattern until you have knitted 108 (124) stitches from the marker, place a second stitch marker, continue in pattern over remaining 57 (65) stitches—222 (254) sts.

Row 2 p1, k1; repeat from * across.
Rows 3–8 Repeat rows 1–2 three times for seed stitch pattern.
Next row (RS) Change to larger needles, put the first 6 stitches on a small stitch holder or waste yarn (these will be picked up later to work the right buttonhole band), and using color B, knit to last 6 stitches, put last 6 stitches on a small stitch holder or waste yarn (these will be picked up later to work the left button band)—210 (242) sts.

Begin skirt stripe pattern, working 7 rows.

Decrease Row (RS) Knit to last 4 stitches before the first stitch marker, k2tog, k2, slip the marker, k2, ssk, knit to last 4 stitches before the second marker, k2tog, k2, slip the marker, k2, ssk, knit to end.

Repeat the last 8 rows 10 (12) times more—166 (190) sts.

Continue to work skirt stripe pattern to completion.

Bind off all stitches.

Decorative ridge

With WS facing (so that a ridge of the bound-off stitches is formed on RS), size 3 needles, and using color F, pick up and knit 168 (192) stitches across the bound-off edge of the work. (This is two stitches more than you just bound off.)

Yoke

Row 1 (RS) Using E, begin yoke stripe pattern AND rib pattern as follows: *k3, p1; repeat from * to last 4 stitches, k4.
Row 2 (WS) p4, *k1, p3; repeat from * to end.
Rows 3–4 Work rib pattern and yoke stripe pattern as established.

Note From this point on, the right front, left front, and back are knitted separately.

Tip

You can easily replace the stripe pattern shown here with your own freestyle mixing of colors. That's how the first Fern was created. Choosing your own color pattern frees you from constantly referring to the pattern. And who knows—your stripe pattern may well please you more than ours.

This is the very forest that inspired Fern.

Right Front Yoke

Shape Armhole

Next row (RS) Continuing yoke stripe pattern, work k3, p1 rib pattern over first 39 (45) stitches. Put all other stitches on a holder.

Next row (WS) Bind off 5 stitches, work in rib pattern to end.

Next row (RS) Work even in rib pattern.

Next row (WS) Bind off 4 stitches, work in rib pattern to end.

Next row (RS) Work even in rib pattern.

Next row (WS) Bind off 1 stitch, work in rib pattern to end—29 (35) sts.

Continue in rib and yoke stripe pattern until the yoke measures 5" (6¼") (12.5 [16]cm) from the decorative ridge, ending with a WS row.

Shape Neck

Next row (RS) Bind off 6 (8) stitches, work to end.

Next and all WS rows Work even in rib pattern.

Next RS row Bind off 3 (3) stitches, work to end.

Next RS row Bind off 2 (2) stitches, work to end.

Next RS row Bind off 2 (0) stitches, work to end.

Next RS row Bind off 1 (1) stitch, work to end.

Next RS row Bind off 1 (1) stitch, work to end.

Next RS row Bind off 0 (1) stitch, work to end—14 (19) sts.

Shape Shoulder

Next row (WS) Bind off 7 (7) stitches. Work to end.

Next row (RS) Work even.

Next row (WS) Bind off 7 (6) stitches.

For medium size only

Next row (RS) Work even.

Next row (WS) Bind off 6 stitches.

Back Yoke

With RS facing, matching the yoke stripe pattern on the right front and, AT THE SAME TIME, continuing in k3, p1 rib pattern as established, pick up and knit the next 90 (102) stitches from the stitch holder, leaving the remaining stitches on the stitch holder or waste yarn.

Bind off 5 stitches at the beginning of the next 2 rows; 4 stitches at the beginning of the next 2 rows; 1 stitch at the beginning of the next 2 rows—70 (82) sts.

Continue in rib and stripe pattern until the yoke measures 6½" (7½") (16.5 [19]cm) from the decorative ridge.

Shape Shoulders

For small size only At the beginning of the next 4 rows, bind off 7 stitches. Place the remaining 42 stitches on a stitch holder or waste yarn.

For medium size only Bind off 7 stitches at the beginning of the next 2 rows; then, bind off 6 stitches at the beginning of the next 4 rows. Place the remaining 44 stitches on a stitch holder or waste yarn.

Left Front Yoke

Shape Armhole

With RS facing, matching the yoke stripe pattern on the right front and back and, AT THE SAME TIME, continuing in k3, p1 rib pattern, place the remaining 39 (45) stitches from the stitch holder on the needle, join yarn, bind off the first 5 stitches, work to end.

Next row (WS) Work even.

Next row (RS) Bind off 4 stitches, work to end.

Next row (WS) Work even.

Next row (RS) Bind off 1 stitch, work to end—29 (35) sts.

Work even until the yoke measures 5" (6¼") (12.5 [16]cm) from the decorative ridge, ending with a RS row.

Shape Neck

Next row (WS) Bind off 6 (8) stitches, work to end.

Next and all RS rows Work even.

Next WS row Bind off 3 (3) stitches, work to end.

Next WS row Bind off 2 (2) stitches, work to end.

Next WS row Bind off 2 (0) stitches, work to end.

Next WS row Bind off 1 (1) stitch, work to end.

Next WS row Bind off 1 (1) stitch, work to end.

Next WS row Bind off 0 (1) stitch, work to end—14 (19) sts.

Shape shoulder

Next row (RS) Bind off 7 (7) stitches, work to end.

Next row (WS) Work even.

Next row (RS) Bind off 7 (6) stitches.

For medium size only

Next row (WS) Work even.

Next row (RS) Bind off 6 stitches.

Sleeve (make 2)

With smaller needles and using color A, cast on 40 (48) stitches.

Row 1 (RS) *k1, p1; repeat from * across.
Row 2 (WS) *p1, k1; repeat from * across.
Rows 3–8 Repeat rows 1–2 three times for seed stitch pattern.

Change to larger needles and beginning the sleeve stripe pattern, work 6 rows.

Next row (RS) k2, m1, knit to last 2 stitches, m1, k2—42 (50) sts.
Work 3 rows even in sleeve stripe pattern.
Next row (RS) k2, m1, knit to last 2 stitches, m1, k2—44 (52) sts.

Repeat the last 4 rows 15 times more—74 (82) sts.

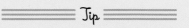

Tip

There are often three things going on at once here: stripe pattern, shaping, and rib pattern. The yoke especially can feel like you are patting your head, rubbing your stomach, and chewing gum at once. Come on—you're so coordinated!

Work even until the sleeve measures 9" (10¾") (23 [27]cm) from the cast-on edge, ending with a WS row.

Shape Sleeve Cap

Bind off 5 stitches at the beginning of the next 2 rows, then 4 stitches at the beginning of the next 2 rows—56 (64) sts.

Decrease Row (RS) k2, ssk, knit to last 4 stitches, k2tog, k2—54 (62) sts.

Work 3 rows even.

Repeat the last 4 rows once more, then work the Decrease Row on every RS row 12 (16) times more—28 (28) sts.

Next row (WS) Work even.

Bind off 2 stitches at the beginning of the next 8 rows, bind off the remaining 12 (12) stitches.

Left Front Button Band

Transfer the 6 stitches from the holder to a size 2 (2.75mm) needle. With RS facing, using color A, using a firm hand to avoid unevenness, work even in seed stitch. When the button band is the same length as the left front to the beginning of the neck shaping, place the stitches on a holder. Leave a nice long tail in case you need to add a few rows of button band when you're sewing it on. Sew the button

band to the front edge. Pin 8 (9) safety pins evenly along the button band to mark button placement.

Right Front Buttonhole Band

Transfer the 6 stitches from the holder to a size 2 (2.75mm) needle. With WS facing, using color A, work in seed stitch to end. Work even in seed stitch, making a buttonhole to correspond to each button marker on the button band as follows:

Buttonhole Row (RS) Work seed stitch for 2 stitches, yo, k2tog, work to end.

Work in seed stitch until the buttonhole band is the same length as the right front to the beginning of the neck shaping, ending with a WS row. Place the stitches on a holder. Do not break the yarn— you will be using it to make the collar.

Sew Button Band and Buttonhole Band in place.

Finishing

Block all pieces.

Sew the shoulder seams.

Collar

With RS facing and smaller needles and using the color A yarn from the buttonhole band, work in seed stitch as

established across the first 6 stitches of the buttonhole band. Pick up and knit 19 (22) stitches along the right front neck shaping, 42 (44) stitches across the back neck, 19 (22) stitches along the left front neck shaping. Work the 6 button band stitches in seed stitch.—92 (100) sts.

Work 18 (22) rows even in seed stitch on all stitches.

Continuing in pattern, begin short-row shaping as follows:

Next 2 rows Work to last 5 stitches, w&t.

Next 2 rows Work to last 7 stitches, w&t.

Next 2 rows Work to last 9 stitches, w&t.

Next 2 rows Work to last 11 stitches, w&t.

Next 2 rows Work to last 13 stitches, w&t.

Next 2 rows Work to last 15 stitches, w&t.

Next 2 rows Work to end of row.

Bind off all stitches.

Embroidery

Using chartreuse yarn and the tapestry needle, chain-stitch fiddleheads all around the lower edge of the coat, as shown in photograph on page 107.

Sew on buttons. Find a small girl. Dress her up and head for the woods.

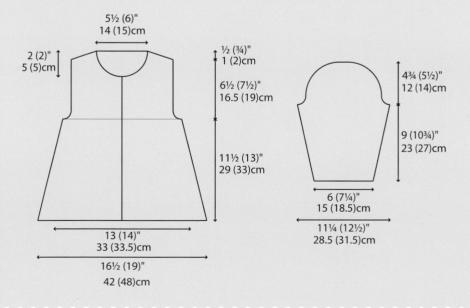

Chapter Four

Occasional KNITTING

Ann ✳ Like occasional poetry—poems written for a special occasion, you know, Walt Whitman writing about Lincoln dying or Maya Angelou going on about the pulse of morning at Bill Clinton's inauguration—there is such a thing as occasional knitting. Babies are the all-time greatest generator of occasional knitting. Who doesn't want to cover a newborn with a handknit?

What newborn doesn't want to receive it? But there are all sorts of other occasions that can be improved with some event-specific knitting, and we turn now to this rich zone of inspiration.

We begin with the occasion that has generated more crafts than any other: Christmas. From Fra Angelico's *Annunciation* to My Little Pony tree skirts, there is a lot of room for imaginative interpretation of this holiday. We go here with a careful step, because the terrain is rugged, the chance of a misstep high. We won't stay long in the land of Christmas knitting, but we have a couple of missions we must complete.

The crucial time window for making a Christmas stocking is not all that wide—the stocking has to be made early enough that the child has no memory of life without that Christmas stocking and, more important, early enough that the child is photographed as a baby in front of the fireplace with the stocking visible in the background. It is best made at birth so it can be said, "Your Aunt Sissy made this for you before you were even born."

When the frenzy of present-opening is done, the fellas always discover the stocking last—where the small surprises are sometimes the best.

Mission Number 1: Overcoming Christmas Guilt

Christmas is the sort of holiday that often involves long-observed family traditions. My family's Christmas, growing up in Alabama, was no exception.

The Christmas tree, for example, was full of tradition. And decay. The tree skirt was cotton batting with glitter sparkles. We used that tree skirt for so long that *it wore out*. Who wears out a tree skirt? My sister Buffy and I treated that tree skirt like it was the Shroud of Turin. It was only years later that Buffy called me, in a tizz, announcing that she'd seen a similar tree skirt at Walgreen's for $1.99. "I thought that thing was *precious*," she howled. "I thought it was *rare*."

It was rare. It was the Tree Skirt. It was almost as special as our Christmas stockings. I can hardly express how important our Christmas stockings were. Back in the 1960s, the Christmas season did not begin in September; it actually bore some correlation to the calendar. If you went to Loveman's department store, you didn't see a Christmas decoration until Thanksgiving week. It was compressed into a couple of weeks of insane wishyness and magic, wildly intoxicating to us. At our house, the Christmas stockings were hung a few days before Christmas. The appearance of the Christmas stockings meant one thing: Christmas is imminent. Christmas is TOMORROW.

Our stockings were made for us by our great-aunt Elizabeth Kirkpatrick. She made them for everyone in the family. My sister has long stated that if her house caught on fire, she would go back for her Christmas stocking and baby book.

I blew it.

I never made the Ancestral Stocking Pattern for my two boys. I believe this is my most shameful Failure to Knit—worse than No Sweater for Hubbo, lower than No Blanket for Baby Named for Me, even more appalling than attending a baby shower without a handknit present. There are reasons why I blew it—I was in a long period of knitting dormancy, I didn't have the pattern—but still. I'm pretty sure that Aunt Elizabeth, looking down from the yarn store in the sky, is still waving that pattern at me and yelling, "Honey! Honey! *The stocking!* You haven't made the stocking!"

The stockings that my fellas hang by the chimney with care are knitted, true, but not by me and quite likely by a machine. I don't think I can quite get over this gaffe, this abuse of family responsibility, but I am going to try. Having broken with tradition, I have resolved to make things right.

I decided to track down a copy of the pattern. My sister Buffy had received one from cousin Suzie Kirkpatrick, who was living a fine life in Alabama seeing as how she had made two dozen stockings and had thus kept the chain intact.

It looks like a chain letter, the Ancestral Christmas Stocking pattern. It has been photocopied so many times that the letters are blurry, and there are faint markings all over it. CAROLINE 1983, 5 5 6 3 1 4 4 4. How many stockings has this pattern spawned? Who was Jason? Do I have a cousin named Cecelia?

The thing is, I never really liked the Ancestral Stocking Pattern. Who are the girl and boy? They look Dutch to me, and we're not Dutch. And Hunchy Santa. What's with him? He's got back trouble. The whole pattern is constructed in a very unsockish way—the top is knit flat in order to accommodate the need for rendering the Dutch Twins and Hunchy Santa in intarsia. Ech! Intarsia! And the ankle is shaped. What's the point of that? It cuts into perfectly good Christmas candy capacity.

There are good things about the pattern, though. It makes a long, skinny sort of stocking, one that might fit an actual foot, not like today's steroid-filled giant stockings. I remember my fourth grade Christmas when my stocking fit my leg. And the colorway is straight-ahead Christmas: red, white, and green, albeit an eye-busting red, white, and green.

So, in the hope that 60 years from now, somebody can use this thing, here is my contribution to Christmas knitting. It's more abstract than the stocking of my youth, but it's still as Christmassy as Bob Cratchit handing a plum pudding to George Bailey who's singing "White Christmas" beside Charlie Brown's Christmas tree.

Please make a dozen or two of these, one for everyone who you are even vaguely related to. You may want to photocopy it 20 or 30 times before you use it, to get some age on it. It does look awfully clear right now. One thing that makes me happy: the colors that I find so cheerful are sure to look utterly 2008, down the road in 2048.

If you have fallen in love with the Dutch Twins and Hunchy Santa, the 1945 Stocking pattern is available online at http://www.knitting-and.com/knitting/patterns/christmas/1945-stocking.htm. If you make it, Aunt Elizabeth will grant you three wishes.

The Rosetta Stone of stocking patterns.

NEW ANCESTRAL CHRISTMAS STOCKING

SIZE

20" (51cm) from top of stocking to heel; 8" (21cm) from toe to heel

MATERIALS

- 🔟 medium/worsted
- Cascade 220, 100% wool, 3½ oz (100g), 220 yd (200m), 1 skein each in red, white, and green
- Two size 3 (3.25mm) circular needles, 24" (60cm) long, or size needed to obtain gauge
- One double-pointed needle (to help redistribute stitches)
- Tapestry needle
- One jingle bell, any size (optional)

GAUGE

26 stitches and 33 rows = 4" (10cm)

The trick (pictured above) will help the strands spread out. After completing the cuff, turn the stocking inside out and work with the inside of the stocking on the outside of your needles. This will cause your floats to spread out more evenly. You will still be able to see the front side of your work; it's just that it will be inside your circular needles.

When you line a stocking with silk, the holiday swag slides right out.

DIFFICULTY

Don't tell anybody, but this is just a really big sock. With a couple of fancy parts.

NOTE

This stocking is made using the Fair Isle technique. (See page 63 for instructions.) It can be tricky to keep the strands inside the stocking from pulling too tight; they want to pull across to the other side of the stocking.

Leg

The stocking is worked in the round from the cuff down. Using red, cast on 64 stitches and divide evenly between the 2 circular needles—32 sts per needle. (See page 116 for instructions on working with two circular needles.) Begin working in the round, taking care not to twist stitches as you join. Work even in k2, p2 ribbing for 8 rounds. Cut red.

Using white, knit 18 rounds.

Work Chart 1. Begin at the bottom right corner and knit from right to left across the chart. Work Chart 1 twice per round, joining in and cutting colors as needed.

For the argyle section, knit only the red and white diamond pattern. The green lines are to be duplicate stitched once the stocking is finished.

On the final row of Chart 1, knit to the last 16 stitches of the round. (You will not complete this last round. Sorry.) Cut green.

Heel

If you've been knitting inside out (doesn't your Fair Isle look fabulous, by the way?), turn your stocking right side out again. Redistribute the stitches to get ready for the exciting heel flap portion of the program. Shift the stitches around so that the pattern on the leg shows flat when viewed from the side. Move the last 16 stitches of the round from Needle 1 (the needle currently in use) to Needle 2. Using a double-pointed needle may help with the maneuvering. Move the last 16

stitches from Needle 2 to Needle 1—32 sts on each needle.

Needle 1 will work the back of the stocking, and Needle 2 will work the instep and top of foot.

Heel flap

The heel flap is worked back and forth in stockinette stitch on Needle 1.

Row 1 Using white, slip 1 as if to purl, knit to end.
Row 2 Slip 1 as if to purl, purl to end.
Row 3 Repeat rows 1–2 11 times more, ending with a completed purl row—32 sts.

Turn the Heel

Work short rows as follows:

Row 1 (RS) k18, k2tog, k1, turn.
Row 2 (WS) Slip 1, p6, ssp, p1, turn.
Row 3 Slip 1, k7, k2tog, k1, turn.
Row 4 Slip 1, p8, ssp, p1, turn.
Row 5 Slip 1, k9, k2tog, k1, turn.
Row 6 Slip 1, p10, ssp, p1, turn.
Row 7 Slip 1, k11, k2tog, k1, turn.
Row 8 Slip 1, p12, ssp, p1, turn.
Row 9 Slip 1, k13, k2tog, k1, turn.
Row 10 Slip 1, p14, ssp, p1, turn.
Row 11 Slip 1, k15, k2tog, k1, turn.
Row 12 Slip 1, p16, ssp, p1, turn.
Row 13 Slip 1, k17, k2tog (no k1), turn.
Row 14 Slip 1, p18, ssp, (no p1), turn.
Row 15 k18 to end. Cut white.

Gusset

Using red, pick up and knit 12 stitches along the edge of the flap, m1 at the intersection of the flap and instep, k16—47 sts on Needle 1, 16 sts on Needle 2.

Transfer the first 9 heel turn stitches on Needle 1 to Needle 2—38 sts on Needle 1, 25 sts on Needle 2.

Using Needle 2, k16, m1 at the intersection of the flap and the instep, pick up and knit 12 stitches along the edge of the heel flap, k9—38 sts.

Knit 1 round as follows: k9, k12 tbl, k2tog tbl, k32, ssk, k12 tbl, k9—76 sts total.

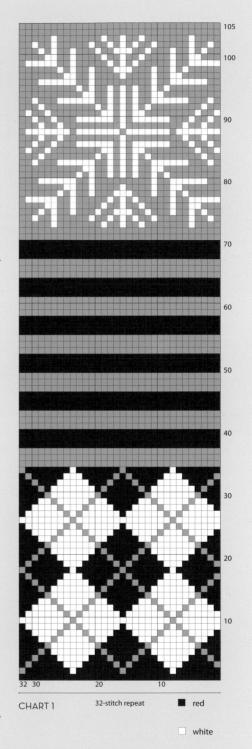

```
32 30          20          10
```

CHART 1   32-stitch repeat   ■ red

□ white

■ green

TWO CIRCULAR NEEDLES: THE ZIPPY WAY TO KNIT IN THE ROUND

We learned this popular technique from Cat Bordhi's classic book, *Socks Soar on Two Circular Needles*.

Here are the basics. You need two *circular needles* of the appropriate needle size. A cable length of 24" (60cm) is ideal. After casting on all the stitches on Circular 1, divide the stitches evenly between Circular 1 and Circular 2. Join the stitches to begin working in the round, taking care not to twist the stitches. Work the first half of the stitches using both tips of Circular 1. When you arrive at the stitches that are on Circular 2, pull on one tip of Circular 1 to move the stitches to the center of the cable, so that the needle tips of Circular 1 dangle limply, out of your way. Now work the other section of stitches using both tips of Circular 2.

Two cardinal rules:

- Always work stitches with the two tips of one circular.

- When a circular is not in use, pull on a tip to move the stitches to the center of the cable.

Decrease Rounds

Round 1 Needle 1: k20, k2tog, k16. Needle 2: k16, ssk, k20.

Round 2 and following even-numbered rounds Knit.

Round 3 and following odd-numbered rounds Continue decreases as in Round 1, knitting 1 fewer stitch before the k2tog and after the ssk. Continue until there are 64 stitches left, making sure to have 32 stitches on each needle.

Knit a total of 25 rounds in red, including the gusset rounds. Cut red.

Using green, knit 26 rounds. Cut green.

Toe

Join white.

Round 1 k13, k2tog, k2, ssk, k13. Repeat for Needle 2.

Round 2 and all even-numbered rounds Knit.

Round 3 Continue decreasing one stitch fewer before and after decreases. When there are 6 stitches left on each needle, stop. Redistribute

stitches so that there are 6 on the top of the foot and 6 on the bottom.

Finishing

Graft together the tip of the toe.

Duplicate stitch the green lines on the argyle section. Note that the lines will not perfectly align at the seam marking the beginning and end of rounds; it's just a quirk that comes with knitting in the round. Duplicate stitch the name and year of birth.

Create the name and date from Chart 2. If you have a long name, put the year of birth on the heel of the sock. Some letters can be condensed by one stitch—if you're squeezing ALEXANDRA in there. If the name has a Y with a T or an L before it (BETTY, ALLY), do not leave a blank stitch between these two adjacent letters.

Weave in the ends. Attach a double strand of red at the top of the stocking and use it to crochet a loop of 25 chains. Fasten down the end of the loop tightly. Block the stocking using as much steam as you can gather. The Fair Isle starts to behave when it's damp.

Sew on that jingle bell FAST. Christmas is COMING. It is practically HERE.

Variation

This stocking would be pretty much adorable done in the stripe pattern alone. And we don't use the word *adorable* lightly.

CHART 2

We love an Advent calendar, don't get us wrong, but there's just no knitting to be done in an Advent calendar. A forest of Advent trees seems a perfectly sensible thing to do.

Mission Number 2: Really Great Christmas Decorations

Ann ✳ I'm sitting in the parking lot, talking to Kay on the phone, having just survived a trip inside the mall for some Christmas gifts. We're discussing Christmas decorations, and how we don't really like Christmas decorations except for really great ones, and I hang up the phone realizing that I don't actually have any "really great Christmas decorations."

Which is what makes this next pattern a welcome addition to our mantelpiece.

Instant handmade Christmas spirit. Little is required in the way of wool or time.

FELTED TREES

SIZE AFTER FELTING

Small Tree: 6½" (16.5cm) high x 7½" (19cm) diameter at base

Medium Tree: 11½" (29cm) high x 9" (23cm) diameter at base

Large Tree: 14" (36cm) high x 8" (20cm) diameter at base

MATERIALS, FOR SET OF THREE

-  medium/worsted
- 3 skeins Berroco Ultra Alpaca, 50% wool, 50% alpaca, 3½ oz (100g), 215 yd (198m), in shades of green
- One set of 4 size 8 (5mm) double-pointed needles
- Tapestry needle
- Pillow case for felting
- Decorative buttons and findings (optional)

GAUGE BEFORE FELTING

14 stitches and 20 rows = 4" (10cm) using yarn doubled

DIFFICULTY

A festive holiday snack.

NOTE

skp: With the yarn in back, slip one stitch knitwise, knit the next stitch, insert the left needle into the front of the slipped stitch, pull it over the knit stitch and off the needle.

Small Tree

Holding yarn double stranded, cast on 60 stitches and divide evenly among 3 needles—20 sts per needle.

Rounds 1 and 2 Knit.
Round 3 (Decrease Round) skp, knit remaining stitches on first needle, skp, knit remaining stitches on second needle, skp, knit remaining stitches on third needle.

Alternate Round 1 and the Decrease Round until 3 stitches remain. Break yarn, thread end through a tapestry needle and run needle through remaining stitches. Weave in ends.

Medium Tree

Holding yarn double stranded, cast on 75 stitches and divide evenly among 3 needles—25 sts per needle.

Rounds 1 and 2 Knit.
Round 3 (Decrease Round) skp, knit remaining stitches on first needle, skp, knit remaining stitches on second needle, skp, knit remaining stitches on third needle.

Work the Decrease Round every third round until 12 stitches remain. Alternate Round 1 with Decrease Round until 3 stitches remain, and finish as described in instructions for Small Tree.

Large Tree

Holding yarn double stranded, cast on 99 stitches and divide evenly among three needles—33 sts per needle.

Rounds 1, 2, and 3 Knit.
Round 4 (Decrease Round) skp, knit remaining stitches on first needle, skp, knit remaining stitches on second needle, skp, knit remaining stitches on third needle.

Work the Decrease Round every fourth round until 3 stitches remain. Finish as described in instructions for Small Tree.

To Felt the Trees

Place trees in a zippered or safety-pinned pillowcase and run through two hot water washing machine cycles with mild detergent. Stuff the damp trees with plastic grocery bags, shaping and allowing them to air dry. Embellish as desired. We went nuts with a bag of shell buttons. You go nuts with whatever makes you nuts. (We would like to see pictures. Just saying.)

A Forest of Advent Trees

To create your very own forest of trees that will help you and your family count down the days until Christmas, make 24 of the Small Trees, following any or all of the patterns above but using Size 6 (4mm) needles and a single strand of yarn. Adding numbers to the trees is a chance for you to get creative. We used linen buttons with tiny chain stitched numbers, handmade by crafter Stephanie Sykes (rubycrownedkinglette.typepad.com). Rubber stamping numbers on patches of cloth would look nice, too. Kits to cover buttons with fabric are available at sewing and craft stores.

Tips

Don't let an aversion to sewing on buttons suck the joy out of this project. Using one long thread, anchor each button with a few stitches and move on to the next button without cutting or knotting. Even easier: No buttons. (We know you're thinking, "Hot Glue." No comment.)

If you dislike working on double-pointed needles, you can work these little trees flat and use mattress stitch to seam them into conical perfection before felting. Felting will melt away any imperfections in your sewing.

A Knitting Project That Answers to a Higher Authority

Kay ✳ Kippah (plural: kippot) is the Hebrew word for a skullcap or yarmulke, the traditional Jewish head covering. Orthodox men cover their heads wherever they go, while non-Orthodox men (and women, if they wish) cover their heads for prayer, and in sacred places. At Jewish celebrations, the host provides a basket of lovely new kippot for the guests, stamped inside with the date and the name of the bride and groom, the bar mitzvah boy, or the bat mitzvah girl. The sea of festively matching noggins in the synagogue is a lovely sight.

Non-Jewish by birth, I first learned about souvenir skullcaps at a Passover seder. (One of the funny things about life in New York City is that, come springtime, even non-Jews ask each other, "So what are you doing for Passover?") Not wanting to seem like I didn't know what I was doing (which I didn't), when the basket of kippot went around, I took one. Inside it said, "Michael Finkelstein, January 27, 1968." Wow. Who is this Michael Finkelstein? I wondered; he must be someone very special if the family has cherished this relic for so long. As it turns out, Michael Finkelstein was one of many 13 year olds my friend knew in 1968, when he was 13 (and therefore attending a lot of bar mitzvahs himself). But Michael Finkelstein's bar mitzvah lives on whenever the kippah basket is passed. For sentimental fools of any religious persuasion, the souvenir kippah is a cool custom. With no disrespect, I think it gives the personalized Christmas stocking a run for its money.

I had not been a member of my own Jewish family for very long when I saw that there was a knitterly opportunity in kippot. Growing up in Nebraska, I was schooled in the pioneer lore of community barn-raisings and quilting bees. Wouldn't it be fun to gather my knitting friends and whip up a basket of handknit kippot for a special life-cycle event? I fully intend to do it for my own kids' coming-of-age parties. Consider yourself warned.

There are no hard-and-fast rules about how kippot are made. You see them in sober black velvet and lurid polyester satin. Little boys wear New York Yankees or Thomas the Tank Engine kippot. Teenage girls crochet them in bright colors and patterns for their sweethearts. You don't see a knitted one very often, but there's no rule against it (I checked). The standard pie-wedge pinwheel (dear to knitters' hearts for making rugs and finishing hats), in shiny cotton stripes, makes a beautiful kippah. It knits up quickly, so plan on getting two of them out of every guest at your kippah-knitting bee.

One size fits all. There is no requirement that a kippah cover the whole head.

MASON-DIXON KIPPAH

There is not a lot of knitting to a kippah. Kippot are a great way to use up small amounts of brightly colored worsted weight yarn. Take a basic short-row pinwheel recipe, add a cro-Kay edging, (page 152) and you've got a happy head covering for a Jewish friend.

SIZE
5" (12.5 cm) diameter

MATERIALS
- **(4)** medium/worsted
- Tahki/Stacy Charles Cotton Classic, 100% mercerized cotton, 1¾ oz (50g), 108 yd (100m), 1 skein each in colors of your choice: A and B and a small amount of C for edging
- Size 4 (3.5mm) needles, or size needed to obtain gauge
- Tapestry needle

GAUGE
22 stitches and 44 rows = 4" (10cm) in garter stitch

DIFFICULTY
So easy that you can crank 200 of these in, um, 300 hours.

NOTE
This pattern employs short rows to shape the pinwheel. When the term "row" is used in these instructions, it means both the RS and WS portions of a short row. Alternate yarns A and B to stripe the garter ridges, changing colors at the outer edge of the pinwheel.

Cast on 13 stitches in A.

Row 1 (WS) Slip 1 with yarn in back (wyib), knit to end of row.
Row 2 Knit all stitches except last 2, w&t, knit to end of row.
Row 3 Knit all stitches except last 3, w&t, knit to end of row.
Row 4 Knit all stitches except last 4, w&t, knit to end of row.
Row 5 Knit all stitches except last 5, w&t, knit to end of row.
Row 6 Knit all stitches except last 6, w&t, knit to end of row.
Row 7 Knit all stitches except last 7, w&t, knit to end of row.
Row 8 Knit all stitches except last 8, w&t, knit to end of row.
Row 9 Knit all stitches except last 9, w&t, knit to end of row.
Row 10 Knit all stitches except last 10, w&t, knit to end of row.
Row 11 k3, *insert the point of the right needle from the front under the wrap, lift the wrap, and place it on the left needle behind the stitch that it was wrapping, knit the wrap and the stitch together through the back loops; repeat from * to last stitch, k1.

You have now knit 1 of the 6 wedges that will form the pinwheel. Repeat these instructions 5 more times. Bind off. Using mattress stitch, seam the first and last wedges together to complete the pinwheel.

Finish the kippah by working 2 rounds of cro-Kay (see page 152) edging around the outside. Weave in ends. The edging will cause the pinwheel to dome slightly, like the human head. If your kippah-wearer wants to use a hairclip to secure it, we think it's a nice touch to sew the clip to the underside of the kippah.

Mastering the Art of Poached Wool

Kay ✳ When making a felted project, the knitting part is only a prelude. The fun part is seeing what happens to the knitting when you plunge it into the hot wash cycle. Since I felt for fun, I usually agree with myself in advance that I don't care if the finished product closely resembles what I expected when I started out.

This project is different from most knit-to-felt items. The inspiration came from a shadow of a doubt about felted bags. I love, love, love a felted bag. But no matter how thick the felt, I find them a bit sloppy and poochy-outy for daily use. I carry a lot of stuff. Heavy items, misshapen items, and delicate items, such as a camera and a phone. I like a sturdy bag. Top-stitching is always good—rivets even better.

Several years ago, I was visiting Ann Buechner in Berkeley, California, and she gave me the Knitters VIP Tour of her home. One item was an old canvas tote bag that Ann had reupholstered in knitting. She called it a cozy for the tote. (The cozy is an organizing principle of Ann's creative universe. When you think about it, most knitting is a cozy for *something*.) The wonderful thing was that the bag looked like it was knitted, but underneath, it had all the fortitude of marine canvas. Back in '45, General Eisenhower used this wonderfully tough material to land soldiers on the beaches of Normandy; it can handle anything I'm hauling.

Ann's inspiration morphed into a plan to make a felted cozy for a canvas tote bag. It starts with a medium-sized tote bag in heavy-duty canvas. (Ours is from the L.L. Bean catalog, the classic Boat and Tote® bag.) You knit a huge overbag for it, and you embellish it with a cool graphic designed by Cristina Shiffman. You toss this jumbo wad of wool into the washing machine, felt it like crazy, take it out, put it on the bag, and pat yourself on the back. Can anybody see a problem with this plan? I sure couldn't.

So I knit the bag (full commitment to project at this stage), got out my tapestry needle and chart, and ran smack into a major problem. Duplicate stitching onto such large, open stitches is a nightmare. Lacking a firm foundation, the duplicate stitches twist, recede into nothingness, make you scream in agony and snap at loved ones. I didn't give up too quickly, though. First I made a swatch, performed Bad Duplicate Stitch on it, and felted it to see if the felting cured the Bad Duplicate Stitch. It did, but only a little, and now there was another problem: the swatch had felted unevenly, shrinking less in areas that had been duplicate stitched, and more in the plain background areas. I started considering a plain, brown, slightly striped bag. I could get behind that, couldn't I? I decided to put the thing aside while I made dinner. (Shocking, but true. I, Kay Gardiner, made dinner.) Dinner included a salad with green beans in it.

As I was blanching the green beans to ensure that they were tender-crisp and maintained their lovely green color and nutrients, the idea hit me. What if I blanched the bag? What if I felted it lightly—parboiled it—to firm up the fabric but not erase the stitches entirely? Wouldn't I then have a lovely, al dente surface for my duplicate stitch?

Yes, indeed I would, and indeed I did. And indeed this bag is very fun to knit, embellish, and felt. And it makes me smile to think that Julia Child, who has always been such a friend to me in the kitchen, helped me solve a knitting problem. When in doubt, blanch it.

The canvas bag "lining" makes it really possible to tote a whole picnic in this bag.

PICNIC BAG

FINISHED SIZE AFTER FELTING
Measurements are given for the individual components that were knitted for the purchased bag we used. If you are using a different canvas bag for the base, the size of the components can be adjusted.

Bottom: 13" x 8" (33cm x 10cm)

Gussets: 5" x 12½" (12.5cm x 32cm)

Sides (stockinette stitch): 13" x 11" (33cm x 28cm)

MATERIALS
- (5) bulky
- Manos del Uruguay, 100% wool, 3½ oz (100g), 138 yd (126m), 3 hanks in chocolate brown, 2 hanks in chartreuse green, and 1 hank each in orange and turquoise
- Size 15 (10mm) circular needle, 32" (80cm), or size needed to obtain gauge
- L.L. Bean Boat and Tote® Bag, size medium
- Tapestry needle
- Stitch markers
- Pillowcase for felting

GAUGE
Before felting
10 stitches and 14 rows = 4" (10cm) in stockinette stitch

After felting
17 stitches and 20 rows = 4" (10cm) in stockinette stitch

DIFFICULTY
This is an easy, fast knit with minimal shaping. HOWEVER, the felting part requires undivided attention. Nerves of steel and a high score for nonchalance are recommended.

Bottom
With size 13 (9mm) needles and using green, cast on 39 stitches.

Row 1 (RS) Purl.
Row 2 Knit.

Repeat rows 1 and 2 twice, for a total of 6 rows of reverse stockinette stitch. Work 15 ridges of garter stitch (knit every row for 30 rows). With RS facing, repeat rows 1 and 2 three times, for a total of 6 rows of reverse stockinette stitch, and bind off in purl.

Gussets
With RS of the bottom facing and using turquoise, pick up and knit 15 stitches in the row ends of the garter stitch along one of the short ends of the bottom. (Do not pick up any stitches in the reverse stockinette stitch borders.) Work the next row as follows: *kfb, k2, repeat from * to last 3 stitches, kfb, k1, kfb—21 sts. Work 4 rows of reverse stockinette stitch as you did to begin and end the bottom.

With RS facing, work stockinette stitch stripes as follows:

Row 1 Using orange, knit.
Row 2 Using orange, purl.
Row 3 Using turquoise, knit.
Row 4 Using turquoise, purl.

Repeat Rows 1–4 until you have 32 stripes, then repeat Rows 1 and 2 once more, for a total of 33 stripes— 66 rows.

Bind off in purl.

Make a second gusset on the opposite end of the bottom in the same way.

Sides
With RS of the bottom facing and using brown, pick up and knit 39 stitches. Purl the next row. Work in stockinette stitch (knit the RS rows; purl the WS rows), working an increase row on the 9th row from the beginning and every following 8th row as follows:

Increase row (RS) k2, m1, knit to last 2 stitches, m1, k2.

Continue until you have 55 stitches— 65 rows.

Next row (WS) Purl 1 row, and bind off in purl.

Make a second side, and sew the side seams using mattress stitch (page 153).

Flange with Handle Openings
With RS facing, starting at the beginning of the top edge of a gusset and using brown, pick up and knit 21 stitches from the gusset, 55 stitches from the side, 21 stitches from the other gusset, and 55 stitches from the other side—152 sts. Place a marker to indicate the beginning of the round.

Purl 3 rounds.

Bind off for handle openings On the next round, p31, bind off 35 in purl, p41, bind off 35 in purl, p10.

Cast on for handle openings On the next round, p31, cast on 32 using the knitted cast-on method, p41, cast on 32 using the knitted cast-on method (page 153), p10—146 sts.

Purl 3 rounds even. Cut brown.

Using green, k21, place a marker, k52, place a marker, k21, place a marker, k52. You now have 4 markers.

Next round (decrease round) k2tog, knit to 2 stitches before marker, ssk, slip marker, k2tog, knit to 2 stitches before marker, ssk.

Continue knitting every row, working a decrease round every 4th round until 118 stitches remain. Cut green.

Using brown, knit 3 rounds. Bind off in purl, and weave in all ends.

Pause
At this point in any felted knit, it is traditional to see how many small children will fit in the thing you have just knitted. The gauge on this fella is that one 8-year-old and one 10-year-old can put it over their heads and it will reach below their knees. Lying flat, the official measurements are 24" (62cm) wide by 25" (65cm) tall (to the handle opening).

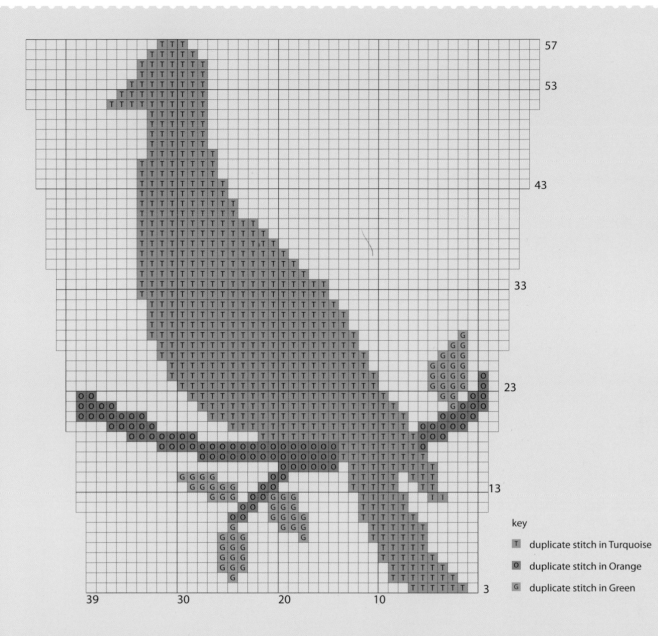

key

T	duplicate stitch in Turquoise
O	duplicate stitch in Orange
G	duplicate stitch in Green

First Felting

Place the bag in a zippered or safety-pinned pillow protector and into a top-loading washing machine set to warm wash. Use a small amount of detergent and place a pair of jeans or a towel in the load with the bag. After 5 minutes, check the bag to see how much it has felted. In this first felting, you do not want the bag to felt so completely that the stitches become invisible. You do want the bag to shrink somewhat, and for the stitches to become firmer and smaller than they were before.

This is a judgment call. If you are a nervous felter or it's your first time, get a more experienced felter to keep watch with you and help decide when to pull the bag out. Err on the side of pulling it out too soon. You can always felt something more, but as the prophets say, "Whatsoever shall be felted shall not be unfelted, though the earth tremble and the knitter gnash her teeth."

When the bag is felted as described, stop the cycle and spin until most of the water is out. Do not rinse before spinning, as

this will felt the bag more. Lay the bag on a flat surface to dry. It should still be quite a bit bigger than the canvas base bag.

Duplicate Stitch

When the bag is dry, work the duplicate stitch chart on one side. Work loosely and evenly and don't worry about it too much. Avoid pulling too tightly on your yarn. There is no need to weave in the ends. Trim to 2" (5cm) and let them hang on the back; those ends are not going anywhere.

kaycam

Before

After first felting

Duplicate stitch makes for a tweedy bird.

Final Felting

Repeat the instructions for the first felting, this time setting the machine to hot wash. Check the bag every 5 minutes and avoid overfelting it. When it has felted more, but still looks like it is a bit too big, stop the washer, remove the bag, and squeeze as much water out of it as you can. Check the size against the canvas bag. If it needs more felting, put it back in the washer, but oh dear, be very careful you don't overfelt it. When it's ready, stop the cycle, spin most of the water out. (If you spin it too dry, you risk crease formation.)

Place the damp bag over the canvas base bag. Smooth it, straighten it, fuss with it, and steam it with a steam iron if you think it needs it (and it probably does). Let it dry. When it is dry, use matching yarn to sew the handle openings closed between the straps.

Have a strong cup of tea (or something). This has been nerve-wracking, but soul-satisfying, hasn't it?

The Anti-Antimacassar

The occasion: You need a housewarming present. The mission: a handknit table runner that would not look like somebody left a mohair shawl lying on the table. In our personal collections of old issues of *Workbasket* (an American needlecraft magazine that had a glorious run from the Anglican Antimacassar '30s to the Needlepoint '90s), table runners and place mats abound, but they often have a doilyish vibe that seems inappropriate to modern lifestyles. We identified the problem—the Hobson's choice of naked table or overdressed table—but didn't have a clue to the solution. That's when we lobbed the whole project over to Cristina Shiffman. Cristina refused to divulge her secret plan. She requested linen yarn and clammed up for what seemed like a long time.

A table runner that doesn't look like a scarf (but go ahead and wrap it around your neck if it's chilly).

VIA VENETO TABLE RUNNER *by Cristina Bernardi Shiffman*

This is the result of Cristina's mad-scientist tinkering with the DNA of the table runner. That stitch that looks like weaving? It *is* weaving. You drop a stitch all the way down the runner, and then weave a contrasting yarn (we used linen, but coarse twine would be nice), potholder-loom style, back through the ladders of the dropped stitch. So simple, and such a nice break from, you know, knitting.

The irony of it all is that although this elegant, understated runner definitely does not look like a Victorian stole abandoned on the table, its flat, reversible pattern would make a stunning, unusual-but-not-weird scarf. And unusual-but-not-weird is always a good look.

SIZE
49" x 12" (124.5cm x cm)

MATERIALS
- (2) fine
- 4 hanks Louet Euroflax Sport, 100% linen, 3½ oz (100g), 270 yd (246m); 2 hanks aqua (Main color—MC), 1 hank each of brick (A) and mustard (B)
- Size 2 (2.75mm) straight and circular needles, 32" (80cm), or size needed to obtain gauge
- Tapestry needle

GAUGE
24 stitches and 30 rows = 4" (10cm) measured over pattern

DIFFICULTY
An easy, pretty stitch pattern and a field trip to weaving.

Runner
Using MC, cast on 57 stitches in the main color.

Row 1 (RS) p4, *k1 tbl, p7; repeat from * 5 times more; k1 tbl, p4.
Row 2 (WS) k4, *p1 tbl, k7; repeat from * 5 times more; p1 tbl, k4.
Row 3 (RS) p4, *k1 tbl, m1, p7; repeat from * 5 times more; k1 tbl, m1, p4—64 sts.
Row 4 (WS) k4, *p2 tbl, k7; repeat from * 5 times more; p2 tbl, k4.
Row 5 (RS) p4, *k2tog tbl, p7; repeat from * 5 times more; k2tog tbl, p4—57 sts.
Row 6 (WS) Repeat Row 2.

Work Rows 1–6 until the piece measures 48" (120cm) from the cast-on edge, ending with Row 5.

Drop Stitch Row With WS facing, work Row 2, dropping the central stitch of each 7-stitch panel of reverse stockinette from the needle as you go—6 sts dropped. Bind off all stitches very loosely.

Pulling from top to bottom and from side to side of the piece, let the dropped stitches form runs to the cast-on edge. Weave in all MC ends.

Garter Stitch Eyelet Border
With RS facing and using A, pick up and knit 188 stitches along one of the long sides of the piece from right to left.

Rows 1-3 Knit.
Row 4 (RS) k2, *yo, k2tog; repeat from * to last two stitches; yo, k2.
Rows 5 and 6 Knit.

Bind off all stitches loosely.

Work Garter Stitch Eyelet Border in the same way along the second long side.

To work the Border along the short sides, using A, pick up and knit 64 stitches starting from the short edge of one long side border you just knit, across the short side of the runner, and over the short edge of the other long side border, and follow the instructions above. Weave in all A ends.

Woven Stripes
Before weaving color B into the "warp" formed by the dropped stitches, block the piece thoroughly by wetting it, spinning it in the washer, and laying it flat to dry, pulling the piece gently from the long sides to straighten the "warp."

For each stripe, thread a blunt tapestry needle with a 5¼ yd (5m) strand of color B (4 times as long as the runner). Lay the piece flat on a work surface so that one of the long sides is nearest you. (The bars formed by the dropped stitches are perpendicular to you and look like the warp threads in a piece of weaving.) Working from right to left, run the needle over and under the warp formed by the dropped stitches, pulling the thread through at intervals to straighten the weft you are making as you weave. When you reach the end, anchor the thread by running it through the seam formed on the wrong side where the border meets the main body of the runner. Turn the runner 180 degrees so that the line just made is at the top of the warp and weave a second line just below it from right to left making certain to run the needle *under* the warp where you went over on the first pass and vice versa. Anchor at the edge as before. Turn the piece 180 degrees again and weave a third line above the second running the thread as you did for the first line. Weave in the ends.

This runner would look great in many plant-based yarns, or combinations of yarns. Linen is a practical choice for the table, because it washes and dries beautifully.

This sturdy bag collapses into a tiny puddle, making it simple to take to the grocery store. So much more convenient than a big, canvas bag. And the knitting makes for the best kind of puzzle: crazy stitch patterns that work up fast.

Bid Farewell to Plastic Grocery Bags Forever (And Say Hello to 1971 While You're at It)

What is it about knitters that makes us think we always have to have a knitted present for someone? A bag is always a welcome present, even if it's a present for yourself. String bags are handy, ecological things to carry around in your purse or the trunk of your car, but they generally have a crunchy granola "I compost in my kitchen" feeling. Not this one. When Ann Buechner sent us a snapshot of this bag hanging over the back of a chair, we mistook it for a scarf, it's so pretty.

This bag is great fun to knit because it's a sampler of stitches that will seem crazy and new to most knitters. Ann was inspired by Mary Walker Phillips's book *Creative Knitting, A New Art Form* (Van Nostrand Reinhold, 1971) which is full of extraordinary wall hangings with a macramé vibe. Walker Phillips uses stitches composed of multiple wraps that open up the fabric of her pieces when the wraps are dropped. The bag's rim is worked with Debbie New's bind-off stitch, first used in her Cast-Off Sweater in *The Natural Knitter* by Barbara Albright. We named the bag after the Monteagle Sunday School Assembly in Grundy County, Tennessee, where the fashions of 1971 (and 1878) are alive on cottage porches.

MONTEAGLE BAG

by Ann Hahn Buechner

SIZE
About 12" (30.5cm) across and 13" (33cm) long; when stretched strap measures 20" (51cm) and bag stretches up to 22" (56cm) in length.

MATERIALS
- **(2)** fine
- 1 skein of Louet Euroflax Sport, 100% linen, 3½ oz (100g), 270 yd (247m) in berry red
- Size 10 (6mm) 20" (50cm) circular needle, or size needed to obtain gauge
- Stitch marker
- Stitch holder or piece of string
- Extra knitting needle for the 3-needle bind-off
- Tapestry needle

GAUGE
11 stitches over 4" (10cm) in stockinette stitch in the round

DIFFICULTY
A sampler of trippy stitches that will call for your concentration the first time around. You will want to crank out many more.

Give yourself a good 6-foot (1.8m) tail to cast on and still have enough to sew up the bottom seam.

Loosely cast on 72 stitches and join in the round, taking care not to twist. Place a marker to mark the beginning of the round.

Rounds 1–3 Knit

Round 4 Knit into the front and back of every sixth stitch—84 sts.

Twisted cross stitch

Round 5 *Right cross.* Knit two together with a double wrap, but do not transfer to the right needle. Knit the first stitch again with a double wrap, and transfer both stitches to the right needle. Repeat on each following pair of stitches for the entire round.

Round 6 Knit each stitch of the round by inserting the right needle knitwise between the two wraps on the left needle, knit the stitch and drop the second wrap on the left needle as you pull each stitch off. Remove the marker, slip the first stitch of the round, and replace the marker.

Round 7 *Left cross.* *Knit into the back of the second stitch with a double wrap, but do not transfer to the right needle; knit the first and second stitches together through the back loops with a double wrap and transfer both stitches to the right needle; repeat from * around on each following pair of stitches.

Round 8 Repeat Round 6.

Rounds 9–12 Repeat Rounds 5–8.

Rounds 13–14 Repeat Rounds 5–6.

Horizontal stitch

Round 15 To begin the round, knit into the front and back of the first stitch and slip the left-most of the new stitches back onto the left needle; * *left cross:* knit into the back of the second stitch, then knit the first and second stitches together through the backs and lift both stitches off the needle; slip the left-most of the new stitches back onto the left needle; repeat from * for each following pair of stitches in the round. When you reach the marker, slip it to the right needle, slip the first stitch of the round to the right needle and pass the last stitch of the round over the marker and over the first stitch, slip the first stitch back to the left needle.

Round 16 Repeat Round 15.

Note The next stitch, fancy crossed throw, or veil stitch is a long, twisted stitch made by wrapping the yarn around the outside of the needles and pulling the last wrap through the stitch.

Round 17 Insert right needle into first stitch on left needle as if to knit. Holding the needles crossed in this position, wrap yarn counterclockwise around the outside of both of the crossed needles—like you're lassoing the needles—4 times. Wrap yarn around the right needle, then slip the yarn between the crossed needles and pull this yarn through the wraps to complete the knit stitch, letting all the wraps fall below the new stitch.

Rounds 18–20 Knit all stitches.

Round 21 Repeat Round 17.

Round 22 Knit until the last stitch of the round; knit the last stitch with a double wrap.

Note Cast-off stitch: This stitch looks like macramé and is created by knitting each stitch with a double wrap and passing one of the previous wraps over the new stitch.

Round 23 Knit the first stitch with a double wrap, reach back with the left needle and pull one of the wraps from the previous stitch over the marker and the new stitch; repeat until you reach the last stitch; knit the last stitch with one wrap, pass one of the wraps of the previous stitch over it.

Rounds 24–25 Repeat Rounds 22–23.

Bind off for straps.

Round 26 Purl 14, bind off 28, knit 14 (and place on holder or string), bind off 28.

Strap

Work back and forth on the 14 stitches on the needle in garter stitch until the strap measures 20" (51cm) when stretched. When complete, join the strap with a 3-needle bind off to the 14 stitches on the holder.

Finishing

Sew up the bottom seam and fill with something heavy to stretch out the stitches.

Dept. of This Little Light of Mine

"You come in here and you sprinkle the place with powder and you spray perfume and you stick a paper lantern over the light bulb—and, lo and behold, the place has turned to Egypt and you are the Queen of the Nile, sitting on your throne, swilling down my liquor."

—Stanley Kowalski, in a crabby moment, to Blanche DuBois,
from *A Streetcar Named Desire* by Tennessee Williams

Cleopatra here, reporting on the paper lantern situation in rural Tennessee.

Suppose you had a summer community of 160 cottages, in the woods, most of which were long on porches and eaves. Wouldn't you at some point realize that you could cover them in lanterns?

This is what happened recently at my summer getaway, the Monteagle Sunday School Assembly, not too far from Nashville. To celebrate this chautauqua's 125th anniversary (a sasquatchcentennial—OK, it's quasquicentennial, but what a mouthful), a group of big-thinking Assemblywomen hatched a plan to illuminate the Assembly, much in the way a group of Martha's Vineyard folks light up their village of Oak Bluffs. The goal was to get everybody to decorate their cottages with colorful lanterns—but no candles because houses burn down all the time in the Assembly, and an Illumination Night like that would put people off lanterns for a good while.

For the Assembly, this was as urgent a mission as it gets; lantern sales began a scant 13 months before Illumination Night.

I immediately thought illumination would be fun, but as I look back, I realize I didn't see the light on this project until my friend Frannie sat on the porch with me one morning, looking at all the paper lanterns I had bought from the Good Women Marketing Lanterns.

"Aren't they colorful?" I said, gazing at the fruits of two solid hours' labor rigging up extension cords and cup hooks. It was the hardest work I had ever done.

She looked at me with puzzlement. "You mean . . . you're not going to make your lanterns?" Frannie was as close to incredulous as I've ever seen her.

I'm thinking, *OK, Miss Architecture School Fancypants, not all of us can engineer lanterns that look like Frank Gehry took over a paper lantern factory. Not all of us—*

"You know," she said. "Knit them?"

SUPERFESTIVE LANTERN

SIZE
To fit paper lantern 14" (36cm) high x 32" (80cm) circumference at widest point

MATERIALS
- (3) light/DK
- Judi & Co. Cordé, 100% rayon over cotton core, 144 yd (131m), in Sunset
- Size 13 (9mm) 16" (40cm) circular needle
- Tapestry needle
- 1 paper lantern (the lantern shown is from www.paperlanternstore.com)

GAUGE
One of the few situations where the gauge you get is, in fact, the right gauge

DIFFICULTY
A few hundred stitches, total. Cake!

Cast on 36 stitches and join stitches to begin knitting in the round, taking care not to twist the stitches.

Round 1 and 2 Knit 2 rounds.

Round 3 *k1, wrap yarn 3 times around needle; repeat from * to end.

Round 4 *k1, drop the yarn wraps; repeat from * to end.

Repeat Rounds 1–4. Bind off when the tube of knitting is a bit shorter than the lantern. It will stretch to fit.

Finishing
Place the lantern cover on your lantern. Using a tapestry needle and a length of yarn, thread yarn through the top and bottom of lantern cover, drawstring style. Tighten the top and bottom for the best fit, then tie knots.

Tip

Fitting a Lantern Shaped Like a Cube, a Ball, or Otherwise Not Shaped Like a Pod

This is a forgiving stitch pattern. It's very stretchy. To fit your lantern, measure its widest part, then figure out the number of stitches to cast on based on that measurement. Figure on 1.25 stitches per inch.

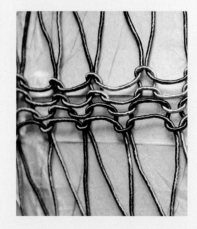

The soft glow of a paper lampshade is perfect for a baby's room.

Chapter Five

The Sophisticated KITCHEN

Kay ✳ Everybody has a kitchen, or a wretched rathole that serves as their kitchen. Judging from the lifestyle magazines and home improvement mega-stores, our culture is on a quest for the perfect kitchen. Once as dowdy as a utility closet, the kitchen is now a status symbol, crammed with oversized appliances and often sporting a family room complete with television.

There is no pricey fridge or range that will draw your friends and family to your kitchen faster than the smell of a casserole in the oven. Particularly if it has crushed potato chips on top.

I am serious about this. Use your kitchen, and you will be surrounded by family and friends. The neighborhood strays (canine and human) will be sniffing at your screen door. Baking an apple pie—or putting a cinnamon Pop-Tart in the toaster—can save boatloads on the renovation budget.

What does this have to do with knitting? Everything. Knitters, some of us are guilty of being a bit too precious about our craft. We will devote time and expensive yarn to socks that we stick in our shoes all day, but we turn up our nose at knitting the humble household items that our grandmas made. I may be the prophet of dishrag knitting, but I have flat-out lied to people who see me knitting on the subway and ask me "What are you making?" It's usually a dishcloth— God's perfect subway knitting, so portable, so memorizable,

so not necessary to have light or space or quiet to concentrate—but I usually say, "I'm swatching a stitch pattern" or "It's a square for a blanket." Why? It's not illegal to knit a dishrag. It just doesn't seem like a good use of time for the Modern Woman.

But the thing is, it is really nice to have knitted things in the kitchen. Handknits are homey. Handknits are bright. Handknits remind us of how clever we are, how self-reliant and ecological. A handknit towel is as uplifting as a flower arrangement or hand-thrown piece of pottery.

Another bonus is that kitchen knits are quick and fun. If you are slogging through a sweater, don't be tempted to cast on another sweater just for a change of pace . . . that way lies madness. Knit a palate-cleansing item for the kitchen and return, refreshed, to your more complex knitting. Use these small projects to play with colors and experiment with stitch patterns. Also use them to clean up your kitchen.

Knitting As an Alternative to Renovation (It's Less Messy and You Don't Need a Home Equity Loan)

think about kitchens a lot, and about one kitchen in particular. This kitchen, my Grandma Mabel's, doesn't exist anymore. In childhood, this kitchen was my home away from home. If I ran, and jumped over the steps between our adjoining backyards, I could get from our back stoop to a seat on one of Grandma's vinyl chairs in 20 seconds flat.

Such a short distance to another world. Our kitchen was Brady Bunch Provincial; it had aspirations, or at least cabinets. We had an army of small appliances, gleaming and chrome-y, plugged into every outlet. In Grandma's kitchen, it was 1937, now and forever.

The aesthetic of Grandma's kitchen was Danish-American Ruthless. The decorative principle was this: nothing should be in the kitchen that did not need to be in the kitchen. Cabinets were not needed because there was a separate pantry. There was a cast-iron sink, which bathed babies and dishes. A gas range. A refrigerator known as The Icebox. There was a dinette table with a red Bakelite top. The tubular steel chairs no longer matched, because they had been reupholstered in pebbly beige vinyl.

There was nothing intentionally cozy about this kitchen. No tiles saying "No Matter Where I Serve My Guests They Seem to Like the Kitchen Best." No souvenir salt & pepper shakers. Grandma's blue transferware dishes, which shuttled back and forth from table to pantry, had been acquired one piece at a time, as free gifts with purchase from the Safeway grocery store.

Why I am so nostalgic about this bare-bones kitchen? Because that kitchen was the Grandma Place. She was always there, glad—but not over-glad—to see you, waiting to ask you some intrusive questions. She prepared quaint dishes like fresh vegetables and boiled beef. She showed you how she crimped the pie crust with her thumb. She had Mason jars full of homemade chili sauce. She let you eat bits of this and that as she cooked. It was a good place to be.

When I grew up and moved to New York City, I followed the typical outsider's real-estate journey. I went from airless hovel to slightly-less-bad walkup, to almost-habitable elevator building, to decent-but-illegal-sublet, until finally, after a character-building string of roommates and landlords, I found myself in the cheaply renovated co-op of my dreams. Since then, to test the strength of our marriage, Hubby and I have renovated two kitchens. We have spent more money than I care to think about to satisfy my quest for the perfect kitchen.

It was upon completion of Kitchen the Second, as I gazed upon the Pietra Whatever stone countertops from Italy and the Salute to 1929 green glass backsplash, that it hit me: all I really wanted was Grandma Mabel's kitchen. A plain, scary-clean room in which someone was actually cooking something. A place with vinyl chairs, where my kids could hear "Hello sweetie" and "Are you hungry?" when they came rushing in, banging the door. It really wasn't complicated at all.

"*Now* you tell me," said Hubby.

Aw c'mon, save the world! Make a reusable mop cover. You know you want to!

A Perfectly Good Use of a Law Degree

This is a project that makes people wonder why I bothered with higher education. (At my law school reunion, they were whispering, "Poor Kay—she's making *mop covers* now.") But I ask you: Is this, or is this not, the cutest mop cover ever? Loosen up! Every time you open the broom closet, you'll laugh to think that you knitted a mop cover. That's good for your mental health, if nothing else.

The world's greatest stitch pattern, now and forever.

SWIFTY

SIZE
Approximately 9¼" x 4" (23.5cm x 10cm), when buttoned

MATERIALS
- ▣ medium/worsted
- Peaches & Creme worsted weight, 100% cotton, 2½ oz (70g), 122 yd (112m), 1 ball each in colors Lemon (A), Olive (B), Silver Grey (C), Shrimp (D)
- Note on yarn quantities: Although the pattern calls for four balls of yarn, it requires a total yarn weight of only 2 ounces. You can use up odds and ends from your most recent dishrag-knitting binge by changing colors at will. The pattern indicates where we changed colors on the mop covers pictured.

- Size 7 (4.5mm) needles, or size needed to obtain gauge
- Stitch holder
- Tapestry needle
- Two large (1" [2.5cm] diameter) buttons

GAUGE
20 stitches and 32 rows = 4" (10cm) in pattern stitch

DIFFICULTY
If you've never knit this slip-stitch pattern, you will have to pay attention for the first repeat to get the rhythm of it. After that, this pattern clicks along like magic.

Main Section
With A, cast on 45 stitches.

Row 1 (RS) Using A, purl.

Row 2 (WS) Knit.

Row 3 Join B, k4, slip 1 purlwise *k5, slip 1 purlwise; repeat from * to last 4 stitches, k4.

Row 4 k4, yarn forward (yf), slip 1 purlwise, yarn back (yb), *k5, yf, slip 1 purlwise, yb; repeat from * to last 4 stitches, k4.

Row 5 p4, yb, slip 1 purlwise, yf, *p5, yb, slip 1 purlwise, yf; repeat from * to last 4 stitches, p4.

Row 6 Repeat Row 4.

Row 7 Using A, knit.

Row 8 Purl.

Row 9 Using B, k1, slip 1 purlwise, *k5, slip 1 purlwise; repeat from * to last stitch, k1.

Row 10 k1, yf, slip 1 purlwise, yb, *k5, yf, slip 1 purlwise, yb; repeat from * to last stitch, k1.

Row 11 p1, yb, slip 1 purlwise, yf, *p5, yb, slip 1 purlwise, yf; repeat from * to last stitch, p1.

Row 12 Repeat Row 10.

When you have finished these 12 rows, you will see two sections of a brick pattern. Repeat these 12 rows twice more (for a total of 6 sections of bricks). Change to C in Row 9 of the third repeat of Rows 1 through 12. Then repeat rows 1 through 6 again, and then, using A, knit 2 rows. You now have 7 sections of bricks.

Button Flaps

Without cutting A and with RS facing, purl 17 stitches. Place remaining stitches on a holder and work the first 17 stitches only.

***Next row (WS)** Knit.

Work 10 ridges of garter stitch (knit every row for 20 rows).

Bind off in purl on the RS. Cut yarn.

Rejoin A to the remaining stitches.

Bind off 11 stitches in purl, then purl to the end of the row—17 sts.

Repeat from * to complete the second button flap.

Buttonhole Flaps

On the other side of the mop cover (opposite the side with the button flaps), with RS facing and using D, pick up and knit 45 stitches.

Next row (WS) Knit.

Next row (RS) Purl 17 stitches. Place remaining stitches on a holder and work the first 17 stitches only.

***Next row (WS)** Knit.

Work 5 ridges of garter stitch (knit every row for 10 rows).

Buttonhole Row (RS) k7, bind off 3 stitches, knit to the end of the row.

Next row (WS) k7, turn work and cast on 3 stitches using the knitted cast-on method, turn work back to WS, knit 7—17 sts.

Work 5 more ridges of garter stitch (knit every row for 10 rows).

Bind off in purl on the RS. Cut yarn.

With RS facing, rejoin D to the remaining stitches.

Bind off 11 stitches in purl, then purl to the end of the row—17 sts.

Repeat from * to complete the second

Free Pattern!

Does this stitch pattern look familiar? It's the same one used for the universally beloved Ballband Dishcloth. Our double-blind, peer-reviewed testing has revealed that no other stitch pattern comes close to the Ballband in the vital categories of Pet-Hair Adhesion and Overall Moppability.

To make a dishcloth instead of a mop cover, simply continue the slip stitch pattern until you have 13 sections of bricks. Then knit a row, purl a row, and bind off.

We know that some people are going to feel compelled to knit matching mop cover and dishcloth sets. Do what you need to do. No judgments.

Tip

We cannot overemphasize how much freedom you have with the color changes. A mop cover is no place to be dignified. We're aiming for "cheerful" here.

Extra credit for using mismatched buttons! Just make sure they are plastic or another machine-washable material. You are going to be washing this thing a lot.

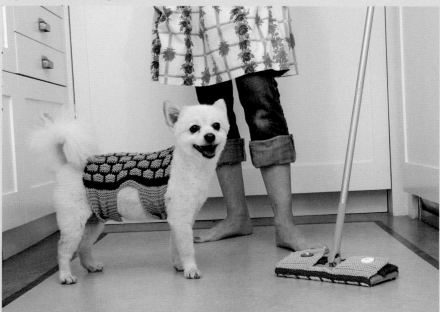

Flip him on his back, give him a push, and that dog is earning his keep.

An Excellent Lady Gift

Back to our roots: the beauty of simplicity and usefulness.

My grandma and her frugal ladyfriends made each other gifts for the kitchen: home-made aprons, embroidered napkins, or terrycloth towels with fabric loops sewn on for hanging. While she may have preferred not to have seven embroidered kittens doing household chores, Grandma did appreciate having a clean dishtowel for every day of the week. This vintagey hand towel makes a sweet housewarming gift with a dishrag and a bottle of aromatherapy dishwashing liquid. (Grandma would not have wanted to live to see aromatherapy dishwashing liquid.)

MITERED HANGING TOWEL

by Cristina Bernardi Shiffman

This pattern is a miter, but by making fewer decreases, you give it a wide, towelly shape. The hanging tab is knitted with a double strand of yarn for durability. We're not going to have a soggy hanging tab, now are we?

SIZE
Approximately 18" x 15" (45.5cm x 38cm), measured at widest point with hanging loop buttoned

MATERIALS
- (4) medium/worsted
- Peaches & Creme worsted weight, 100% cotton, 2½ oz (70g), 122 yd (112m), 1 ball each in colors A and B (We used Yellow, Lemon, Baby Green, Silver Grey, and Ecru.)
- Size 7 (4.5mm) needle, or size needed to obtain gauge
- One 1" button
- Stitch marker
- Tapestry needle

GAUGE
18 stitches and 28 rows = 4" (10cm) in stockinette stitch

DIFFICULTY
Actually easier than pie.

NOTE
The main section of the dishtowel is made with one strand of yarn; the hanging loop is made with the yarn used double.

Cast on 90 stitches, placing a stitch marker between the 45th and 46th stitch to mark the center of the row.

Bottom Border

Rows 1 and 3 (RS) Knit to 2 stitches before the marker, ssk, slip marker, k2tog, knit to the end of the row.

Rows 2 and 4 (WS) Knit.

Main Section

Row 1 and all RS rows Knit to 2 stitches before the marker, ssk, k2tog, knit to the end of the row.

Rows 2, 4, 6, and 8 k1, purl to the last stitch, k1.

Rows 10, 12, and 14 Knit—72 sts.

Repeat rows 1–14 twice more—44 sts.

Repeat rows 1–8—36 sts.

Cut A. Join B and work in garter stitch (knit every row), decreasing 2 stitches at the center of each RS row as established, until 24 stitches remain. Knit one row.

Hanging Loop

Using a double strand of B but without changing the needle size, continue working in garter stitch, decreasing 2 stitches at the center of each RS row as established, until 8 stitches remain. Knit one row, ending with a WS row.

Starting with RS facing, knit 9 garter ridges (18 rows), ending with a WS row.

Form a folding line as follows

Row 1 (RS) Knit.
Row 2 k1, purl to last stitch, k1.

Repeat Rows 1 and 2 four times more.

Knit 8 garter ridges (16 rows), ending with a WS row.

Buttonhole and End of Hanging Loop

Row 1 (RS) k2, bind off 4, k1.
Row 2 k2, turn, cast on 4 using the cable cast-on method (page 152), turn, k2.
Rows 3 and 4 Knit.
Row 5 ssk, k4, k2tog—6 sts.
Row 6 Knit.
Row 7 ssk, k2, k2tog—4 sts.
Row 8 Knit.

Bind off remaining 4 stitches in purl.

Finishing
Weave in ends. Sew the button in place.

THE STITCH MARKER NEXT DOOR

Stitch markers are like ballpoint pens: You have a million of them but you can never find one when you need one. Here is a woefully incomplete list of things you can use in place of an official stitch marker. There is no need to run out to buy stitch markers when you are surrounded by them.

* **Short length of string or yarn,** tied in a loop

* **Piece of plastic or paper** torn from the nearest supermarket bag, with hole poked in it by knitting needle

* **Twist tie** (trust me, there are 8 million of these in a drawer in your kitchen)

* **Strip of foil** from takeout sandwich, sculpted into a ring

* **Mylar wrapper** from a Pop-Tart, with needle-poked hole

* **Citrus peel,** with needle-poked hole (for those who feed their children fruit that is not in the form of a Pop-Tart)

* **Key ring** (works better if you remove the keys, but whatever)

* **Hoop earring** (remove any precious gems that are removable; you know how you keep losing those stitch markers?)

* Take apart mate's Mont Blanc pen

* Salvaged parts of other items of sentimental value to your spouse

---

Tip

To work with a double strand of yarn without using two skeins, use both ends of yarn from the same skein. Take the outside end and hold it together with the end that is inside the skein. It may take a bit of digging to find the inside end, but it's there.

Audrey Hepburn would so wear these. She would. She's looking down at these, from heaven, wishing she'd brought some with her.

No More Dishpan Hands

Walking past one of the Duane Reade chain drugstores found on every other block in New York City, and thinking of kitchen knits (as you do), I had a sudden flash of inspiration. I went straight into the store, bought a pair of kitchen gloves, and before you could say "Playtex Living Bra," I was doing minor surgery to make holes in the cuffs so I could pick up stitches.

We like to imagine that when Audrey Hepburn did the dishes, her elegant arms were sheathed in stylishly embellished rubber gloves. While the highest and best use of these gloves is a gift for the groom at a newfangled co-ed bridal shower, there is a dab of practicality to this project. The dishcloth cotton cuffs will catch those annoying drips that would otherwise run into the crook of your elbow when you lift your hands out of a bucket of water. We have fixed that clammy curse, once and for all. We feel real good about it.

GOLIGHTLY GLOVES

This is fully as much a scissoring project as a knitting project.

LENGTH OF KNITTED CUFF
Approximately 6¾" (17cm), unfolded

MATERIALS
- (4) medium/worsted
- Peaches & Creme worsted weight, 100% cotton, 2½ oz (70g), 122 yd (112m), 1 ball in Olive (A); small amounts of Chocolate (B) and Baby Green (C)
- Two size 7 (4.5mm), 24" circular needles (preferred), OR 1 set of 5 double-pointed needles, or size needed to obtain gauge
- One pair rubber gloves
- Small sharp scissors
- Tapestry needle
- Stitch marker

GAUGE
26 stitches and 24 rows = 4" (10cm) in rib stitch, measured without stretching.

DIFFICULTY RATING [1 drop of water.]
These are so easy you can knit them in the bath. A lightning fast, happy knit.

Prepare your gloves.
Preparation is the main event of this project. One of our bedrock beliefs is that You Can Pick Up a Stitch from Anything. Figure out how to make a hole, and you're on your way.

Turn the cuff of the glove back approximately 2" (5cm), as shown in the photograph. With a ballpoint pen or permanent marker, mark 23 dots evenly around the fold. Using sharp scissors and taking care not to cut yourself, make a cut at each dot that is big enough to pull a loop of yarn through with a yarn needle, approximately ⅕ inch (5mm).

Thread a yarn needle with a length of cotton yarn approximately 36" (91cm). Do not knot the end. With the inside of

the glove facing and leaving a 4" (10cm) tail, back-stitch (photo below) all the way around through the holes. You will sew 24 stitches. Cut yarn, leaving a 4" (10cm) tail.

Using A and continuing to work inside the glove (photo below), pick up and knit one stitch loosely in the front and back of each sewn stitch, for a total of 48 stitches.

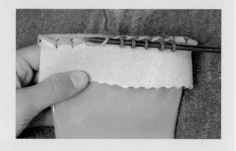

Join, place a marker, and work in the round, distributing the stitches evenly over 2 circular needles or 4 double-pointed needles.

Round 1 *k2, p2; repeat from * to the end of the round.

Round 1 establishes k2, p2 rib stitch, which you will work for the entire cuff. Work 14 rounds in A. Then work 2 rounds B, 2 rounds A, 4 rounds B, 2 rounds A, 2 rounds B, 6 rounds A, end with 4 rounds C. Bind off in C in rib pattern. Weave in ends.

Make a second glove cuff, same as the first.

To guard against tearing, we recommend using rubber gloves that have a bonded fabric lining. We found these tough, brightly colored gloves at www.williamssonoma.com.

The combination of double strands of yarn and Fair Isle knitting make Toto superthick and sturdy. Excellent protection against the cruel heat of your pots and pans.

Breaking New Ground

Oven mitts have one big advantage over regular knitted mittens: since you have to make only one, there is no danger of Second Mitten Syndrome. It's nice to have two, though. Go ahead and knit a second one. They don't have to match, if that's what's stopping you. Nothing ever has to match, OK?

The challenge here was to make a mitt that was cotton, and therefore washable, dryable, and—most important—knittable, but thick enough to protect the hands from hot dishes. Inspired by molded silicone oven mitts, I also wanted to create a smaller, handier shape that would stand up on the counter, the better to find and grab in that moment after the lid of the pot starts to rise and before it boils over. Toto is all that—and more.

TOTO THE EXTREMELY USEFUL AND CUTE POTHOLDER

SIZE
Approximately 5" x 5" (12.5cm x 12.5cm)

MATERIALS
- (4) medium/worsted
- Peaches & Creme worsted weight, 100% cotton, 2½ oz (70g) ball, 122 yd (112m), 1 ball each in colors A and B (We used Olive, Chocolate, Light Green and Baby Green.)
- Two size 8 (5mm) 24" circular needles (preferred), or size needed to obtain gauge
- OR 1 set of 5 double-pointed needles, plus 2 extra double-pointed needles (size is not important as the 2 extra needles are for holding stitches and knitting just one row)
- Stitch marker
- Tapestry needle

GAUGE
16 stitches and 18 rows = 4" (10cm) in stockinette stitch, holding yarn doubled

DIFFICULTY
The construction is a fun puzzle. The doubled yarns take a little getting used to.

NOTE
The yarn is used doubled throughout.

Base of Pocket
Holding 2 strands of A together, loosely cast on 10 stitches.

Working back and forth, and slipping the first stitch of each row, knit 3 rows to form a small rectangle.

Pick Up Stitches
At the end of the third row, pick up and knit 2 stitches from the adjacent short side of the rectangle, 10 stitches from the cast-on edge, and 2 stitches from the other short side—24 sts.

Arrange Stitches to Work in the Round
Distribute the stitches as follows: If using 2 circular needles, place 12 stitches (10 from one of the long sides and 1 from each of the short sides of the rectangle) on each of the 2 circular needles. If using double-pointed needles, place 6 stitches (5 long-side stitches and 1 short-side stitch on each needle) on each of 4 double-pointed needles.

Pocket

First Side

Place a marker at the beginning of the round, join and knit in the round as follows:

Rounds 1, 3, and 5 Knit.
Round 2 k1, *m1, k10, m1* knit 2; repeat from * to * once more, k1—28 sts.
Round 4 k1, *m1, k12, m1* knit 2; repeat from * to * once, k1—32 sts.
Round 6 k1, *m1, k14, m1* knit 2; repeat from * to * once, k1—36 sts.
Round 7 Join a double strand of B and start Fair Isle stripes as follows: k 2A, *2B, 2A, 2B, 2A, 2B, 2A, 2B*, 4A; repeat from * to * once more, 2A.

Repeat Round 7 seven more times, then cut both yarns.

Set the pocket aside on 2 spare double-pointed needles, or stitch holders.

Second Side

Make a second pocket, same as the first, but do not cut A.

Join the Pockets
Each pocket has 2 sides of 18 stitches each. Align the two pockets, on their needles, so that 18 stitches from each pocket are side by side. Continuing with A, work a three-needle bind-off (see page 154) across these 18 stitches, leaving the last stitch live and not cutting the yarn.

Cuff
Now the two pockets are joined at the center, with 18 live stitches on the outside edge of each pocket, plus the 1 stitch left live after joining the pockets. Starting after the live stitch from joining the pockets, knit 18 stitches from one pocket, which will place you at the other end of the stitches you just bound off. Pick up and knit 1 stitch in this spot, and work the remaining 18 stitches, from the other pocket, to the end of the round, which now has 38 stitches. Place a marker at the start of the round and knit 5 rounds of stockinette stitch (knit every round). Cut A.

I-Cord Bind-Off
Bind-off all stitches using a double strand of B and the I-cord bind-off (new technique alert!) as follows:

The stitches to be bound off are on the left needle.

Using the knitted cast-on method, cast on 3 stitches onto the left needle.

*Knit 2, knit the third stitch together with the next stitch on the left needle, slip the 3 stitches just formed back onto the left needle; repeat from * until 3 stitches remain, which you bind off normally.

Weave in ends. Immediately use potholder as a hand puppet, to get this urge out of your system.

Nothing to see here: we were just out for a walk with a large, unidentified handknit. (Oh, like you don't ever do that.)

Superfoxy Matrons Flee, Dragging Handknits Behind Them

t's always good, either in battle or in knitting, to close with Sir Winston Churchill: "Every day you may make progress. Every step may be fruitful. Yet there will stretch out before you an ever-lengthening, ever-ascending, ever-improving path. You know you will never get to the end of the journey. But this, so far from discouraging, only adds to the joy and glory of the climb."

While the joy and the glory of the climb sounds like an awful lot of hiking to us, we think Sir Winston is on to something. The ever-lengthening ball of yarn never runs out, right? The path ever improves, and we keep learning new things.

As you continue you on your way, let us know how it's going. State fair triumphs, the words you put on your Margaret Sweater, your aha moments—please visit us at masondixonknitting.com. We'll be there, trying out new ideas and keeping a spot for you on the busted-out corduroy sofa.

ACKNOWLEDGMENTS

The honorary citizens of the township of Mason-Dixon Knitting are as bighearted as they are talented, and their generosity is here on every page. Thank you for your beautiful work, and for making it fun.

Thank you thank you!

To the readers of our blog, masondixonknitting.com, whose chat and chatter crack us up, inspire us, and keep us looking for the next great thing to knit. Thanks for hanging out with us even when we're knitting something doggish, and for reminding us that the important thing is the laughter that happens on the way to a finished object.

To Anna Bell, Ann Hahn Buechner, Bonne Marie Burns, Mary Neal Meador, Cristina Shiffman, and Mercedes Tarasovich-Clark, designers who are friends, and friends who are designers. Thank you for taking so many ideas and running with them.

To our adventurous, stoic, and exquisitely skilled knitters: Charisse Baer, Cheryl Carpenter, Suzanne deSalme, Yvonne Fisher, Frances Jago, Tara Lynchard, Meg Manning, Amanda Mitchell-Boyask, Susan Mitz, Liana Morris, Jennifer Munkelwitz, Erica O'Rourke, Polly Outhwaite, Francie Owens, Julie Schneider, Robin Smith, Kelly Sundberg, Mary Sue Taylor, and Audrey Yates.

To our models, who exhibited grace while wearing handknits in June, and gamely complied with our wacky stage directions: Carrie Bergmann, Joseph Bergmann, Colby Black, Charlotte Lola Burke, Boo Davidson, Danielle Davidson, Onslow Falcone, Jon Gardiner, Fionnuala "Finn" Goodale, Rose Hassel, Isaac Kruger, Julia Kruger, Lacy Lovell, Heather McLaughlin, Ava Monske, Ilana Monske, Ruth Nardini, Nicolas Paul, Jacob Pfeifer, Yvette Postelle, Luke Robinson, Clifton Shayne, David Shayne, Bridget Uzzelle, Julia Webb, Meara Wilson.

To Hannah Dawes, Heather McLaughlin, Jill Clark, and Mary Elizabeth Long, for their professional skills, cheerful impromptu modeling, and companionship at our photo shoots.

To the citizens of Monteagle, Tennessee, and Southampton, New York, for sharing their stunning locations, people, babies, and props. We would also like to thank the professional dog walkers of New York City for their important contribution.

To Julie Fraenkel, for her tidy drawings.

To Belinda Boaden, for her beautiful design and editing work and her many contributions to our British slang vocabulary.

To our photographer, Gale Zucker, for her amazing eye. She captured what we love about our real people in real places, and especially our real knitting.

To the brilliant professionals at Potter Craft: Jenny Frost, Lauren Shakely, Rosy Ngo, Erin Slonaker, Erica Smith, Chi Ling Moy, Isa Loudon, La Tricia Watford, and Amy Sly. It is exhilarating and scary to write about knitting for editors who are passionate knitters themselves. We can't wait to see what they knit from this book.

To Chalkley Calderwood, for her patience and truly beautiful book design.

To our long-suffering civilian friends in Nashville and New York.

To our sweet children, who touch us so much by being proud of us, and tolerating all the knitting and typing.

To our husbands, for forbearance, wise counsel, encouragement, and for being the loudest voices in our cheering section. We know they have zero-point-zero interest in knitting, and we think that's so cute.

And finally, to Joy Tutela, our agent, friend, and champion.

Anna Bell

Lifetime Londoner . . . sophisticated . . . voted Most Likely to Design a Pullover for the Queen . . . First book of patterns due soon . . . perfectly perfect taste . . . online at My Fashionable Life (http://needleandhook.co.uk/journal/)

Ann Hahn Buechner

Missouri-born, living the dream in Berkeley, California . . . lives three blocks from Chez Panisse . . . tweed nut . . . online at The Runcible Bin (http://runciblebin.blogspot.com)

Bonne Marie Burns

Wears many hats, including her own famous Bucket o' Chic Hat . . . Coco Chanel reincarnated as a hard-workin' television camerawoman . . . online at Chic Knits (http://chicknits.com/)

Mary Neal Meador

That hair! . . . Book designer during the day, knitter by night . . . too cool to blog . . . lofty lifestyle in Chicago . . . voted Least Likely to Use a Pattern

Cristina Bernardi Shiffman

Waldorf mom . . . what's this Chicago girl doing in Philly? . . . indigo vat in her basement . . . seen quilting . . . . . .most likely to e-mail you a link that will make you buy something . . . will send you a Sigrid Undset trilogy in a blink . . . online at Philacraft (http://philacraft .blogspot.com/)

Mercedes Tarasovich-Clark

Birmingham, Alabama . . . coolest yarn shop owner . . . art school grad . . . puts the hip in hip knitting . . . known to run very long distances for good causes . . . online at Knit Nouveau (http://knitn.com)

SOURCES: DELECTABLE, ROAD-TESTED YARNS

Picking yarns for this book was hard work. All those hours hanging out in our favorite local yarn stores, petting skeins, chatting up yarn reps, and knitting swatches left us limp as a dishrag, but somebody had to do it.

Here are our old and new yarn friends, each of which was specified for one or more of our patterns. The websites give current information on where the yarns are sold.

Berroco
www.berroco.com

Brown Sheep Company, Inc.
www.brownsheep.com

Cascade Yarns
www.cascadeyarns.com

Classic Elite Yarns
www.classiceliteyarns.com

Crystal Palace Yarns
www.crystalpalaceyarns.com

Harrisville Designs
www.harrisville.com

Hemp for Knitting
www.hempforknitting.com

Judi & Co.
www.judiandco.com

Koigu Wool Designs
www.koigu.com

Lorna's Laces
www.lornaslaces.net

Louet Sales
www.louet.com

Manos del Uruguay
www.manos.com.uy

Muench Yarns
www.muenchyarns.com

Nature's Palette
www.handjiveknits.com

Noro Yarns
www.knittingfever.com

Peaches & Crème
www.elmore-pisgah.com

Rowan
www.knitrowan.com

Tahki Yarns/Tahki•Stacy Charles, Inc.
www.tahkistacycharles.com

STANDARD YARN WEIGHT SYSTEM

* GUIDELINES ONLY: The above reflects the most commonly used gauges and needle or hook sizes for specific yarn categories.

Yarn Weight Symbol and Category names	**1** SUPER FINE	**2** FINE	**3** LIGHT	**4** MEDIUM	**5** BULKY	**6** SUPER BULKY
Type of Yarns in Category	Sock, Fingering, Baby	Sport, Baby	DK, Light Worsted	Worsted, Afghan, Aran	Chunky, Craft, Rug	Bulky, Roving
Knit Gauge Range* in Stockinette Stitch to 4 inches	27-32 sts	23-26 sts	21-24 sts	16-20 sts	12-15 sts	6-11 sts
Recommended Needle in Metric Size Range	2.25–3.25 mm	3.25–3.75 mm	3.75–4.5 mm	4.5–5.5 mm	5.5–8 mm	8 mm and larger
Recommended Needle in U.S. Size Range	1 3	3-5	5-7	7-9	9-11	11 and larger
Crochet Gauge* Ranges in Single Crochet to 4 Inches	21-32 sts	16-20 sts	12-17 sts	11-14 sts	8-11 sts	5-9 sts
Recommended Hook in Metric Size Range	2.25–3.25 mm	3.5–4.4 mm	4.5–5.5 mm	5.5–6.5 mm	6.5–9 mm	9 mm and larger
Recommended Hook in U.S. Size Range	B-1 to E-4	E-4 to 7	7 to I-9	I-9 to K-10 ½	K-10 ½ to M-13	M-13 and larger

This is where we give brief explanations of techniques, terms, and abbreviations that you might not already know. Because knitting is rooted in a long oral tradition, and is practiced by speakers of many languages (including variations of English), we may use a term that you already know, but it means something slightly different to us. We are not saying that our definitions are definitive, but that this is what we mean when we use these terms. Remember: there are no knitting police, only knitters trying to get to the end of their projects with a minimum of cussing and throwing needles around.

Backstitch A sewing stitch in which you pull thread through fabric and then take a small backward stitch. Pull the needle through again, this time a little in front of the first stitch; then take another stitch, inserting the needle at the point at which the thread first came through.

c4b Slip the next 2 stitches to the cable needle and hold at back of work, k2, k2 from cable needle.

c4f Slip the next 2 stitches to the cable needle and hold at front of work, k2, k2 from cable needle.

Cro-Kay edging This is an improvised single-crochet edging made with knitting needles that can be used around armholes, neck openings, blanket edges or wherever there is a need for a non-bulky finish. With WS facing, start at the far right end of the edge to be finished, or in the case of a circular opening, at the bottom center. Pick up and knit two stitches, *bind off one stitch, pick up and knit 1 stitch; repeat from * until the edging is complete.

Crossed stockinette stitch Knit all RS stitches through the back loops, and purl all WS stitches in the usual way.

Cable cast-on Make a slip knot and place it on the left needle tip. Insert the right needle tip into the stitch as if to knit, pull a new stitch through the loop of the slip knot and place it on the left needle. *Insert the right needle tip into the space between the previous two stitches on left needle, pull a new stitch through and place it on the left needle; repeat from * until the required number of stitches have been cast on.

Duplicate stitch Known to some knitters as Swiss darning, this embroidery stitch mimics knitting.

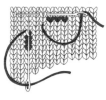

Garter stitch Knit every row.

I-cord Using 2 double-pointed needles, cast on the required number of stitches. *Without turning work, slide stitches to the right end of needle, pull yarn around back of stitches and knit; repeat from * until the cord is the required length. (What you are doing, essentially, is knitting in the round on a very small number of stitches.)

I-cord bind-off The stitches to be bound off are on the left needle. Using the knitted cast-on method, cast on 3 stitches onto the left needle. *Knit 2, knit the third stitch together with the next stitch on the left needle, slip the 3 stitches just formed back onto the left needle; repeat from * until 3 stitches remain, which you bind off normally.

I-cord border Using a circular needle, pick up and knit the appropriate number of stitches from the edge to be bordered. With RS facing, pull needle through so that you are ready to work from the beginning of the picked up stitches. Work I-cord edging as follows: On separate needle, cast on 2 stitches. Transfer them to the circular needle holding the edge stitches. Work as follows: *k1, slip 1, yo, k1 (from edge stitches), pass the slipped stitch and the yo over the last knit stitch, replace the 2 stitches on the right needle to the left needle; repeat from * to end of stitches. The border can be eased around corners (on collars or blankets) by working the first 2 stitches only once or twice before continuing from *.

k Knit.

kfb Knit into the front and back of the next stitch.

k2tog Knit 2 stitches together.

Knitted cast-on Make a slip knot and place it on the left needle tip. Insert the right needle tip into the stitch as if to knit, pull a new stitch through the loop of the slip knot and place it on the left needle. *Knit into the first stitch on the left needle, then place the new loop back onto the left needle; repeat from * until the required number of stitches have been cast on.

LT left twist. Knit into the back of the second stitch, but do not transfer to the right needle. Knit the first and second stitches together through the back loops and transfer both stitches to the right needle.

m1 Pick up strand that lies between the stitch just worked and the next stitch, knit (or purl) into the back of it.

Mattress stitch This is a sewn seam that is invisible on one side; it is also called *ladder stitch* or *invisible stitch*. While mattress stitch can be used to join any two pieces of knitting, it is most easily worked when joining row ends to row ends (as for the sides or sleeves of a sweater), or stitches to stitches (as for shoulder seams). Align the edges to be joined with RS facing on a flat surface. Using a tapestry needle and a length of yarn that is approximately 8" (20cm) longer than the seam you are sewing, take the needle up from the wrong side of the garment through the first stitch, either one stitch or one half-stitch in from the edge. Now go to the corresponding stitch on the other piece, and take your needle in from front to back. *Now go back across to the other piece, and take your needle into the SAME STITCH YOU CAME OUT OF, from front to back. Repeat from * until the seam is joined. After a few stitches, you will see a ladder pattern emerging as your stitches criss-cross from one piece to the other. Every few inches, pull the yarn snug, gently and smoothly. When the seam is completed, pull on it to ensure that the length of yarn is lying straight and all the stitches have been snugged up, but that there are no places where the seam is bunched up.

pfb Purl into front and back of next stitch.

Phony seam A technique that we learned from Elizabeth Zim-

mermann, a phony seam creates the appearance of a seam in a seamless garment, usually at the sides of a sweater that is knit in the round, but anywhere a vertical fold in the fabric would be attractive. Work across the piece to the point where you want the seam to appear (in some cases, you have pre-marked the stitch by always purling it on the rows below). Drop the next stitch from left needle and unravel down to the row where you want the seam to end. Using a spare knitting needle, pick up the "ladders" of the dropped stitch again, but instead of picking up each ladder individually as you normally would to repair a dropped stitch, pick up 1 ladder, then 2 ladders together, repeating this sequence until you have picked up all the ladders. When you have picked up all the way back to the top, place the dropped stitch back on the left needle and work to the end of the row.

Provisional cast-on (crochet chain method) There are several ways to do this. The easiest for us is as follows: Using waste yarn and a crochet hook, make a loose crochet chain several stitches longer than the numebr of stitches you need to cast on. Switch to a needle and the working yarn. Pick up and knit one stitch in the back loop of each crochet chain until you have the number of stitches you need. When it's time to activate those stitches, pull out the waste yarn to expose the live stitches.

p Purl.

RS Right side.

RT right twist. Knit 2 stitches together, but do not transfer to the right needle. Knit the first stitch again and transfer both stitches to the right needle.

Seed stitch When worked over an odd number of stitches, work every row as follows: k1, *p1, k1; repeat from * to the end of the row. When worked over an even number of stitches, alternate rows as follows: Row 1: *k1, p1; repeat from * to the end of the row. Row 2: *p1, k1; repeat from * to the end of the row. The idea is, you alternate knit and purl stitches across each row. When a stitch presents itself to you as a knit stitch, you purl it. When the stitch presents itself to you as a purl stitch, you knit it.

skp Slip, knit, pass. Slip the first stitch knitwise, knit the second stitch, and pass the slipped stitch over the knitted stitch, thus decreasing one stitch.

Sewn bind-off Break yarn, leaving a tail at least 3 times longer than the edge you are binding off. Thread yarn tail on a tapestry needle, and work as follows: *Draw tapestry needle through first 2 stitches purlwise, and draw back through first stitch knitwise, drop first stitch from knitting needle; repeat from * until all stitches are bound off.

Slip Transfer the stitch from the left needle to the right needle without working it. Unless otherwise specified, stitches are always slipped purlwise, which means that you insert the needle into the stitch as if you were going to purl it.

ssk Slip, slip, knit. This instruction typically means to slip 2 stitches separately knitwise, then insert the left needle into the front of these stitches, and knit them together from this position. We also like a variation in which you slip the first stitch knitwise and the second stitch purlwise before knitting them together. This variation is a bit tidier in appearance than the traditional version, and also it seems to be smoother to work.

sssk Slip the next 3 stitches knitwise, one at a time, to the right needle. Insert the left needle into the front of these 3 stitches. Knit them together.

ssp On a purl row, slip 1 stitch knitwise, slip another stitch knitwise. Return slipped stitches to left needle. Purl these 2 stitches together as follows: insert right needle into the back loops of the two stitches—inserting the needle from left to right in the back of the second stitch on the left needle, then the first stitch—and purl them together from this position.

Three-needle bind-off This technique is used to join 2 edges containing an equal number of stitches, without sewing a seam. The most common use is to join the front and back pieces of a sweater at the shoulders. The stitches for both pieces are left live on their separate needles. Arrange the two needles so that the points are facing to the right, and the RS or WS surfaces of the knitting are facing each other. (If you want the bind-off to show on the right side of the garment, as in Margaret on page 54, the wrong side of the pieces should be facing each other; if you want the bind-off to show on the wrong side of the garment, the right side of the pieces should be facing each other.) Using a third needle as the right needle, and a new strand of yarn, insert the right needle into the front loops of the first stitch on each of the 2 left needles, pull a single loop through both stitches, and place it on the right needle. *Insert the right needle into the front loops of the first stitch on each of the 2 left needles, pull a single loop through both stitches, and place it on the right needle, lift the first stitch on the right needle over the second stitch; repeat from * until 1 stitch remains on the right needle, pull the yarn through this last stitch, and fasten off.

WS wrong side

w&t wrap and turn. On a knit row, move yarn to the front of work, slip next stitch, take yarn to the back of work, slip wrapped stitch to left needle. Turn work. On a purl row, move yarn to the back of work, slip next stitch, bring yarn to the front of work, slip wrapped stitch back to left needle, turn work.

Whipstitch This is a classic, intuitive sewing stitch used to sew on buttonbands and generally to attach things, like plastic bag handles, to knitting. Using a tapestry needle and a length of yarn, take the needle around and around, back and forth between the 2 pieces you are joining, as neatly as possible. Fun fact: When you give a small child a needle and yarn and tell them to sew 2 things together, 99 times out of 100 they will whipstitch it, proving that whipstitch is part of the human genome.

yo yarn over. The most common type of yarn over is made after a knit stitch and before another knit stitch. Move yarn from back of work to the front, and knit the next stitch from this position. Then on the next row, work this yarn over as if it were a normal stitch. A yarn over results in an increase of one stitch, and looks like a hole or eyelet in the fabric.

yf yarn forward. Move yarn to front of work.

yb yarn back. Move yarn to back of work.

The Art of Fair Isle Knitting: History, Technique, Color & Patterns by Ann Feitelson (Interweave Press, 1996)

The Avengers: The Complete Emma Peel Megaset (2006 Collector's Edition DVD)

Cables Untangled: An Exploration of Cable Knitting by Melissa Leapman (Potter Craft, 2006)

A Charlie Brown Christmas by Charles M. Schulz (Running Press, 2003)

Charlotte's Web by E. B. White (HarperTrophy, 2004 edition)

Charted Knitting Designs: A Third Treasury of Knitting Patterns by Barbara Walker (Schoolhouse Press, 1998)

Color Me Beautiful: Discover Your Natural Beauty through the Colors That Make You Look Great and Feel Fabulous by Carole Jackson (Ballantine, 1987)

Creative Knitting by Mary Walker Phillips (Van Nostrand Reinhold, 1971)

EastEnders (BBC Television)

Elizabeth Zimmermann's Knitter's Almanac by Elizabeth Zimmermann (Dover Publications, 1981)

Emma by Jane Austen (Oxford University Press, 2003 edition)

Erica Wilson's Embroidery Book by Erica Wilson (Charles Scribner's Sons, 1973)

Fair Isle Sweaters Simplified by Ann Bourgeois and Eugene Bourgeois (Martingale, 2000)

Fitted Knits: 25 Designs for the Fashionable Knitter by Stefanie Japel (North Light Books, 2007)

Fire and Ice: The Story of Charles Revson, the Man Who Built the Revlon Empire by Andrew Tobias (Warner Books, 1977)

The Harmony Guide to Aran and Fair Isle Knitting by Debra Mountford, Editor (Crown, 1995)

I Feel Bad About My Neck: And Other Thoughts on Being a Woman by Nora Ephron (Knopf, 2006)

Icky Thump by The White Stripes (Warner Brothers, 2007)

Indigo Knits: The Quintessential Guide to Denim Yarn by the Founders of Artwork by Jane and Patrick Gottelier (Potter Craft, 2007)

In the Hebrides by Alice Starmore (Broad Bay Company, 1995)

Kaffe Knits Again: 24 Original Designs Updated for Today's Knitters by Kaffe Fassett (Potter Craft, 2007)

Knitting Ganseys by Beth Brown-Reinsel (Interweave Press, 1993)

The Knitter's Handy Book of Patterns: Basic Designs in Multiple Sizes by Ann Budd (Interweave Press, 2002)

Knitting Essentials I and II (DVDs) by Lucy Neatby (Tradewind Knitwear Designs)

Knitting from the Top by Barbara G. Walker (Schoolhouse Press, 1996 edition)

Knitting on the Edge by Nicky Epstein (Sixth&Spring Books, 2004)

Knitting Over the Edge by Nicky Epstein (Sixth&Spring Books, 2005)

Knitting Beyond the Edge by Nicky Epstein (Sixth&Spring Books, 2006)

Knitting Outside the Limits of the Known Universe by Nicky Epstein (OK, we're kidding, but we do hope Nicky keeps writing these books.)

Knitting Vintage Socks: New Twists on Old Patterns by Nancy Bush (Interweave Press, 2005)

Mastering the Art of French Cooking, Volume 1 by Julia Child, Louisette Bertholle, and Simone Beck (Knopf, 2001 edition)

The McCall's Book of Handcrafts (Random House, 1972)

The Natural Knitter: How to Choose, Use, and Knit Natural Fibers from Alpaca to Yak by Barbara Albright (Potter Craft, 2007)

Outlander by Diana Gabaldon (Dell, 2005 edition)

Pride and Prejudice by Jane Austen (Penguin Popular Classics, 2007 edition)

Rocky Mountain High by John Denver (1972, RCA)

Sensational Knitted Socks by Charlene Schurch (Martingale and Company, 2005)

Sense and Sensibility by Jane Austen (Oxford University Press, 2004 edition)

Socks Soar on Two Circular Needles: A Manual of Elegant Knitting Techniques and Patterns by Cat Bordhi (Passing Paws Press, 2001)

A Streetcar Named Desire by Tennessee Williams (Signet, 1986 edition)

That Girl—Season One (1966) (Shout Factory Theatre DVD, 2006)

A Treasury of Knitting Patterns (four volumes) by Barbara G. Walker (Schoolhouse Press, 1998–2001 editions)

Take Your Time: Finding Balance in a Hurried World by Eknath Easwaran (Hyperion, 1998)

Woman's Home Companion, August 1935 issue

Workbasket magazine, various editions from 1940s

Mason-Dixon Knitting Hall of Shame

Tito Puente Percussion Instrument

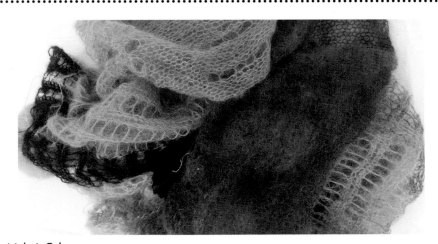

Mohair Odyssey

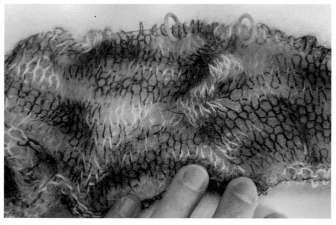

O! Possum! My possum!

Fantasy: If you turn the pattern sideways, and knit it in wool, it will make a toasty, insulating coat.
Reality: Hey lady! There's a dishcloth stuck to your—oh, that is your coat.

Mason-Dixon Knitting Hall of Shame (continued)

Nuclear Power Plant Glove

Fantasy: If you knit a tube of Fair Isle long enough, it will eventually look pretty. Reality: Fair Isle yoga mat cover.

Fantasy: If you knit a tube of Christmassy Fair Isle long enough, it will turn into a cool Christmas stocking. Reality: What? Doesn't everybody have a Christmas yoga mat holder?

Poorly Executed Tribute to the Cherokee People, Or, A Horse Blanket for a Very Tiny Horse

Embelished Kitchen Gloves. Oh, wait—we put that one in the book!

JILL THE MONKEY

*As you walk your knitting path, remember
Mason-Dixon Rule Number 61: Never say never.*

*Jill Goes to The Oscars, created by Rhonda Tesch of Waconia, Minnesota.
Winner of masondixonknitting.com's Teeny Project Runway.*